The Development Factory

The
Development
Factory

Unlocking the Potential of Process Innovation

Gary P. Pisano

HARVARD BUSINESS SCHOOL PRESS
BOSTON, MASSACHUSETTS

01   5 4 3

Library of Congress Cataloging-in-Publication Data

Pisano, Gary P.
The development factory : unlocking the potential of process innovation / Gary P.
Pisano.
p.   cm.
Includes bibliographical references and index.
ISBN 0-87584-650-5 (alk. paper)
1. Technological innovations—Economic aspects. 2. Pharmaceutical industry—Technological innovations—Case studies. 3. Chemical industry—Technological innovations—Case studies. 4. Biotechnology industries—Technological innovations—Case
studies. 5. New products. 6. Manufacturing processes. 7. Economic development.
8. Competition, International. I. Title.
HC79.T4P57 1996
338'064—dc20   96-4073
                                                                              CIP

The paper used in this publication meets the requirements of the American National
Standard for Permanence of Paper for Printed Library Materials Z39.49-1984

To my parents,
who were the most important teachers
during much of my own development.

C O N T E N T S

Preface

The Development Factory is about managing process development in the pharmaceutical industry. Because some might be surprised that anyone would choose to write an entire book about process development (and equally astounded that it should focus on the pharmaceutical industry), let me offer a few words about the genesis of and motivation for this book.

During Autumn 1990 my colleague Steven Wheelwright and I began a project at a biotechnology firm renowned for its world-class capabilities in genetic engineering and biomedical research. Nevertheless, because of problems developing a viable manufacturing process, the company was struggling to get its first product through clinical trials and to market. Moreover, although the technical challenges of process development were significant, many of the company's problems seemed to be organizational in nature (miscommunication, lack of coordination, poor planning, and so forth). A number of concepts from manufacturing strategy and product development literature could clearly help the company with its more basic problems. But as we probed deeper into the company's problems over the course of several months it became evident that process development involved specific technical and managerial challenges that remained unaddressed by the existing bodies of literature. I thus began seeking research on process development that dealt with the specific issues faced by high-tech organizations. What I found—or, perhaps more accurately, what I did not find—was surprising.

Although there was a vast body of literature on process development in mature industries (such as commodity chemicals) and an increasing focus on design for manufacturability in assembled products, there was virtually nothing on process development in high-tech environments, where organizations must deal with rapidly changing technical frontiers, a great deal of uncertainty in development, and enormously complex product technologies, which often create significant challenges for process development. As I began to explore other high-tech companies both inside and outside of pharmaceuticals, it became apparent that superior process development capabilities—if developed and managed properly—could be a hidden advantage for companies competing on the basis of product innovation. Understanding how to unlock this potential became the starting point for this research. As I delved deeper into the problem, I also began to realize that process development offered a window into a broader array of important issues related to managing knowledge and organizational learning.

Because I was primarily interested in how process development might influence product development performance, I chose to carry out this research in pharmaceuticals, where product development is central to competition. Pharmaceutical companies also must compete in an environment undergoing rapid and profound technological and institutional changes. In the wake of these changes, established and young companies alike have pursued various strategies for improving and exploiting their process development capabilities. The quantitative and qualitative data, statistical analyses, and case studies presented in the following chapters—based on three years of in-depth field research—reflect my attempt to capture the learning from these natural experiments and to distill their many implications for both management practice and scholarly research. My goal has been to present the material in a way that not only proves stimulating and convincing to scholars interested in innovation, the management of knowledge, and organizational learning, but also remains accessible to and useful for practitioners interested in unlocking the potential of process development in their own organizations. Although some parts of the book are clearly targeted more to one audience than to the other, I have made every effort to present an integrated body of concepts and findings.

A project of this magnitude would not have been possible without the help and support of many people and organizations. My first debt of thanks is to the companies and more than 200 scientists, engineers, and managers who participated in the field research. Guarantees of confidentiality prevent me from mentioning their names, but I cannot stress enough how grateful I am for their willingness to participate and to share their time and information so generously with me. I am also deeply grateful to a number of my colleagues here at the Harvard Business School. Steve Wheelwright, who collaborated on parts of this study, was there from the beginning. He gave me the initial encouragement (and courage!) to do this project, helped open doors at pharmaceutical companies, listened to my ideas, sharpened my thinking, and provided extremely helpful comments on early drafts of this manuscript. Kim Clark, now Dean of the Harvard Business School, was chair of the Technology and Operations Management area for most of the duration of this project. He not only structured my assignments so that I would have the needed time to undertake fieldwork and writing, but also provided valuable comments, criticisms, and suggestions throughout the project. I am grateful to John McArthur, former Dean of the Harvard Business School, who provided support for this research project and whose warm words of encouragement were truly a source of inspiration. I am indebted to the Harvard Business School Division of Research and to my research directors over the past several years (Warren McFarlan, Jai Jaikumar, Steve Wheelwright, and Dwight Crane) for ensuring that I had generous funding and support. I also benefited enormously from discussions with and comments from Bob Hayes, Kent Bowen, Dave Garvin, Dorothy Leonard-Barton, Roy Shapiro, Richard Rosenbloom, Richard Walton, Dave Upton, Marco Iansiti, Alan MacCormack, and numerous faculty and doctoral students who attended the Technology and Operations Management workshops where pieces of this research were presented over the past few years.

I am also grateful to Richard Nelson and Rebecca Henderson, who provided valuable comments and suggestions on the manuscript, and to Eric von Hippel, Keith Pavitt, David Mowery, Ed Zajac, Jay Barney, and seminar and conference participants at the University of California at Berkeley, the Wharton School, the Academy of Management, and TIMS/ORSA for helpful suggestions along the way. Sharon Rossi provided two years of outstanding research assistance during the field data collection phase and helped develop a number of the case studies presented in chapter 9. Brent Omdahl, my research assistant for six months, did an excellent job tracking down much of the data used in chapter 3. Jerome Meier, Kevin Moran, Farzan Riza, and Scott Walton, MBA students at the Harvard Business School (Class of 1994), did a first-rate field study project that provided some very important data used in chapter 4. I want to thank Nick Philipson, my editor at the Harvard Business School Press, for encouraging me to do this book and for providing support and enthusiasm throughout, and Jean Smith, who was responsible for editing the manuscript, designing graphics, handling revisions, and seeing that everything was in order.

Finally, I wish to thank my wife, Ingrid, and my two children, Stefan and Melanie. The love and fun they put into my life made writing this book a much more enjoyable experience.

The Development Factory

CHAPTER 1

Introduction: Process Development as a Competitive Weapon

TODAY, WHEN MERCK reports promising results for a potential "blockbuster" drug, the story makes the evening news. Similarly, automobile aficionados snap up the latest issues of *Road & Track* to catch glimpses of next year's BMW sport coupe, and the Internet buzzes with rumors of Sun's latest Netra or Intel's next-generation microprocessor. Popular business magazines such as *Fortune* and *Forbes* contain articles on new products in almost every issue, and *Business Week* publishes an annual issue on its choice of best product designs. Both academics and practitioners alike have come to recognize the competitive power of new product development. In the past few years alone, a flood of articles and books has been written on how to make product development cycles both faster and more effective.[1] MBA and executive-level courses on new product development are oversubscribed across the country. Major consulting firms such as McKinsey, Booz-Allen, and Bain have made product development a staple of their client services, while hundreds of "boutique" consultancies now specialize in managing product development. Across a wide range of industries, it would be hard to find senior managers who are not actively trying to improve their companies' product development performance. Today, the improvement of product development attracts the kind of resources and attention that productivity and quality management attracted during the 1980s.

Perhaps not surprisingly, the development of new manufacturing *process* technologies generates less excitement among academics and practitioners, much less the public at large. This is partly because we, as consumers, often come into direct contact with innovative new products in our daily lives but rarely glimpse the manufacturing processes hidden behind factory walls. But the reasons run still deeper. Following a decade in which companies began to take manufacturing seriously, there is a growing perception that manufacturing is no longer a necessary strategic competency, at least for companies that compete in technologically dynamic contexts. Process development and manufacturing prowess are viewed as strategic competencies in precisely those "mature" industries in which U.S., European, and increasingly even Japanese companies find themselves at a comparative disadvantage relative to rivals from newly industrialized countries. Indeed, during the 1980s many U.S. companies turned to new product development as a way to compete against offshore rivals with stronger manufacturing competencies.

In an effort to focus resources on "core competencies," many companies in industries such as computers, pharmaceuticals, biotechnology, and electronics are increasingly turning over manufacturing of entire products, not just components, to third-party contract manufacturers. A growing number of senior executives in high-tech industries appear to agree with William Joy, cofounder of Sun Microsystems, who notes, "The creative path of design is going to add value. . . . [Because manufacturing prowess can be bought from any number of vendors], intellectual property is the asset for the 1990s."[2] Moreover, a recent article in *Fortune,* citing numerous examples of how innovative companies successfully outsource production, concludes, "In the new economy, the most successful 'industrial' companies will often be those that don't make their own products."[3]

This dichotomy between "high-tech" or "knowledge-intensive" industries, where R&D capabilities predominate, and more "mature," manufacturing-intensive industries is very apparent in the academic literature. Despite rapid growth in both over the past decade, the literature on high-tech competition (e.g., Nelson 1984, and Scherer 1992) and manufacturing strategy (Hayes and Wheelwright 1984; and Hayes, Wheelwright, and Clark 1988) generally have not intersected. A perusal of the leading texts and casebooks on manufacturing strategy (such as Hayes and Wheelwright 1984, Schmenner 1987, and Garvin 1992) unearths a plethora of examples and cases from traditional fabrication and assembly industries, as well as from mature, capital-intensive, process industries (such as chemicals or steel), but relatively few from technologically dynamic contexts. Similarly, research on manufacturing productivity, quality, flexibility, and process innovation has tended to focus on technologically mature contexts, such as petrochemicals, automobiles, air conditioners, and paper.[4]

Likewise, the strategic role of manufacturing is barely mentioned in discussions of high-tech competition. Here the focus tends to be on the determinants of R&D performance as measured by patents, number of innovations, R&D productivity, or lead times to launch new products. Beyond rectifying serious deficiencies in manufacturing performance through better communication between R&D and plants, and through adopting design-for-manufacturability (DFM) practices and philosophies, there is little discussion of how strong *process* development capabilities might lead to better competitive outcomes or might enhance a company's product development performance.

It is hard to argue with the principle that different types of capabilities may be important in different industries and that managers should focus on those activities offering the greatest competitive leverage. Yet the perception that manufacturing competency fails to contribute to—or may even hinder—product development performance may mask a deeper reality: lurking behind many new product introductions is the development of complex, novel, and enormously costly production technologies. The latest generations of computer memory chips, for example, require production facilities ("fabs") costing over $1 billion but with useful economic lives of just a few years. Moreover, the true value of these facilities lies not in the mere physical artifacts (the buildings, tooling, and machinery), but in the intellectual capital (information about tool designs, reaction conditions, assembly sequences, and quality assurance methods) created by scores of process development scientists and engineers. Even some relatively low-tech new product introductions can require the development of highly sophisticated process technologies. Gillette engineers, for example, spent seven years, $75 million in R&D, and $125 million in capital to develop the manufacturing process for the Sensor razor system. The novel product design required the development of an entirely new process technology for making the cartridge heads, including a laser spot-welder that could operate at unprecedented speeds.[5]

From high-tech to low-tech environments, commercializing innovative and complex product designs often requires the development and successful implementation of novel process technologies. How quickly and effectively a company can develop and implement such process technologies increasingly shapes the overall cost, timeliness, and results of new product introductions, and the overall competitive success of the company. Process development, then, can be the hidden leverage in product development performance. This book investigates the role of process development capabilities in product development within one industry—pharmaceuticals—and the patterns of organizational behavior and managerial actions that help build such capabilities over time. A central theme is that effective process development capability is rooted in how organizations create, manage, and integrate knowledge.

The Hidden Leverage: An Illustration

Two examples below, drawn from the pharmaceutical industry, illustrate the integral role of process development capabilities in the product development performance of high-tech companies. In many ways, pharmaceuticals is a classic high-tech industry: R&D intensity is high; product development is long, costly, and risky; and profitability depends critically on launching new products in a timely fashion. Given the potentially high profit margins, many people inside and outside the industry believe that manufacturing is not a significant concern.[6] After all, if you discover a pathbreaking drug and can charge a high price for it, why should manufacturing costs be important? The two vignettes below, however, illustrate how process development capabilities can exert a significant influence (either positive or negative) on the competitive fortunes of pharmaceutical companies and firms in other industries like it. In both cases, information has been disguised to protect confidentiality.

AlphaGene

AlphaGene was one of several pioneers in the biotechnology industry. Founded by a world-renowned scientist, the company spent five years conducting research on proteins with potential therapeutic effects. During this period, it discovered a molecule that, after extensive laboratory analysis and animal experiments, looked like a promising treatment for a serious infectious disease. Given the molecule's complexity, developing a manufacturing process capable of making even small quantities of a drug based on it was a major challenge. Over the next eighteen months, an AlphaGene scientist, working in close cooperation with chemical engineers from the company's newly built pilot plant, developed a small-scale process capable of producing enough highly pure material to supply initial clinical trials. As patient enrollment in clinical trials expanded and demand for the drug escalated, process developers implemented a new version of the process at a tenfold increase in scale.

It was at this point, about two years after the start of clinical trials, that the program began to bog down. Initial clinical results on the drug were not promising, and there was serious discussion of killing the project completely. Given the uncertainty surrounding the project, all work on process development ceased, and personnel were transferred to another project with more pressing needs. When preliminary tests suggested that the drug might be effective against a certain type of cancer, however, clinical trials were reinitiated. A multiyear, large-scale (Phase III) trial was undertaken which would ultimately lead to the drug's approval.

During this Phase III trial, however, no additional process development work was conducted. As one scientist on the project explained, "After all the trouble with clinical trials early on, and the uncertainty over whether a product would ever be approved, senior management was very hesitant to invest in additional process development or manufacturing capacity. Another of our products was coming to market, and it was much more pressing for us to get the process scaled up for it." After four years of clinical tests, the data looked favorable enough to file an application with the Food and Drug Administration (FDA) to market the drug commercially.

By most accounts, this should be considered a highly successful project; very few drugs make it to the FDA review phase. At this point, however, the company discovered that it would face a serious capacity shortfall with the current low-yielding process. As one process developer explained it, "The process was only intended to meet the needs of clinical trials. The yields and throughput were way too low to supply the market." The company began a crash effort to improve yields and capacity in time for commercial launch. Unfortunately, process developers had little latitude to change the process, because FDA guidelines required that the process used to conduct clinical trials be representative of the process used to supply the market. Any significant changes would require costly and time-consuming trials to demonstrate equivalency. The company had no choice but to go to market with its existing process. As a result, it could not meet initial demand without major investments in new capacity—a task that took nearly two years to complete and drained a significant share of the cash flow from sales of the drug. Even worse, AlphaGene lost its opportunity to penetrate the market while it had an exclusive position.

BetaGene

Like AlphaGene, BetaGene was a pioneer in the biotechnology industry and had spent several years trying to discover therapeutically active proteins. One of its first development projects was a new drug to treat a life-threatening infection. BetaGene, however, was not alone. Several other companies had cloned the same molecule within weeks, and because the patent status was uncertain, all were racing to start clinical trials. As is often the case in biotechnology projects, the lead time for developing a pilot manufacturing process was on the critical path for starting clinical trials. Adding to the pressure in this case was the molecule's enormous complexity. Because conventional process techniques yielded a biologically inactive molecule, the company's scientists had to invent an entirely new approach to manufacturing proteins on a large scale. One scientist noted, "At the time, many people thought our proposed approach was scientifically impossible."

In order to start clinical trials as quickly as possible, BetaGene focused on developing a simple small-scale process that would meet all FDA quality requirements and make enough product to satisfy initial clinical demands. It was suspected from the beginning that this process might be unsuitable for very large-scale manufacturing; thus the process development group continued to explore alternative approaches in parallel. As clinical trials progressed, it became apparent that the drug was effective, but only at much higher doses than originally expected. This meant that the final phase of clinical trials and future commercial requirements (if the drug were approved) would require much greater volumes of the molecule than could feasibly be produced with the first-generation process.

Fortunately, because the company had continued to work on alternative versions of the process during initial trials, it had a prototype high-volume process ready and was able to commence the final phase of clinical testing without delay. Additional work over a three-month period led to a two-fold increase in yields. One year later, clinical trials ended, and the company filed an application with the FDA for commercial marketing. By this time, BetaGene's lead over its nearest rival—which at the outset of the project had been two weeks—had grown to two years. The company's ability to rapidly develop and scale up its manufacturing process played a critical role in enabling its rapid completion of the project. Once approval came, the company had no trouble meeting demand (which escalated rapidly in the first several years). Perhaps more importantly, the technical and organizational capabilities built during this project provided a foundation for a stream of future product development projects.

The examples of AlphaGene and BetaGene illustrate the strategic role that superior process development capabilities can play in an emerging technology. In neither case were manufacturing costs a major issue. Instead, process development capabilities were required to solve extremely difficult manufacturing problems. Each company had very capable scientists, but senior management took different perspectives on the role of process development. The cases of AlphaGene and BetaGene also illustrate a tension within many firms. At a time when new product development has become critical to success in a multitude of industries, and as such has received significant managerial attention, strong process capabilities have come to play an even greater strategic role than in the past.

The Role of Process Development in Context

To understand the strategic role of the process development capability, it is crucial to explore and establish its context—from roots in the product life cycle model to a more expanded view of its interaction with product innovation in various industries.

The Product Life Cycle Model

The idea that process development becomes increasingly important as industries mature dates back almost twenty years to the work of Abernathy and Utterback (1978), who developed the product life cycle model of innovation (see figure 1.1).[7] Their model posited that, in the earliest phases of an industry's life, when basic product concepts are still being formed, the rate of product innovation will exceed the rate of process innovation. Once producers and consumers have gained enough experience with alternative versions of the product, a "dominant design" will emerge (such as the piston, gasoline-powered, steel-body automobile), and opportunities for radical product innovation will begin to recede. At this point, competitors will shift to producing similar designs at lower cost, and firms will focus on process innovation. Thus, according to the product life cycle model, process innovation becomes important only later in the life of an industry.

The product life cycle model provides compelling logic that helps explain patterns of innovation in several industries (Utterback 1994). It also draws attention to the critical competitive impact of the emergence of dominant designs and has provided insight into why established firms tend to experience difficulties adopting radical innovations.[8] Yet the experiences of AlphaGene and BetaGene highlight three critical assumptions of the model which may not always apply. First, the model focuses on cost reduction as the primary benefit of process innovation. It holds that firms have an incentive to develop new

FIGURE 1.1 The Product Cycle Model of Innovation

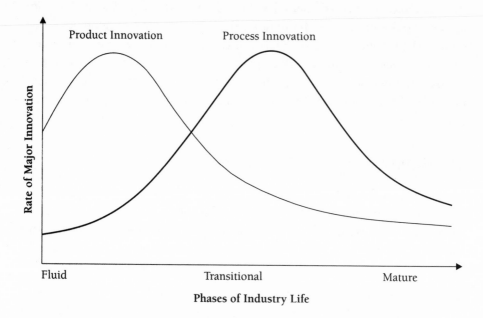

Source: William J. Abernathy and James M. Utterback, "Patterns of Industrial Innovation,"
Technology Review 80, no. 7 (June–July 1978). Reprinted with permission from
Technology Review, copyright 1978.

processes only in the intermediate phases of an industry's life, when opportunities for product innovation have been depleted and production volumes are sufficiently high, and are hesitant to invest in specialized process technology until the product design is stable. However, other potential advantages illustrated in the AlphaGene and BetaGene cases, such as time to market and production ramp-up, are ignored. Second, lurking beneath the product life cycle model is an assumption that the organizational competencies required for product innovation are fundamentally different from—and at odds with—those competencies required for process innovation. Abernathy, in *The Productivity Dilemma,* notes:

> Special, but different, conditions are required for steady cumulative progress in high-volume established products, and production processes: to reduce costs, improve productivity, perfect product features, and assure quality. These capabilities are found in a productive unit's more advanced stage of development. They are much different from those needed to achieve a high rate of major product innovation.[9]

Yet in the case of BetaGene, strong product and process R&D capabilities not only coexisted peacefully, they actually complemented one another. Beta's continued success with new product introduction and the strength of its process development capabilities provide a strong counterexample to the notion that product and process capabilities are mutually exclusive. Finally, the product life cycle model assumes that specialized process innovation is not needed to enable product innovation. Indeed, if anything, investment in specialized process technologies is viewed as a potential hindrance to further product innovation (as firms become hesitant to introduce new products that make existing process technologies obsolete) and thus needs to be avoided early on. In the context in which AlphaGene and BetaGene operated, this was clearly not the case. The products could not have been commercialized without breakthroughs in process technology.

The AlphaGene and BetaGene examples suggest the need for an expanded view of the role of process development—one that recognizes how process development capabilities can be valuable outside the confines of mature, cost-driven industries and can proactively contribute to, rather than conflict with, an organization's ability to compete on the basis of product innovation. They also suggest that the challenges and opportunities run deeper than ensuring compatibility of product and process design, or achieving manufacturability. Process development represents a technically difficult and organizationally complex undertaking in its own right.

Mapping the Context

Figure 1.2 provides a matrix in which to consider the role of process development in different industries. The upper left-hand corner ("Process Driven") encompasses traditional mature industries, such as commodity chemicals, steel, and paper. In these sectors, there is relatively little product innovation, but relatively intense process innovation focused on producing existing products at lower costs. The lower right-hand corner ("Product Driven") captures industries in which product innovation is rampant but process technologies are relatively stable. Many assembled goods fall into this category; perhaps the most extreme example is software, in which the development of physical transformation processes is virtually nonexistent. In this quadrant, the critical challenge for manufacturing process technology is ensuring that product designs are compatible with existing process capabilities. Design-for-manufacturing principles and methods are well suited to these situations.[10] These two quadrants of the matrix represent the perspective of the product life cycle

FIGURE 1.2   Relationships between Product and Process Innovation

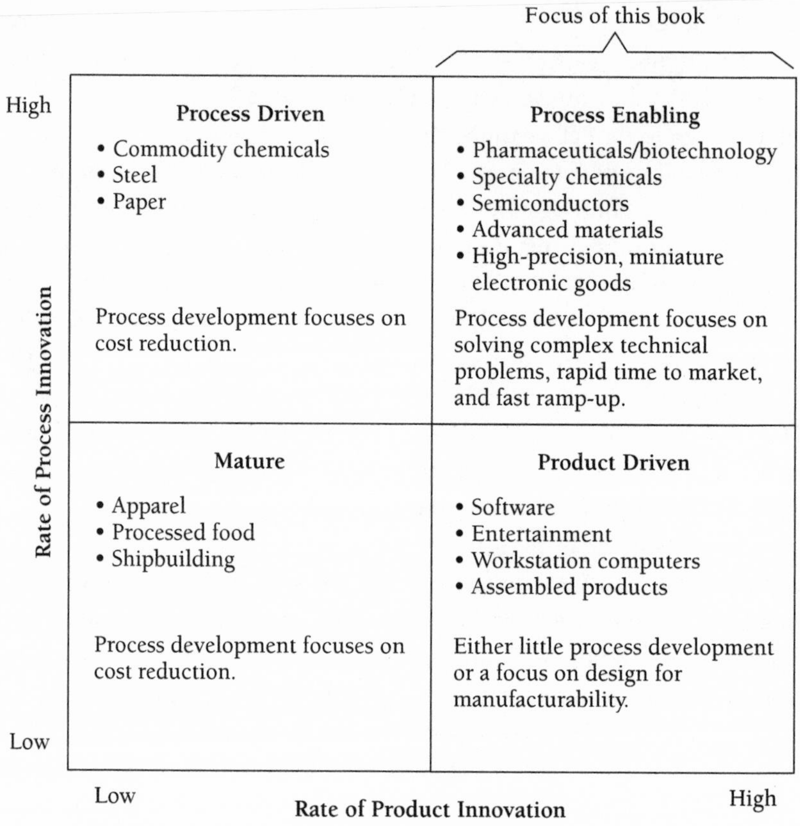

Focus of this book

	Process Driven	**Process Enabling**
High	• Commodity chemicals • Steel • Paper	• Pharmaceuticals/biotechnology • Specialty chemicals • Semiconductors • Advanced materials • High-precision, miniature electronic goods
	Process development focuses on cost reduction.	Process development focuses on solving complex technical problems, rapid time to market, and fast ramp-up.
	Mature	**Product Driven**
	• Apparel • Processed food • Shipbuilding	• Software • Entertainment • Workstation computers • Assembled products
Low	Process development focuses on cost reduction.	Either little process development or a focus on design for manufacturability.

Rate of Process Innovation (vertical axis)

Low   **Rate of Product Innovation**   **High**

model, with "product-driven" industries in the emerging or fluid phases and "process-driven" industries in the post-dominant design phase.

The upper right-hand corner ("Process Enabling") encompasses industries such as pharmaceuticals, specialty chemicals, semiconductors, and advanced materials, where both product and process technologies not only evolve rapidly, but also must be well synchronized. Even in some assembled products, the connection between product and process may be tighter than is assumed by the product life cycle model. For example, producing miniaturized product designs in medical devices, instrumentation, and consumer electronics often requires the development of extremely high-precision processes.[11] It is in this quadrant that the capability for fast, efficient, and high-quality process development has a direct impact on the commercial success of new product introductions. Product and process capabilities, far from being at odds with one another, are mutually dependent. The capabilities required for high-performance process development in this quadrant are the main focus of this book.

Leveraging Process Development Capabilities

Although superior process development can reduce manufacturing costs, in itself an important dimension of competition, the power of process development more often lies in how it helps companies achieve accelerated time to market, rapid production ramp-up, enhanced customer acceptance of new products, and a stronger proprietary position.

Accelerated Time to Market

Perhaps no issue has drawn more attention in both the academic literature and the popular business press in recent years than the strategic value of getting new products to market faster.[12] The benefits of reducing development lead times are well known. In some contexts, even short delays in product introduction can be deadly if first movers have been able to gain a stronghold in the market. In an attempt to shorten lead times, many companies have adopted simultaneous engineering approaches and overlapping product and process design cycles. There is compelling evidence that, if managed properly, simultaneous product and process design offers significantly shorter development lead times than a purely sequential approach.[13] However less attention is generally given to reducing the time required for *process* development, despite the fact that decreasing process development lead times may translate into shorter overall product development lead times. Even with significantly overlapping product and process design, process development can remain on the critical path for product launch. This is particularly true where process technologies are relatively complex and need to be customized to product designs. In these contexts, further shortening of product development lead times hinges directly on the capability of rapid process development.

Moreover, companies usually find that successfully undertaking product and process design in parallel requires a far more responsive process development capability than was necessary under the traditional sequential approach. With sequential product and process design, process developers begin their task with relatively complete knowledge of product specifications. Although they face intense time pressures, they also have the luxury of working around a relatively fixed set of product specifications. Under simultaneous engineering, process developers must be able to respond quickly to an almost-continuous flow of information about evolving product specifications.[14]

Process development may also influence total product development lead time in more subtle ways. For example, in contexts such as those for pharmaceuticals, semiconductors, and automobiles, some process development must occur so that functional prototypes or representative product samples can be fabricated. Slow process development at this stage can lead to long lead times for development of prototypes, which can in turn delay an entire project. Similarly, a process technology incapable of producing sufficient quantities of test materials can severely restrict a company's ability to conduct needed tests. Even worse, where problems in process technology result in low- or variable-quality prototypes, test results may be inaccurate or unreliable. This is a particularly important issue in industries, such as pharmaceuticals and certain specialty chemicals, where relatively large volumes of test batches must be manufactured to allow for thorough product evaluation by future customers, users, or regulatory agencies.

Another strategic advantage for the company with rapid process development capabilities is that it can afford to wait longer before starting process development, without delaying the product's launch. In essence, fast process development makes it less imperative for an organization to adopt simultaneous engineering. In environments where commercial success is far from guaranteed and complete technical failure is a serious possibility, the ability to carry out development more sequentially, without extending the new product introduction date, can offer a company security against the financial risks of development. Drug companies, for example, know this well: only a tiny fraction of newly discovered molecular entities ever reach market. By holding off on process development and engineering until late in the development cycle, a firm may reduce the risk of investing resources in a project that may be terminated or of making commitments to process technologies that may be made obsolete by unanticipated product design changes. But to be able to afford to wait, the company must have fast cycle process R&D capabilities.

Rapid Ramp-up

When a new product is first manufactured, it may take days, weeks, or even months before productivity, capacity, quality, and yields reach what might be considered normal long-term levels. This period is generally known as "ramp-up." In the automobile industry, for example, it may be six months or more before a factory produces a new model at full-scale production volumes. In semiconductors, initial manufacturing yields for new devices may be less than 5 percent but climb to 80 percent within several months (Hatch and Mowery 1994). Ramp-up occurs for two reasons. First, as operators become familiar with a process, they become more effective at carrying out necessary production tasks. Second, it is during this initial period of production that many process problems are identified and fixed. As discussed in more depth later, effective and thorough process development before commercial launch can contribute significantly to a smooth and rapid ramp-up.

Rapid and effective ramp-up is valuable for three reasons. First, the faster a firm can expand production capacity (without adding new capital), the faster it can generate sales revenues and recoup development investments. This clearly has implications for the numerator of return on net assets (RONA). Quick ramp-up can also enhance RONA by reducing the size of the denominator. Typically, capital expenditures for manufacturing a new product are determined by a combination of the process's productivity (output per unit of capital) and estimated demand. For any given forecast of demand, higher productivity requires lower investment in capital. All else being equal, a firm with the capability to increase yields or productivity quickly will need to invest less capital in manufacturing capacity than will a firm with a more gradual ramp-up.

Beyond these financial reasons, however, rapid ramp-up can play a critical strategic role. The faster and more effectively a firm can ramp up production, the faster it can penetrate the market, gain broad acceptance of its product, and begin to accumulate high-volume production experience that may lead to lower future production costs. There are many examples of companies that have been first to market with innovative product designs, but for which problematic ramp-ups led to poor quality and severe product shortages, which in turn opened the door to competitors. Flaherty (1992) has shown that one key to Japanese companies' success in DRAM semiconductors was their ability to ramp up new processes to full production volumes more quickly than their U.S. counterparts. Similarly, Plus Development was able to capture and hold 65 percent of the market for "plug-in" hard disk drives, despite the entry of dozens of competitors. Because Plus and its manufacturing joint venture partner focused on designing the product and process for quick ramp-up and reliable production, Plus was able to reach factory yields of over 99 percent within three months of starting commercial production (compared to an industry norm of about six months) and to achieve much higher levels of reliability than its competitors. Fast ramp-up not only gave Plus the ability to penetrate the market more deeply than its competition, it also proved critical in building the company's reputation for reliable delivery and products.

Enhanced Customer Acceptance

Most consumers, unless they are production/operations management buffs, are not concerned with the details of the process used to make a product. Prospective car buyers, for example, generally want to learn about the engine, the size of the trunk, and how well the car rides; beyond the location of production, they probably do not care at all about the nature of the production control system (JIT versus MRP), whether the company uses empowered cross-functional teams, or which software was used in the factory's programmable logic controllers. Yet, in many contexts, the product features they do care about (such as size, weight, reliability, and environmental impact) are directly affected by the specifics of the production process. The Kodak FunSaver, a single-use disposable camera, is an excellent example. To appeal to environmentally conscious consumers, Kodak integrated recycling into its main production process for the FunSaver.

In some cases, a strong process development capability will allow an organization to fundamentally alter its basic product concept. In 1988 Johnson & Johnson's Vistakon division introduced the first disposable contact lens—the Acuvue.[15] Although the concept of a disposable lens was novel, the product design was not. The Acuvue was fabricated from the same basic type of polymer used for other soft lenses, and although the lens was thinner (to permit greater oxygen transmissibility to the eye), its basic design was similar to that of existing lenses. What was novel was its manufacturing process. To make the concept of weekly disposability a reality, Vistakon developed (over a five-year period) a process technology that reduced manufacturing costs by an order of magnitude and dramatically tightened tolerances. Thus, the lenses could be sold profitably at a price that permitted weekly disposal, and consistency was high enough that users did not perceive differences in fit or corrective power from one week to the next. Rapid production ramp-up allowed Vistakon to market Acuvue nationally within just a few months. Although major competitors soon introduced their own disposable lenses, it took them from six months to one year to ramp up production and begin national marketing, and Vistakon was able to maintain its lead in the disposable market. Within three years of its introduction, Acuvue had achieved worldwide sales of more than $225 million (compared to Vistakon's total sales of $20 million before introducing this product), captured approximately 25 percent of the

U.S. market for contact lenses, and catapulted Vistakon into a leading position in the contact lens industry.

Stronger Proprietary Position

Great new products are a two-edged sword. On the one hand, they attract buyers willing to pay premium prices, generate profits, and make a company the envy of all its competitors. On the other, the better and more successful the product, the more competitors will strive to imitate it. And imitators can be swift and ruthless. EMI, for example, invented the diagnostic imaging technology known as CAT scanning but was knocked out of the market within years by established imaging companies. Bowmar may have invented the calculator, but it was Texas Instruments, Hewlett Packard, and (later) Sharp that came to dominate the business. Survey data from Levin et al. (1987) suggest that only in industries such as chemicals and pharmaceuticals do product patents play any significant role in protecting intellectual property. Even where patents do provide protection, long lead times between the discovery of the patentable technology and its commercialization may mean that patent protection expires relatively early in (or even before the start of) the product's commercial life.

Innovative process technologies are one way for organizations to extend the proprietary position of a product. Would-be imitators might be able to reverse-engineer a product but can still be blocked from entry if they cannot determine how to manufacture the product at competitive cost and quality levels. In some sense, product designs that are inherently difficult to manufacture create opportunities to use manufacturing as a barrier to imitation. The Gillette Sensor mentioned earlier is an excellent example. The Sensor has proven to be one of the most successful products in Gillette's history and a major driver of its earnings growth in recent years. Yet despite licensing of the Sensor's *product* patents, no generic versions of the Sensor have reached the market. The complex manufacturing process (which was not shared with others) has proven a major barrier to entry.

Driving Forces behind Process Development's Strategic Value

The above discussion suggests that process development capabilities create competitive leverage that extends well beyond the confines of mature, highly cost-competitive industries. A company with the ability to develop and implement new process technologies quickly and effectively is in a position to beat competitors to market with new products, sustain lower development risks, achieve rapid product market penetration, offer more innovative and attractive product designs, and protect its position from would-be imitators. These benefits have always existed, but a number of relatively recent technological and competitive forces are shifting the nature of competition in high-tech industries and in turn elevating the strategic value of process development capabilities (see Table 1.1).

Growing Technological Parity

During the 1960s, many U.S. high-tech firms were able to dominate world markets solely on the basis of their technological prowess. By virtually any indicator—including patents, relative R&D spending, share of innovations, sources of pioneering inventions, and number of scientists employed—U.S. high-tech industries held a commanding lead. Indeed, some European observers worried that the U.S. lead posed a serious long-term threat to the economic well-being of Europe.[16] By the 1980s the picture had changed dramatically. Major technology gaps, between the United States and Japan in particular, had closed substantially. For instance, the share of U.S. patents granted to non-U.S. companies rose from approximately 38 percent in 1978 to 47 percent in 1991. More noteworthy, perhaps, was the increase in patent share of Japanese companies from 11 percent in 1978 to 22 percent in 1991.[17] In several areas, U.S. companies found themselves at a technological disadvantage compared to their Japanese or European competitors.[18] One study found, for example, that by 1986 Japan had a technological lead in seven major areas critical to electronics and optics.[19] Today, even newly industrialized countries such as Singapore and Taiwan are home to world-class R&D facilities in electronics.

As technological capabilities diffuse globally, geographic origin may no longer be a significant barrier to accessing basic technology. Larger firms can locate their R&D facilities to tap local technological expertise in other areas. Japanese electronics firms have R&D facilities in Silicon Valley, and U.S. electronics firms have established design centers in Japan. European pharmaceutical companies undertake a significant share of their R&D in the United States. American automobile companies have design studios in Europe. Further, when firms cannot physically invest in new facilities, they can form collaborative relationships with firms or universities around the world.[20]

Table 1.1 Process Development Capabilities: Driving Forces and Competitive Implications

	Driving Forces		
	Growing Technological Parity	Product Complexity	Shorter Product Life Cycles
Competitive Implications	Difficult to sustain advantage on product functionality or performance alone	Costly/uncertain development	Rapid obsolescence of physical and intellectual capital
Source of Advantage	First to market; rapid market penetration; barrier to imitation/entry	Sophisticated technical problem-solving capabilities; capability to push the envelope of both product and process technology	Short development lead time; rapid market penetration; lower fixed development and manufacturing costs
Potential Strategic Contribution of Process Development Capabilities	Rapid process development increases time to market; fast manufacturing ramp-up supports market penetration; process technology enhances customer acceptance; proprietary process technology used as barrier to imitation	Rapid process development reduces risk and complexity of development by allowing later start; strong problem-solving capabilities provide technical degrees of freedom for product design	Rapid process development facilitates quick time to market; rapid manufacturing ramp-up supports market penetration; efficient process development increases returns to R&D; development of processes that economize on capital expenditures increase return on net assets (RONA)

Paralleling this trend in parity across countries is the growing parity of technological competencies within industries. With the exception of personal computers, where Intel and Microsoft thus far have been able to set the agenda, there are relatively few instances in high-tech industries of firms' having a monopoly on technological competence. Broad access to basic technological know-how, a highly mobile scientific and engineering workforce, and relatively weak intellectual property protections in many industries are some of the factors leading to rapid diffusion of technological know-how and competencies across firms within the United States. Growing parity in basic design capabilities among competitors makes it difficult to sustain an advantage on the basis of performance and functionality alone. Although these attributes continue to be critical (and in some cases paramount in the eyes of customers), technological parity elevates the importance of time to market, rapid ramp-up, and a proprietary process position.

Product Complexity

To gain a slim edge in product performance or functionality, firms must increasingly work at the frontiers of technology and, in industries such as biotechnology or advanced materials, at the frontiers of science. It was once thought that a key to successful product development was to separate invention from development; that is, a firm should use only proven technologies in developing new products. Unfortunately, in rapidly changing technical environments, such as high-performance workstations, flat-panel displays, and semiconductors, such a conservative approach is not possible. Firms find themselves pushing the envelope of technology within each product development project. For some types of technologies, this creates significant challenges and uncertainty for process development and manufacturing. For example, in flat-panel displays (the type used on notebook computers), size increases, improvements in clarity, and the addition of color—all critical product characteristics in the eyes of customers—have required companies to push the envelope of semiconductor process knowledge and process control. In such environments, practices such as design for manufacturability simply are not practical. The product technology, by its very nature, is difficult to manufacture. Although an organization might find ways to avoid unnecessary complexity in the process, organizations with strong process development and manufacturing capabilities will have more degrees of freedom in developing products than those organizations forced to stick with a more manufacturable design.

Shorter Product Life Cycles

Intense competition in product development and technological change lead to shorter product life cycles. Although managers in high-tech companies are keenly aware of this trend, its implications for process development are less well understood. Indeed, many companies view short product life cycles as a primary reason to eschew manufacturing. Yet, in many ways, shorter product life cycles are elevating the importance of strong process development capabilities. For example, short product life cycles raise the stakes for quick time to market and rapid ramp-up. In markets such as DRAMS, being slightly late to market or slow to ramp up is tantamount to death. In addition, because firms have less time to recoup investments in fixed manufacturing assets (before those assets are made obsolete), developing processes that have high capital productivity at the start of commercial production are imperative. Semiconductor fabrication facilities incur weekly depreciation costs running into the millions of dollars. This is one reason why yield improvement and rapid ramp-up play such a critical role in semiconductor manufacturing. In these contexts, the strategy of commencing commercial production with poorly developed or unstable processes and improving over time is too costly. Long before the plant gets to the bottom of the learning curve, the technology may be obsolete and the firm may find itself at the top of a new learning curve. In environments with short product development life cycles, the capability to develop highly efficient processes before launch is a strategic imperative.

The Research

This book is based on a multiyear research project on process development strategies, capabilities, and performance in the pharmaceutical industry. The study focused on three questions which now constitute the central themes explored here. The first question concerns the strategic value of strong process development capabilities. As discussed above, the prevailing wisdom holds that, where new product introductions are the name of the game, process development and manufacturing competence are of secondary importance. Because pharmaceuticals compete largely on the basis of product innovation, we can explore in detail whether this is a valid assumption or whether there is hidden leverage in process development and manufacturing competencies.

The second question concerns the management practices, organizational approaches, and strategies that underpin superior process development capabilities. The analysis focuses largely on three aspects of process development performance: lead time (calendar months to complete projects), development costs (scientific and engineering person-hours needed to complete the project), and development process quality. The study explored such potential determinants of process development performance as organizational structure, the timing of technology transfer into the manufacturing setting, manufacturing's involvement in the process development cycle, the role of process research laboratories, and the nature and timing of investments in process development.

The third issue explored in this book relates to organizational learning. Many researchers now agree that an organization's unique capabilities are embedded in the myriad organizational and business processes used to control everything from research, product development, and manufacturing to customer service, distribution, and logistics. The notion that firms are essentially vast reservoirs of processes underlies much of the thinking in evolutionary theories of economics (Nelson and Winter 1982) and capabilities-based views of strategy (Teece and Pisano 1994), as well as practices associated with such popular movements as total quality management (TQM) and business process reengineering. From this perspective, production processes of the type examined in this study are but part of a larger class of organizational processes. Studying their development opens a window on this more general phenomenon and sheds light on questions of central importance to both academics and practitioners; namely, how do organizations learn?

Pharmaceuticals as a Research Context

A firm's technical and organizational capabilities are rooted in how things get done. To understand them, one must study in great depth how problems are framed and solved, how information is transferred and processed, and how knowledge is integrated across people, functions, places, and time. The need for such depth dictated a focus on a single industry, rather than a cross-industry study. Although several industries might have made excellent research venues, this study draws on the pharmaceutical industry.

The pharmaceutical industry provides a useful and interesting context for several reasons. First, the pharmaceutical industry—which includes classic synthetic chemical drugs, as well as new genetically engineered products—is important in its own right. It has been a major employer and contributor to economic growth in the United States and Europe. In addition, since the invention of aspirin in the late nineteenth century, it has had a major impact on public health. New product development continues to be central to competition in the industry. How process technology interacts with and affects product development performance clearly has implications for the industry and for public health.

Second, the pharmaceutical industry is in the midst of major structural upheaval. The growing role of managed care networks as buyers of drugs, intensifying competition from new biotechnology entrants and generic manufacturers, and the shadow of potential government reform in health care provision have profound implications for the costs of developing and manufacturing new therapeutic entities, and thus for approaches to process development. Pharmaceutical companies, however, must cope with more than just economic change. During the past fifteen years, they have seen the scientific and technical foundations of the industry begin to shift in the wake of advances in molecular biology, biochemistry, and medicinal sciences. The industry's economic structure is changing at the very same time that its scientific and technical foundations are shifting. As they seek to cope with the dual forces of economic and technical change, pharmaceutical companies are searching for and attempting to develop the organizational capabilities necessary in an environment that offers growing opportunities while demanding increasing cost discipline. The study of process development in these firms, at this point in time, is a window on how organizations cope with dramatic environmental changes.

Third, the pharmaceutical industry offers a rich diversity of firms. It comprises some of the largest and oldest industrial enterprises in the world, as well as some of the smallest and fastest-growing entrepreneurial startup companies.[21] Such diversity provides an almost-unparalleled opportunity to glean insights about the impact of different organizational forms, approaches, and management practices on performance.

Finally, although the pharmaceutical industry has certain unique features, such as the regulatory environment, it also shares many characteristics with other technology-intensive industries. As in a high-tech industry such as semiconductors, the development of a process for a new molecular entity is both technically and organizationally complex. Process development in this context must deal simultaneously with the uncertainty surrounding the eventual commercialization of the product and the technical uncertainty surrounding the choice of process technology itself. In addition, because successful process development in pharmaceuticals requires an organization to couple the worlds of leading-edge science with the realities of plant operations, it reflects the special challenges of managing development in science-based industries in general.[22]

Data Collection

Data for this research project were drawn from a number of sources. Although publicly available data often are helpful for analyzing industry trends in competition and technology, answering the main questions of interest here required far more depth than such information could provide. Carrying out research on capabilities requires detailed investigation of internal processes and organizational routines at the level of individual development projects. Central to such an inquiry are "blow-by-blow" data on the problems, solutions, events, and, perhaps most importantly, management decisions shaping outcomes. At the same time, to be able to identify patterns of behavior, actions, and strategies that might underlie superior performance, enough projects needed to be studied to permit the use of statistical methods. Thus, over a period of three years, systematic data were collected on twenty-three process development projects. All the projects were associated with the development of a new process technology required to manufacture a new molecular entity. Thirteen of the projects involved the development of traditional chemical processes, whereas ten involved processes based on biotechnology. A total of eleven organizations participated in the study: five established drug companies, five new biotechnology companies, and one biotechnology division of a major pharmaceutical firm.

Two additional criteria were used to select projects for the sample. Process development had to have been completed through successful transfer to the plant (all took place between 1980 and 1994), and the company had to agree to provide access to data on the project's history and performance, as well as to the personnel involved.[23] Relying on in-depth interviews with project participants, questionnaires, and proprietary company documents, data were collected on the history and timing of critical project events, on resources expended, and on the approaches used to identify and solve problems. To ensure accuracy and consistency, data on each project were checked and cross-checked with multiple sources within the company. When discrepancies were found, these were brought to the attention of the company, and further data were collected to resolve them. During the course of this project, approximately 200 people were interviewed from participating R&D sites and manufacturing plants in the United States and Europe.

The cost of data collection, in terms of time and resources, is one reason for the relatively small sample size. A second factor limiting the sample size was the population of potential projects to study. Each process development project in the sample was associated with the development of a new molecular entity. The largest and most productive firms rarely launch more than one new molecular entity in any given year, and many companies have gone several years without launching any. The situation for biotechnology-based drugs, an emerging area in pharmaceuticals, is even more constrained. Since 1982 only about twenty-five biotechnology-based drugs have been developed and approved. Thus, although the sample size is relatively small, it represents a nontrivial share of the total number of projects completed by pharmaceutical companies during the time frame of the study. The small sample size obviously involves trade-offs. On the one hand, a small sample constrains statistical analysis, particularly if one is interested in classic hypothesis testing. On the other, it permits a deep examination of individual projects, which in turn provides insights into the development processes, the nature of problem solving, and the appropriate variables and metrics to include in the analysis. In-depth knowledge of each sample point also facilitates analysis and interpretation of the effects of outliers. Given the main purposes of this study, these trade-offs are not a serious problem. The emphasis here is not on classic hypothesis testing; instead, statistical analysis is used as an efficient way to describe patterns and relationships observed in the data. In this mode of inquiry, outlier cases, rather than being statistical nuisances or sources of bias, are rich sources of information to be mined and explored.

Although statistical methods can be a useful way to gain insights about performance, certain types of issues and questions are not well suited to statistical analysis, either because of the nature of the data available or the nature of phenomenon itself. For example, certain types of organizational behaviors and management practices are difficult to measure or categorize. Therefore, statistical analysis was complemented with rich case study explorations of the experiences of particular companies. Although they may lack some of the generalizability of statistical analysis, these case analyses provided important insights into the central questions of the study.

Outline of This Book

The book is organized in ten chapters. Following this Introduction, chapter 2 develops a framework focusing on the learning that takes place during process development and the role of knowledge in shaping strategies for learning. Essentially, this framework suggests that the structure of knowledge influences both the nature of the technical challenge (what must be learned) and the appropriate learning strategy for solving those problems (how this must be learned). Chapter 3 examines the changing nature of the institutional and technological environments in pharmaceuticals and chapter 4, the resulting implications for approaches to process development. Chapter 5 begins an in-depth exploration of the anatomy of product and process development in pharmaceuticals, and of the differences in the knowledge bases underlying classic chemical process technologies and newer biotechnology-based processes. Chapter 6 presents analyses of the practices and approaches supporting rapid and efficient process development. Chapter 7 turns to the issue of quality in the development process. Then chapter 8 looks at organizational learning and how organizations build specialized knowledge bases over time to improve development performance. Through a series of case studies from the biotechnology subsample of the project, the chapter traces the evolution of knowledge at different companies and analyzes the organizational factors that appear to have the greatest influence on organizational learning. Chapter 9 focuses directly on the managerial implications of the findings. A set of case studies— from both within and outside of the pharmaceutical context—is presented and analyzed. Chapter 10 concludes by discussing the broader research implications beyond process development and the managerial implications beyond pharmaceuticals.

CHAPTER 2

A Framework for Process Development

THIS BOOK WILL explore the determinants of process development performance, as well as the impact of superior performance on a firm's competitive position. One challenge of this task is that process development does not occur in isolation. Process development projects, particularly the type examined in this book, take place within the broader context of product development projects. Second, process development is also intertwined with a firm's manufacturing and operations strategies. A company with a single plant located next to its R&D center, for instance, faces a very different set of challenges than one with a number of plants scattered around the globe. Third, a firm's competitive status has a major impact on required process development capabilities. A firm for which producing a commodity product as inexpensively as possible is a chief competitive priority will need different capabilities and pursue different strategies than one with a goal of introducing technically complex and novel product designs as quickly as possible. Finally, process development itself is organizationally complex and spans multiple functions, from research laboratories to pilot plants to full-scale commercial production environments. The people who shape a process technology range from PhD scientists performing laboratory experiments and running esoteric computer simulations to shop-floor production workers who fine-tune equipment settings.

In exploring a topic as complex as this, researchers face two risks. One is to become lost in a morass of details. In this mode, every project, every event, every organization becomes fascinating in its own right. Although each event may offer its own lessons, projects viewed in this way cannot be meaningfully compared. It becomes virtually impossible to identify or verify systematic determinants of performance, and one gets the uneasy feeling that, were a different project, event, or organization highlighted, a new set of conclusions might emerge. The opposite extreme is to peruse the empirical terrain at 30,000 feet, never getting one's hands too dirty with the specifics. Because this approach permits large sampling conducted across a range of contexts, it may have advantages in terms of generalizability or external validity. The risk, however, is that the researcher becomes so far removed from the phenomenon that both theoretically and managerially relevant elements of the institutional and technological context are ignored. The findings themselves, although potentially credible, also create frustration. One gets the sense that the real action is happening beneath the veil of the data presented.

The challenge is to steer a course between these two levels of abstraction: to mine the richness of the details but also to step back and draw inferences about patterns and systematic relationships.[1] To do this, a framework is needed to organize and highlight the important facts, generate hypotheses, delineate causes, identify critical connections between observations, and acknowledge the limits of the findings. This chapter is devoted to developing such a framework. Although it is applied to the pharmaceutical context in subsequent chapters, the framework is sufficiently general to encompass other industries.

To provide a point of reference, this chapter begins with a brief discussion of two bodies of literature related to process development: those surrounding the learning curve and product development. The second section discusses how process development fits into a firm's larger competitive, technological, organizational, and operational environments. The third section then develops a capabilities-based perspective on process development. This framework is based on the notion that process development is a capability-creating activity involving the translation of technical knowledge into operating routines. Intellectual antecedents of this approach include Newell and Simon's (1972) models of human problem solving and learning; Nelson and Winter's (1982) theories of organizational routines; Clark and Fujimoto's (1991) notion of development as simulation of future consumption and production experience; and a broad range of work that takes an information-processing perspective on development (such as Allen 1966).

Conceptual Foundations

The learning curve literature and the product development literature have applications to process development. Although both have their limits in illuminating process development, they help to inform and motivate the framework discussed later.

The Learning Curve

There is voluminous empirical evidence that manufacturing performance improves with cumulative experience.[2] As workers gain knowledge of a process, they become better able to execute tasks. Cumulative production experience also generates data needed for systematic problem identification and problem solving, through methods such as statistical process control, or SPC (Fine 1986). In addition, cumulative experience induces second-order improvements through such actions as product and process engineering design changes, equipment modifications, and worker training (Adler and Clark 1991). Although there are many sources and drivers of learning, all essentially involve eliminating some type of process problem through a change in either procedures, specific process parameters, or equipment (including the introduction of new equipment). An underlying theme in the existing learning literature is that only through time or experience with the requisite volume of data can an organization identify and solve latent problems.[3]

These findings carry two important implications for the management of process technology. First, the research suggests that learning does not take place automatically, but instead results from management actions and practices. Thus, in most manufacturing contexts today, one would expect to find programs (such as TQM, cross-functional teams, and worker suggestion boxes) or tools (such as SPC) aimed at systematically speeding up the rate of learning. The second implication is perhaps more troubling. The assumption that manufacturing performance improvement requires time or actual production experience may downplay the impact of development activities that shape a process *before* it reaches the plant. Interestingly, in virtually all studies of the learning curve, the earliest starting point for tracking process performance is the start of commercial production. Episodes of learning that take place before commercial production begins—the learning that occurs during process design, refinement, and pilot production—are not covered. Thus, although studies like those by Hollander (1965) indicate that incremental refinements in the production

FIGURE 2.1   The Learning Curve from Two Perspectives

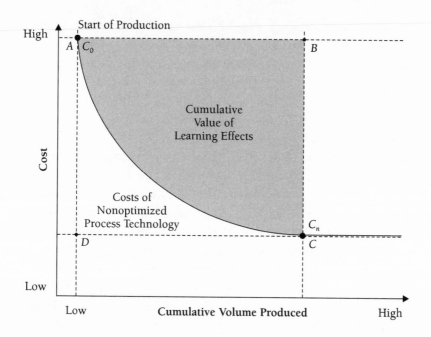

process account for an overwhelming portion of total productivity increases once a plant is built, the data do not shed light on the nature and extent of learning that took place during the plant design and testing phase.

The learning curve framework treats the initial manufacturing performance as given and tends to view performance improvements as unquestionably positive. The framework does not, however, ask the question: What could the initial performance have been with more process development prior to commercial launch? Figure 2.1 shows the contrast in these perspectives. One way to look at a learning curve is to take the initial cost as given, and to consider the benefits that accrue to a firm by reducing costs from C_0 to C_n over a period of time. The cumulative value of this cost reduction is contained in the shaded area ABC. An alternative perspective is to focus on the profits forgone by launching the process with costs at C_0 rather than at C_n. From this perspective, the firm is incurring extra costs of ACD because it has not started production with an "optimized" process. This is a simplistic view, but it raises a number of interesting questions: Could the firm really have launched at the lower cost level? In any given context, how much can a firm expect to reduce its initial production costs through prior process development, and how much improvement must await actual production experience? What would have been the extra development costs of doing so? Would this trade-off of higher development costs versus lower production costs have been worth it? Although these questions are outside the framework of the learning curve, they are probed in more depth later in this book.

Product Development

Research on product development provides a foundation for exploring process development, because development activities—whether aimed at new products or at new processes—share common characteristics. For example, both product and process development are essentially problem-solving activities. Knowledge gleaned in the context of product development can be applied to new processes. Moreover, both types of development require a high degree of cross-functional integration. Knowledge about approaches to integration, from teams to design methodologies, has implications for product and process development. Finally, both product and process development require an ability to probe future user needs.[4] Product designers attempt to understand, anticipate, and simulate how a future customer (whether an individual consumer, industrial user, or organization) will respond to a specific product design (will they like yellow trim, for instance?). Likewise, process designers attempt to understand, anticipate, and simulate how a future process will work in a given organizational context.

Despite the similarities, however, process development involves distinct challenges having to do with the organizational nature of processes. The primary task of product development is to create a detailed characterization of the product and to fully capture information about the design in such media as blueprints, CAD drawings, formulas, specifications, mock-ups, and models. A product design embodies significant information about manufacturing. Indeed, this linkage has become much more explicit with the growing adoption of design-for-manufacturability practices. However, although a well-specified product design might allow a sufficiently skilled person to build a replica of the product, it does not contain explicit instructions for producing large quantities economically. For instance, skilled technicians can construct very accurate prototypes of automobiles using blueprints and CAD drawings, but these may cost up to $1 million each and take several weeks to construct.[5]

Creating and refining an organization's capability to manufacture a product or set of products commercially is the task of process development. It is tempting to think about this capability in terms of the physical artifacts of production (machinery, tooling, buildings, raw materials) and the specific techniques employed (welding, stamping, chemical transformations). Indeed, artifacts and techniques are critical components of any process, and process development must reckon with both. But ultimately production processes involve organizational action. A critical component of process development—one that is often ignored in theory and practice—is the creation and implementation of operating procedures and organizational routines needed to trigger, control, and coordinate the specific set of actions required for production. An illuminating analogy is that of the relationship between computer hardware and software. Just as a computer is completely useless without software, a factory is unable to manufacture products without operating procedures, routines, and instructions.[6] And just as it is difficult to understand the capabilities of a computer without knowing the capabilities of the software, it is difficult to assess the capabilities of a production process strictly in terms of its hardware.

Although product development involves creating new capabilities, these are implemented primarily in the product itself. Unlike products, processes have no life of their own outside an organizational context. The new capabilities created by process development become embedded within the organization. Indeed, process development projects are generally viewed as failures if technical solutions cannot be implemented within the manufacturing organization and do not become part of the normal production routine. The primary task and challenge of process development is to build an organization's capability for production.

Process Development in Context

Many economic models traditionally posit a sharp distinction between *process* innovations (which reduce costs and shift the supply curve) and *product* innovations (which shift the demand curve), viewing process development as an R&D activity unto itself, quite distinct from product R&D. This perspective is quite appropriate for settings in mature industries, where, because of stable product technology, process R&D represents the bulk of total R&D carried out by firms.[7] In such contexts, firms often carry out large-scale process R&D projects unrelated to any change in product technology. Where product and process technology evolve together, however, process development cannot be understood in isolation and must be viewed as part of the total product development process. This fact is clearly recognized in recent product development literature, which has stressed the importance of integrating product and process design through such practices as simultaneous engineering, cross-

FIGURE 2.2 Process Development in Context

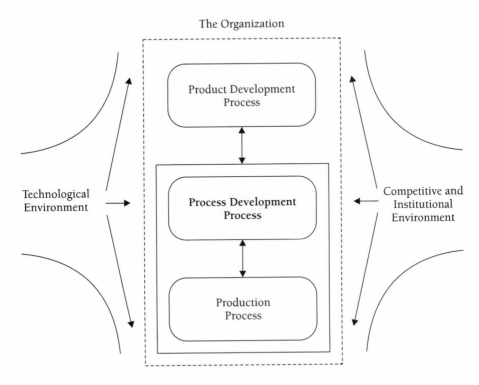

functional project teams, and design for manufacturability.[8] However, much of the focus in this literature has been on *coordinating* product and process design. In the contexts represented in this book, the challenge of process development goes beyond mere alignment with product development (although this is clearly important). Process development is a technically challenging and organizationally complex activity in its own right and operates in a much richer context than is generally portrayed in the simultaneous-engineering literature. Figure 2.2 provides a visual overview of the many internal organizational processes and external forces interacting with process development. Each of these interactions is discussed briefly below.

The Competitive and Institutional Environments

The competitive and institutional environments in which firms operate determine what process development must be able to achieve in terms of speed and efficiency, as well as in performance (in yields, costs, or tolerance). As discussed in chapters 3 and 4, upheaval in the competitive environment has profound implications for process development. Changes in everything from effective patent lives to the systems through which health care is supplied have been fundamentally altering the process development capabilities required to thrive in the pharmaceutical business. And institutional forces—including regulation, controls over intellectual property, financial systems, and political processes—play a central role in shaping competitive outcomes and constraining choices.

The Technological Environment

Available technological knowledge plays a critical role in determining how problems are framed, how potential solutions are generated and tested, and ultimately which solutions are implemented. Technological knowledge includes both "exogenous" public knowledge (such as scientific theories, principles, models, and heuristics) and internal knowledge accumulated through problem-solving experience. The ability to exploit available knowledge and to adapt dynamically to a shifting knowledge base is critical to high performance. Different process development strategies are called for depending on the depth and maturity of technological knowledge available to the organization. A framework for exploring this interaction is developed in the second part of this chapter and is a major theme of chapters 5, 6, and 7.

The Product Development Process

When process development occurs within the context of product development projects, choices of product design and product technology set the technical agenda for process development. A company whose product design strategy emphasizes achieving maximum performance through the use of cutting-edge technology creates technological challenges for process development, which a more conservative strategy would likely avoid. Choices about the product development process also influence the process development cycle from the perspectives of timing of events and information flow. Decisions about the frequency, timing, and goals of prototype tests, for instance, have a direct impact on process development. An organization that wishes to test prototypes built with a highly representative final production process will need to do much more process development up front than will a firm content to use hand-crafted prototypes. In the pharmaceutical industry, clinical trials are a dominant feature of the product development environment, and how trials are conducted has an enormous impact on process development.

It should also be stressed that process development capabilities have the potential to influence the product development process. Returning to our example from Chapter 1, an organization with the capability to rapidly develop a pilot-scale manufacturing process—as did BetaGene—may be in a better position to make larger test batches that are more representative of commercially manufactured product than an organization that can produce only a few laboratory prototypes at an early stage (such as AlphaGene).

The Production Process

The output of an organization's process development effort is a new or improved production process. Process development translates a product design into the technical knowledge, organizational capabilities, and operating processes needed to create the product. Beneath this direct link, however, more subtle interactions influence the effectiveness of process development. For instance, when a new product will be manufactured in an existing plant, new and existing processes must be integrated, and process developers must understand the constraints that existing processes impose on new developments. Process developers also must understand what is operationally feasible and which elements of a process design are hazardous or difficult to carry out consistently. Additionally, the production process itself typically generates new knowledge about the process technology and how it could be improved. In some instances, much of the learning about new process designs comes from cumulative experience with the actual production process. Thus, there are strong feedback loops from the production process to process development.

Although process development must be integrated across all the interfaces just discussed, the linkage with the production process is particularly critical to high performance. The remainder of this chapter develops a framework for exploring this interdependence and the implications for process development strategy.

Process Development: A Capabilities-based Perspective

Figure 2.3 provides a framework for viewing process development, which highlights the multiple avenues through which process capabilities are built,

FIGURE 2.3   A Capabilities-based Perspective on Process Development

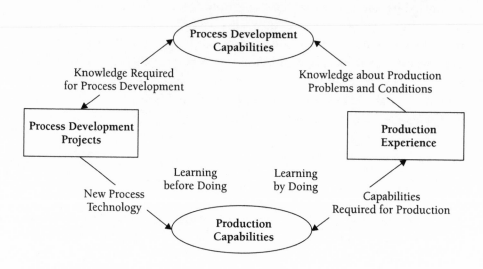

implemented, and evolve over time. It also helps clarify the respective roles of process development and production experience in deepening an organization's capabilities. The lower half of the diagram focuses on two avenues through which production capabilities evolve: process development projects and production experience. In this scheme, process development projects are defined as attempts to create new process architectures, rather than to achieve incremental improvements in an existing technology. Thus a process development project is likely to be associated with the launch of a major new product or the introduction of a next-generation process for an existing product.

Process development focuses on anticipating and attempting to solve problems that might arise in actual production. For example, in specifying the sequence of assembly steps for a new product, process engineers usually model the process to identify bottlenecks. Small-scale pilot runs simulate future production and identify tasks that might be difficult for operators to carry out. Because these problem-solving activities take place before actual production commences, they are referred to as learning *before* doing. Once production starts, additional improvements may occur as operators, technicians, and others become more familiar with the process and with their respective tasks. Production experience also brings about learning by generating data on problems and opportunities for improvement, which can be addressed through changes in the process, the product design, worker skills, or equipment.[9] We refer to these problem-solving activities that take place after production has begun as learning *by* doing.

Just as production performance hinges on the depth of the organization's production capabilities, process development performance rests on the firm's process knowledge base, which provides clues and sometimes answers to problems that arise during a new project. Process engineers who try to specify the design of a piece of production equipment draw from their own and the firm's collective knowledge about what types of design solutions worked well in the past. They may remember (or be reminded by colleagues), for example, that vendor A's design was difficult to operate and broke down frequently during production. The role of process development and production in enhancing this knowledge base is the focus of the upper half of the diagram.

In this framework, each process development project not only creates new production capabilities, but also adds to the firm's stock of knowledge. For example, during a particular project, process engineers might uncover an additional factor affecting process yields. Although this knowledge may be useful for the current project, it may become equally valuable as part of the organization's reservoir of knowledge to be tapped for future projects. It should be stressed that not all of this knowledge need be technical in nature. Projects also generate opportunities to understand and improve the way projects are organized and managed, which further enhances development capabilities.[10]

Figure 2.3 also highlights an interesting symmetry: process development projects and production both have dual roles as users and producers of capabilities. Both process development projects and production create direct feedback through learning-by-doing effects. Production experience augments production capabilities over time; each process development project enhances the firm's process development capabilities. But there are also learning-before-doing effects. Process development projects represent the learning that takes place before the start of commercial production. A successful initial process development project can be thought of as improving the starting point of the learning curve for a new production process. Likewise, prior production experience generates data that contribute to future process development projects—essentially learning that takes place before doing later process development projects.

The framework raises two issues in managing process technology. One concerns the appropriate mode for developing production capabilities. When might a firm want to rely on achieving improvement through production experience, and when would it want to rely more on optimizing the process from the start? On the flip side is a similar set of issues for the evolution of process development capabilities over time. Some organizations might attempt to improve their process development capabilities by making conscious efforts to ensure that lessons from each process development project are incorporated into future efforts. This is learning by doing within process development. Another approach—not necessarily mutually exclusive to the first—is to focus on getting feedback from production back into process development so that developers will become more capable of anticipating process problems. The remainder of the chapter focuses on the first set of issues: improving production capabilities through process development versus doing so through production experience.

Building Production Capabilities: Learning by Doing versus Learning before Doing

Consider the following events, whose analogies routinely take place in virtually every industry:

> A lathe operator on the shop floor of an auto parts manufacturer notices that, in making a certain part, the cutting tool is vibrating slightly and compromising precision. The operator knows from experience that this could be the result of the lathe's excessive speed. In response, the operator gradually reduces the lathe speed until the vibrating stops.

> A PhD chemist in the R&D laboratories of a specialty chemical company runs a series of experiments to investigate the factors affecting production yields of a new polymer. These experiments reveal that, under certain conditions, the reaction takes place most efficiently at 50°. As a result, when the new polymer is put into production, the standard operating procedure specifies that the reaction temperature be set at 50°.

At one level, these two events are worlds apart: they involve very different types of people (operator versus scientist) working in different contexts (shop floor versus laboratory) and using different methods (trial and error versus controlled experiment). Yet, at their roots, both are forms of process development involving problem solving to improve process performance. In fine-tuning the lathe speed for a certain part, the operator has changed the production process for that particular part. In finding the optimal yield, the chemist is helping to write the recipe for a new process. The major difference appears to be in timing. The lathe operator is attempting to improve a current process;

the chemist is seeking to improve a future process. Whereas the operator is engaged in the classic activity of learning by doing highlighted in the learning curve literature, the chemist, in seeking to find a solution to a future process problem, is attempting to learn before doing.

More recent learning curve literature provides a picture of the underlying process by which organizations learn by doing.[11] Learning by doing is largely the result of a series of problem-solving events triggered by either (1) gaps between actual and desired performance or (2) recognition that current performance (even if at desired levels) could be improved. Excluding exogenous factors, such as improvements in the quality of raw materials, components, or equipment supplied by vendors, the downward slope of the learning curve is the result of solving a series of problems. There are two types of problem-solving events. One is a response to problems that were not solved during the development phase (that is, before production started). For example, when a new model of automobile first goes into production, tooling may not be optimized, certain assembly procedures may be awkward to perform, and some parts may be unexpectedly difficult to manufacture at high volume. Debugging, a common problem-solving activity during the initial phases of virtually any production process, can be thought of as mopping up the residual process problems that were not solved during development.

A second class of problem-solving events comes in response to newly discovered opportunities to improve the process. For example, during the development of a particular process, process developers and engineers may have a sense of what the upper bound on performance is. They may believe that a certain type of design can be produced at a minimum of $20 per unit, or that a certain type of molding process will "max out" at 90 percent yields. However, with production experience, data can be generated that suggest alternative methods offering even lower costs.

An interesting example of this phenomenon is McDonald's experience improving its process for making french fries.[12] The basic process is deceptively simple: dip cut potatoes into a vat of hot oil and remove the fries when appropriately crisp. But this process can be very difficult to control, particularly when operated at high volumes. In its early days, McDonald's encountered difficulties with consistency: some batches would be burned while others were undercooked. At first, the company monitored the process in its restaurants and tried to determine the proper temperature and cooking time. In so doing, however, it found that the temperature settings on the fryers had little connection with the temperature of the oil; once cold potatoes were dropped into the oil, the temperature would drop. By sticking temperature sensors on the potatoes and in the vat and charting temperature readings during the cooking process against the quality of fries, McDonald's researchers discovered that the fries would always be perfectly cooked when the oil temperature rose 3° F above the lowest temperature. This led to a new standard operating procedure for cooking fries, as well as a new fryer design. It is unlikely that this opportunity to improve the process could have been discovered without accumulating production experience. This type of problem solving can be viewed as identifying and solving residual opportunities for improvement.

An interesting question is why either problems or opportunities remain unidentified (and thus unsolved) until sufficient production experience has been accumulated. Think about our lathe operator. Why couldn't the production engineers have anticipated the possibility of tool vibration and solved it (through specifying a slower cutting speed) before the operator ever tried the process? Why is actual production experience necessary to identify certain residual problems or opportunities? Recent research on learning by doing, by von Hippel and Tyre (1995), indicates that part of the problem lies in the sheer number of potential factors and interactions that might ultimately affect process performance. As von Hippel and Tyre argue, "The need for learning by doing indicates that the innovation process will often be iterative—and that developers typically *can't* 'get it right the first time.'"[13]

Few people who have studied or been involved in development projects would dispute this claim. Indeed, anyone who has tried to learn a new skill (such as driving a car) would appreciate that practice (driving around in the high school parking lot with an instructor) is no substitute for actually performing the skill repetitively in the actual-use environment (a real road with real Boston drivers). The idea that some forms of learning require doing has important implications for the role of process development in the factory and for how companies manage process technology. It suggests that the appropriate locus of learning production skills is the factory. Some companies have followed this approach successfully. For example, Chaparral Steel, a highly successful minimill known for its innovative steel-making process technology, has no R&D department. According to the company's CEO, Gordon Forward, "Everybody is research and development. The plant is our laboratory" (Leonard-Barton 1992).

Although the notion that you typically cannot get everything right the first time is far from controversial, it does not mean that an organization cannot get many things right before commercial production and marketing begin. Recent empirical studies suggest that some organizations get more things right from the start than others. For example, Clark and Fujimoto's (1991) data from

FIGURE 2.4 Improvement Trajectories

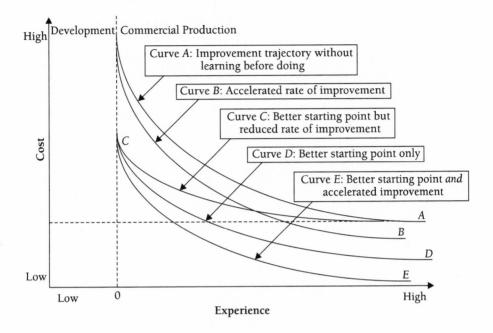

twenty-nine new automobile models reveal wide differences across companies in the number of design problems remaining at different project stages. On average, although the Japanese companies in their sample did not get everything right before market launch, they had a smaller number of remaining design problems at launch than their American counterparts. Similarly, Hatch and Mowery (1994), in a study of semiconductor process performance, found that initial yields for new processes varied significantly across plants.

What organizations learn during the initial development phase clearly has an effect on learning during production. Figure 2.4 depicts the different cost reduction trajectories that might result from process development prior to commercial production. Curve *A* will be our reference point. Assume that it depicts the admittedly extreme case that no process development occurs before the start of commercial production and that all performance improvement occurs as a result of cumulative production experience. Curves *B* through *E* depict how process development might influence the learning curve once commercial production starts. Essentially, process development has two major effects on the learning curve: it can lead to a more cost-effective point and/or it can influence the rate of improvement (steepen the slope of the learning curve).

Curve *B* would result if process development did not lead to a better starting point but did accelerate the rate of improvement once production commenced. Such a trajectory might occur if process development led to a deeper fundamental understanding of the process technology and of critical cause-and-effect relationships. This knowledge could be used to complement problem-solving efforts on the factory floor. Having a better understanding of and control over the key process variables would enhance the productivity of such process improvement tools as statistical process control. This trajectory might also occur if process developers explicitly designed a process with an eye toward enabling future improvements. For example, process designers might initially specify general rather than special-purpose equipment in order to accommodate future process improvements. Similarly, they might specify quality control checks after each stage in the process, so that better future data would be available on the sources of yield losses. At the risk of inventing yet another buzz phrase, this approach might be termed "design for improvability."

Curve C depicts the trajectory of improvement if process development solved problems that otherwise would have to be corrected during production. As a result, the process starts out with better performance, but subsequent improvements are harder to come by. Essentially, all of the "low-hanging fruit" have been picked before the start of production, so that the rate of improvement is slower once commercial production begins. Consider the earlier example of the machine tool operator adjusting the speed of a lathe to reduce tool vibrations. If process engineers had successfully anticipated this problem and specified a slower machine speed, this problem would not have arisen in production. This type of pattern is likely to occur when process development focuses on simulating future production conditions with the aim of identifying and solving potential problems.

In Curve D, process development has the effect of shifting the learning curve downward. As in C, the starting point is better, but in this case, the slope (depicting the rate of improvement) is not affected. Process development will lead to a shift in the learning curve, but will not affect the slope, when it solves problems that could not have been solved simply through the accumulation of production experience. Cumulative production experience generally leads to incremental process changes, such as tweaking reaction conditions, adjusting equipment speeds, modifying tooling and equipment, changing raw material specifications, and refining product designs. These actions generally take place within the confines of a specific technological configuration. Learning by doing does not result in sudden radical changes in the process technology— although the cumulative effects of a series of incremental changes can be quite significant (Hollander 1965). The basic configuration of a process is determined during the process development phase. Where process development leads to better basic technological choices—for example, the use of one type of molding technology which may be superior to another—it can lead to a downward shift in the learning curve. An example of this would be the new molding technology Vistakon used to produce the first disposable contact lens. It was a significant departure from existing technologies (such as lathing) which resulted in dramatically lower manufacturing costs.

Finally, there may be situations in which process development leads to a different basic process architecture, which is both superior to an existing technology at the start and has greater potential for improvement. This is often the case where a process technology based on well-understood scientific principles replaces one that is characteristic of a craft. Because the science-based process can be better controlled, initial performance—in particular, yields—is likely to be better. At the same time, this superior understanding and control over the process provides a foundation for improvement. An example of a case in which the development of a process based on scientific knowledge not only led to initially lower costs, but also triggered more rapid improvement, is the Pilkington float glass process. Initially developed in 1955 and commercially introduced in 1960, the Pilkington process offered more consistent quality and significantly lower manufacturing costs than existing plate glass processes.[14] Initial development of the Pilkington process required extensive trial and error in the factory. But because the Pilkington process was based on deep knowledge of the molecular-level chemical processes that drive glass formation, it was more suitable for systematic improvement (through controlled experiments) than was possible with traditional methods based on mechanical engineering.

The learning curves plotted in figure 2.4 emphasize the various potential benefits of learning before doing. However, all learning—whether accomplished through process R&D in a laboratory or done on the factory floor—is costly. There may be circumstances in which the relative benefits of learning before doing (in terms of either shifting the learning curve down or increasing its slope) are less than the costs of doing process R&D. The converse may also be true: there may be conditions in which the costs of learning by doing are simply too great relative to accomplishing the same amount of learning before the start of commercial production. This raises a question about the appropriate locus of learning: When is it more effective to learn before doing, and when is it more effective to learn by doing? In other words, when is it worth trying to get it right the first time, and when is it worth allowing yourself to get it wrong but improving rapidly through actual manufacturing experience? To get a handle on this issue, a simple model of process development is presented below, focusing on an organization's ability to simulate production experience before the start of commercial production. The framework presented suggests that, when organizations can effectively simulate production experience outside the actual manufacturing environment, process development can result in learning before doing. In contrast, when simulation cannot be accomplished (for reasons discussed below), a better development strategy is to move process technology into the commercial production environment and to learn by doing.

Learning Strategies in Process Development

Despite differences in specific activities, the fundamental challenge of process development is quite similar across industries. The starting point for process development is a description of the product, or a product design. (When process development starts, of course, the description may be incomplete or in a state of flux.) In chemicals, this might be a written description of the molecule, a formula for the set of reactions required to synthesize the molecule, and other data characterizing the molecule. In the model of process development presented here, process developers can be viewed as starting with a set of targets for process performance.[15] These might be framed in terms of unit cost, capacity required, yields, quality levels, critical tolerances, or other operating characteristics. The goal of process development is to find the process parameters (the sequence, timing, and specification of process steps; equipment design and settings; and materials handling procedures) that either optimize performance or achieve a satisfactory target level *when operated under actual production conditions.*[16] In a competitive environment, development goals should include finding this process as quickly and efficiently as possible.

Process development is a technical problem-solving process.[17] Although their activities and nature may vary across contexts, technical problem-solving processes share common characteristics. One is that problem solving is triggered by gaps between desired and actual performance (Newell and Simon 1972, and Iansiti and Clark 1994). As noted above, in the context of process development, this gap can be framed in terms of differences between what existing process technology can achieve (for instance, yields and costs) and what is required to achieve success in the market. The second characteristic of problem solving is that it generally takes place through iterative cycles of search and selection (Frischmuth and Allen 1969, Nelson and Winter 1977, and Nelson 1982). Over a number of cycles, the gap between actual and desired performance becomes progressively narrower, as technical solutions are iden-

FIGURE 2.5 The Locus of Experimentation and Representativeness

Representativeness of Final Production Environment	Locus of Experimentation	Learning Mode
High ↑ ↓ Low	Full-scale commercial factory Pilot plant located at production site Pilot plant located at development site Laboratory Computer-aided simulation Theory, algorithms, heuristics	By Doing ↑ ↓ Before Doing

tified and tested and a subset of solutions is selected. At the heart of this learning process are experiments (both physical and conceptual) that provide feedback about gaps between current and target performance levels.[18] The quality of this feedback plays a critical role in determining development performance.

Experiments can take many forms and be conducted under a variety of conditions. Although the traditional image of an experiment is a laboratory-based analysis of product samples or physical prototypes, advances in technology mean that some product and process designs can be run, tested, and analyzed using computer-aided simulation.[19] Boeing, for example, in developing its most recent generation of wide-body aircraft, the 777, relied heavily on computer-aided design and simulation. Physical experiments can also be conducted in different ways. In process development, some experiments are conducted in laboratories, others are performed in pilot plants, and still others are run in full-scale commercial plants. One way to distinguish between experimental forms is the extent to which they are conducted under conditions representative of the final-use environment (see figure 2.5). An example of an experiment conducted under highly representative conditions would be testing a process technology in a full-scale commercial facility during normal production hours, with regular production operators. At the other end of the representativeness spectrum would be small-scale laboratory tests and computer simulations.

Because experimental conditions affect experimental outcomes, estimates of process performance achieved under laboratory conditions are not always representative of a full-scale run in an actual factory. Most process engineers and manufacturing managers can recount horror stories about the performance of a process dropping precipitously once it was transferred from the laboratory into the factory. Many companies, viewing this as a classic technology transfer problem, respond by instituting new procedures (such as better documentation and cross-functional process startup teams) to ensure that the process technology moves more smoothly from laboratory to factory. Unfortunately, although poor communication between R&D and manufacturing is a common problem, improving it may not address the real issue. Very often, the technology developed and tested in the laboratory is replicated nearly perfectly in the plant. The problem is that specific elements of the plant environment (such as equipment configurations) can cause a deterioration in process performance. This is not a problem of technology *transfer,* but one of technology *development.*

To help the exposition, it is time to introduce some simple notation. Process development can be viewed as the search for the set of process parameters, p^*, that optimize the performance of the process, C, under factory conditions, X_F. Of course, if a developer had complete knowledge of $C(p|X_F)$, there would be no need to experiment to find p^*. In most situations, however, knowledge is incomplete, and experiments must be conducted in order to learn. Laboratory experiments can be viewed as representations of the future commercial manufacturing process. However, although elements of a laboratory experiment may have analogies in the factory—the small glass test tubes represent the stainless steel reaction tanks, the thin glass mixing rods used to stir the reaction simulate the forces of automated steel rotators, and the chemist who sets up and watches over the experiment plays the role of both the future factory operators and the computer-based process control system. Researchers do not actually observe $C(p|X_F)$ under laboratory conditions (X_L); instead, they observe laboratory performance, or what might be called $L(p|X_L)$ (see figure 2.6). (Note that the term *laboratory conditions* is used to encompass a broad range of venues, from computer simulations through pilot-scale production plants.) A major challenge of development is to make predictions about $C(p|X_F)$ based on observations of $L(p|X_L)$.[20]

Learning by Doing versus Learning before Doing. One approach to improving the fidelity of experiments—to reducing the gap between $C(p|X_F)$ and

FIGURE 2.6 A Sample Relationship between Laboratory Data and Production Results

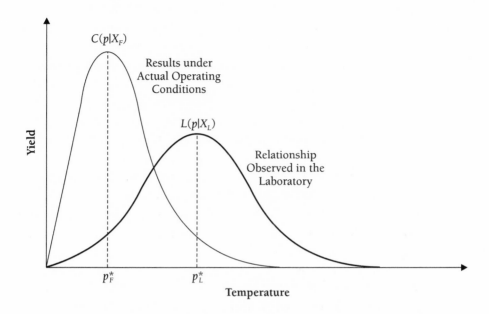

$L(p|X_L)$—is to make test conditions as close as possible to actual operating conditions. At the extreme, test batches might be run in the commercial manufacturing plant rather than in the laboratory or small-scale pilot facility. If all the conditions of the future manufacturing environment are replicated in the test (the same factory, the same equipment, the same workers, the same suppliers, and so forth), X_L should equal X_F, and the test should provide a relatively good indicator of future performance. In reality, given that factory conditions change from day to day or even from minute to minute (people change, equipment wears, humidity fluctuates), it is impossible to exactly replicate future conditions, even in the factory. Nevertheless, the in-factory test should provide the most representative experimental environment. The idea that some things can be learned only by running the process in the factory is consistent with the idea of learning by doing. The power of learning by doing as a problem-solving strategy is that it leads to high-fidelity experimental results. Learning by doing essentially circumvents the problem of predicting $C(p|X_F)$ based on observations of $L(p|X_L)$ by making experimental conditions (X_L) as close as possible to commercial conditions (X_F).

Although learning by doing leads to high-fidelity results, it can be expensive. Direct costs per experiment are typically higher in a factory setting than

in a laboratory setting because of minimum efficient batch sizes and investments in specialized equipment.[21] Factory-based experiments also use manufacturing capacity that might be deployed to make salable product.[22] A higher
cost per experiment means that, for any given number of iterations required
to converge to the desired performance level, an experimental strategy emphasizing in-factory tests will involve higher development costs. In addition,
because factories are complex and sometimes chaotic environments, it can be
difficult to identify and control all the relevant intervening variables. Slight,
but unavoidable batch-to-batch differences in raw materials, equipment, workers, equipment settings, and other process parameters will reduce the signal-
to-noise ratio of factory experiments. Furthermore, in some contexts, extremely costly and delicate high-precision testing equipment that could be used
in laboratory analysis would not be feasible in a production environment.

An alternative and potentially less costly approach is to model future
manufacturing performance using computer simulations, laboratory experiments, or pilot plant tests. These methods can be viewed as attempts to predict
process performance and identify potential problems before the process is
transferred to the factory. Thus, for instance, a process that fails completely in
a test tube will probably not work in the factory either. More subtly, researchers
might be able to identify impurities or sources of process variance through
small-scale models which can be addressed before the process is transferred
to the plant. However, although simulations are generally less costly than
on-line tests in the factory, they may suffer from the fidelity problems discussed
earlier.

Given that most product and process development projects employ the
full spectrum of approaches—from laboratory simulations through "real-life"
tests—the optimal solution may be an appropriate balance between approaches, rather than one or the other. Simulations and other forms of learning
before doing can be used to identify and solve some types of problems; others
for which a representative experiment cannot be designed may be identified
and solved only through learning by doing. Determining the most effective
balance between learning by doing and learning before doing will depend on
a firm's ability to use laboratory experiments and other forms of simulation to
predict future performance and to identify and solve potential problems.

Structure of Knowledge and the Appropriate Learning Strategy. As early as
Polanyi (1958), several writers have distinguished between "tacit" and "codified" knowledge.[23] Although this distinction can be useful, it really only refers
to the *form* in which knowledge is stored. As most writers on the subject have

recognized, beneath this distinction is the extent to which underlying cause-and-effect relationships (or, as Polanyi put it, the "set of rules") have been clearly identified and are well understood.[24]

If problem solvers understand how specific experimental conditions (such as scale, equipment, or humidity) affect outcomes (such as yield), they can use this knowledge to make predictions about performance under a future set of operating conditions. For instance, if a researcher knows, from either scientific theory or experience, that each increase in scale reduces yields by approximately 10 percent, a small-scale experiment can be used to make predictions about performance at larger scale. With deeper knowledge of these cause-and-effect relationships, the researcher can build more complete and accurate models mapping laboratory observations onto expected future performance under some specified set of conditions. In an extreme case, the researcher might have complete knowledge of all the relevant experimental conditions, their impact on process parameters, and the first-and second-order effects of all process parameters on performance.[25]

Take the following simple example of a chemical experiment conducted in a 1-liter glass bottle as a simulation for a commercial process to be run in a 5,000-gallon stainless steel tank. Assume for simplicity that the only relevant experimental conditions are the scale of the process (1 liter versus 5,000 gallons) and the material composition of the reaction vessel (glass versus stainless steel); that temperature is the only relevant process parameter; and that the researcher is interested only in one performance outcome—yield. If the researcher knows all the relevant experimental conditions and process parameters—the independent and interactive relationships between scale, vessel materials, temperature, and yield, for example—an experiment conducted under one set of conditions at one specific temperature point can be used to find the temperature that optimizes yield under a different set of conditions.[26]

For any sufficiently complex process, such complete knowledge is probably impossible to obtain. However, to learn before doing, the researcher needs to have only a global model of how outcomes observed under a specified set of conditions will map onto outcomes under another set of conditions. For instance, through years of testing processes in the laboratory and observing actual performance in the factory, researchers may develop predictive models of the form: "If we observe L in the laboratory, we can expect C in the plant." In this case, the researcher may not be fully aware of how a specific condition affects the process or its performance but will have an overall understanding of how the complete set of experimental conditions jointly influences out-

FIGURE 2.7   The Link between Knowledge and Learning Strategy

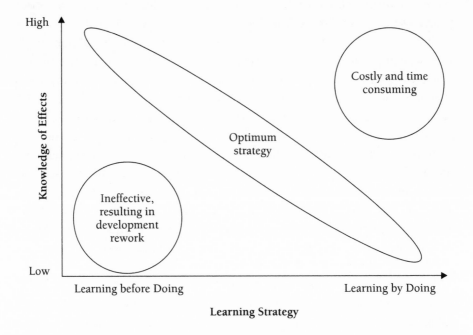

comes. Heuristics may emerge about what to expect based on observations in the laboratory or the pilot plant (for instance, "Multiply the yields observed in the laboratory by 0.75 in order to predict future yields in the factory"). In this case, knowledge takes the form $C(p|X_F) = f[(L(p|X_L)]$, where the functional form of f could be as simple as a constant. When developers talk about a process having a "linear scale-up," they mean that what is learned about the process at small scale (and under other laboratory conditions) can be extrapolated to a larger scale (and other commercial manufacturing conditions).

In any given technological context, opportunities to learn before doing should depend on the degree to which critical cause-and-effect relationships are described by scientific theories or heuristics based on cumulative practical experience. Where underlying theoretical knowledge is strong (and where there is relatively complete knowledge of the conditions in the future production environment), one may know enough about critical variables and their behavior to design highly representative laboratory experiments, which predict expected commercial performance reasonably accurately.[27] Under these conditions, learning before doing should play a greater role in the development process (although the need for some learning by doing in the factory should still be present). In contrast, where theoretical or practical knowledge of scale and other experimental effects is limited, it will be virtually impossible to predict how the process tested in the laboratory will work when run under actual operating conditions. Subtle and often unknown differences between the laboratory and the factory environment could have a major impact on process performance. For this type of technological regime, evaluation of the process needs to be done under conditions as close to actual operating conditions as possible. Transferring the still-immature process to the plant, and developing and refining it there—learning by doing—should be the more efficient approach. Figure 2.7 provides an overview of the link between available knowledge and learning strategies. It suggests that there is no one best approach to development that will be appropriate in all circumstances and highlights the need for managers, scientists, and engineers involved in the development process to come to an explicit understanding of the knowledge environment in which the company operates.

Conclusion

This chapter has provided an overview of the challenges confronting process development. Although process development is rooted in technical problem solving, it is an activity that must be broadly integrated with the external environment and other internal processes of the firm. Next we turn to the changing institutional and technological environments confronting pharmaceutical companies over the past several years, and the implications of these changes for process development.

The Evolving Nature of Competition in Pharmaceuticals

THE EARLY 1990s were a watershed in the evolution of the pharmaceutical industry. After years of relatively stable growth, high profits, and an enviable record of innovation, pharmaceutical firms found themselves struggling against a tide of hostile forces. The molecular biology revolution—in the making for over forty years—finally began to have an impact on the technology of drug R&D. Established pharmaceutical firms, including Merck, Pfizer, and Eli Lilly, intensified their adoption of "rational drug design," while hundreds of biotechnology startup firms, armed with genetic engineering capabilities, struggled to gain a foothold in the industry. Meanwhile, pharmaceutical companies in the United States found themselves in the cross fire of a debate over health care costs and faced growing political pressure to reduce drug prices. At the same time, the rapid emergence of managed care networks radically altered the balance of bargaining power in the drug market, putting even more pressure on drug prices.

Companies grappled with these challenges in a number of ways. Many, such as Merck, Eli Lilly, SmithKline Beecham, Pfizer, Bristol-Myers Squibb, and Rhone-Poulenc, acquired or forged strategic alliances with benefit management companies in an attempt to gain control over distribution channels. Some companies sought scale economies through horizontal mergers with other pharmaceutical firms: Hoffman LaRoche acquired Syntex; American Home

Products acquired American Cyanamid; and Glaxo acquired Wellcome. R&D budgets, once considered sacred, came under intense scrutiny. Many firms sought to control costs by acquiring technology from external sources through licensing agreements, R&D contracts, joint ventures, and other forms of collaboration.

This chapter examines changes in the institutional and technological arenas in which pharmaceutical companies operate, with two purposes. The first is descriptive. Because pharmaceutical companies and development projects are the source of data used in subsequent chapters, it is important to understand the industry's economic, regulatory, and technological context. A second purpose is analytical. New patterns of competition in pharmaceuticals have exposed gaps between existing and required process development capabilities of firms in the industry; these gaps are a focal point of competition. The histories of many industries in transition illustrate how organizations that successfully fill these capability gaps stand a much better chance of survival than those that do not.[1] Thus this chapter is designed to highlight the competitive challenges that both incumbent and new entrants (biotechnology firms) face, as well as the implications of these challenges for development capabilities. The chapter begins with a brief historical background of the pharmaceutical industry. It then turns to the institutional and technological forces that are reshaping the competitive environment.

Historical Background

The pharmaceutical industry defies simple classification. By almost any measure (including R&D intensity, innovative output, and the use of new scientific concepts), pharmaceuticals is a classic "high-technology" or "science-based" industry. Yet drugs are as old as antiquity. For example, the Ebers Papyrus lists 811 prescriptions used in Egypt in 550 B.C. (Mahoney 1959, p. 6). In eighteenth-century France and Germany, pharmacists worked in well-equipped laboratories to produce, on a small scale, therapeutic ingredients of known identity and purity. Mass production of drugs dates back to 1813, when J. B. Trommsdof opened the first specialized pharmaceutical plant in Germany (Statman 1983). In the United States, mass pharmaceutical production began in the second half of the nineteenth century with the founding of such firms as Merck, Squibb, Upjohn, Pfizer, and Eli Lilly. Swiss and German companies such as CIBA, Sandoz, Hoffman LaRoche, Bayer, and Hoescht, leveraging their technical competencies in fine chemicals and dyestuffs, began to manufacture drugs in the late nineteenth century. Salicytic acid (aspirin) was first produced in 1883 by the German company Bayer.

Early History

Although pharmaceuticals might be considered a science-based industry today, it certainly did not begin as such. Until the 1930s, when sulfonamide was discovered, drug companies undertook little formal research on new drugs. Harold Clymer, who joined SmithKline in 1939, noted:

> [Y]ou can judge the magnitude of [SmithKline's] R&D at that time by the fact I was told I would have to consider the position temporary since they had already hired two people within the previous year for their laboratory and were not sure that the business would warrant the continued expenditure.[2]

Wartime needs for antibiotics in World War II spurred the drug industry's transition to an R&D-intensive business. Penicillin and its antibiotic properties had been discovered by Alexander Fleming in 1928; however, throughout the 1930s, it was produced only in laboratory-scale quantities and used almost exclusively for experimental purposes. With the outbreak of World War II, the U.S. government organized a massive research and production effort that focused on commercial production techniques and chemical structure analysis. More than twenty companies, several universities, and the Department of Agriculture took part.[3] Pfizer, which had production experience in fermentation, developed a deep-tank fermentation process for producing large quantities of penicillin. This system led to major gains in productivity and, more importantly, laid out an architecture for the process and created a framework in which future improvements could take place.[4] The largest gains in productivity came about later, through identification, mutation, and selection of higher-yielding penicillin-producing molds. Mass screening of soil samples to find more productive strains of the penicillin mold was a critical aspect of this work.[5]

The early history of the "modern" pharmaceutical industry is interesting in two respects. First, it defies the expected pattern of innovation predicted by product life cycle models. Instead of a period of early product innovation followed by process innovation, we see that both process innovation and product development were absolutely critical from the start. Penicillin simply would not have been commercially feasible without major developments in process technology. Some idea of the impact of process development can be gleaned from data on yield improvements, compiled by the Federal Trade Commission in 1957, which suggest that in 1945 approximately 17,500 gallons of fermentation "broth" were required to produce 1 pound of penicillin. By 1956 yields had improved to such an extent that only 120 to 280 gallons of broth were needed per pound of antibiotics. To put this in perspective, production of all antibiotics increased from 240,000 pounds to 3,081,000 pounds between 1948 and 1956—a factor of nearly 13 times (Federal Trade Commission 1957, p. 7). Had yields remained at 1945 levels, production of 3 million pounds of antibiotics in 1956 would have required 5.25×10^{10} gallons of tank capacity; instead, it required only 840 million gallons. It is difficult to calibrate the exact economic impact of this savings, as no data are available on capital costs per gallon of tank capacity. But considering that average U.S. pharmaceutical companies spent $15 million annually between 1946 and 1950 on new plant and equipment, the financial impact of such productivity improvement was likely quite large.

Second, the early history of the industry is noteworthy in foreshadowing certain themes that reappear during the 1990s. For example, as we will discuss later, process technology was a critical bottleneck in developing genetically engineered drugs. Moreover, we can see how technological changes may require new ways of organizing and managing development. The need for penicillin could be met only if capabilities for process innovation and manufacturing were developed and applied. Even more resonant of current times is the need to integrate across disciplines. Developing new processes for penicillin production required knowledge of both biology (to understand factors affecting cell growth) and engineering (to design plant and equipment). Yet these two disciplines had traditionally operated in very different spheres. At that time, the world of the biologist revolved around the laboratory and the frontiers of science; the engineer was concerned with practical issues of large-scale manufacturing. As one scientist at Squibb in the 1930s noted, "In the early days of the penicillin program, one of the most difficult problems to overcome was the problem of communication between engineer and biologists" (Langlykke 1970, p. 91). As we will discuss later, integrating knowledge across disciplinary specialties is a critical ingredient to high development performance today.

Patterns of Competition: 1950–1990

The period from 1950 to 1990 could be classified as a golden age for the pharmaceutical industry. The industry and its main players—companies such as Merck, Eli Lilly, Bristol-Myers, and Pfizer—grew rapidly and profitably. R&D spending on new drugs literally exploded, producing a steady flow of new drugs. Drug innovation was a highly profitable activity during most of this period. Statman (1983, p. 8), for example, estimated that accounting rates of return on new drugs introduced between 1954 and 1978 averaged 20.9 percent (compared to a cost of capital of 10.7 percent). Between 1982 and 1992, firms in the industry grew at an average annual rate of 18 percent. During the early 1980s, double-digit rates of growth in earnings and return on equity were the norm for most pharmaceutical companies, and the industry as a whole ranked among the most profitable in the United States.[6]

A number of structural factors supported the industry's high average level of performance. One was the sheer magnitude of R&D opportunities and unmet needs. In the early postwar years, there were many physical ailments and diseases for which no drugs existed. In every major therapeutic category—from painkillers and anti-inflammatories to cardiovascular and central nervous system products—pharmaceutical companies faced a completely open field (it must be kept in mind that, before the discovery of penicillin, there were precious few drugs that effectively cured diseases). Faced with such a target-rich environment but very little detailed knowledge of the biological underpinnings of specific diseases, pharmaceutical companies invented an approach to R&D now referred to as "random screening." Under this approach, natural and chemically derived compounds were randomly screened in test tube experiments and laboratory animals for potential therapeutic activity. Pharmaceutical companies maintained enormous "libraries" of chemical compounds and added to their collections by searching for new compounds in swamps, streams, and soil samples. Thousands, if not tens of thousands, of compounds might be subjected to multiple screens before researchers honed in on a promising substance. Serendipity played a key role. In fact, it was not uncommon for companies to discover a drug to treat one disease while searching for a treatment for another.[7] Although random screening may appear ineffective, it worked extremely well for many years. Several hundred chemical entities were introduced in the 1950s and 1960s and, as Henderson notes, "Several important classes of hypertensive drug were discovered in this way, including a number of important diuretics, all of the early vasodilators, and a number of centrally acting agents including reserpine and guanethidine" (1994, p. 613).

As is well known to both practitioners and scholars of innovation, new products do not ensure profits. Rents from innovation can be competed away unless isolating mechanisms are in place to inhibit imitators and new entrants (Rumelt 1984, Teece 1986). For most of the postwar period, U.S. pharmaceutical companies had a number of isolating mechanisms working in their favor. One of these was the process of random screening itself. As an organizational process, random screening was anything but random. Over time, early entrants into the pharmaceutical industry developed highly disciplined processes for carrying out mass screening programs. Because random screening capabilities were based on internal organizational processes and tacit skills, they were difficult for potential entrants to imitate and thus became a source of first-mover advantage. These advantages, combined with the presence of scale economies in pharmaceutical research (Henderson and Cockburn 1992), may help to explain the dearth of new entry. Until the mid-1970s, only one company—Syntex, the developer of the oral contraceptive—succeeded in entering the industry during the postwar era.

A second set of isolating mechanisms helped buffer incumbents from competition among themselves. In many industries, successful new products quickly attract imitators. But rapid imitation may be difficult in pharmaceuticals for two reasons. First, pharmaceuticals has historically been one of the few industries in which patents provide solid protection against imitation (Levin et al. 1987). Because small variants in a molecule's structure can drastically alter its pharmacological properties, potential imitators find it hard to work around the patent. In addition, with random screening, spillovers of knowledge between firms was relatively small (Henderson 1994). When firms essentially rely on the law of large numbers, there is little to be learned from the competition—it is hard to copy luck. Thus, although other firms might undertake R&D in the same therapeutic class as an innovator, their probability of finding another compound with the same therapeutic properties, which did not infringe on the original patent, was quite small.

A third isolating mechanism was the regulatory environment—in particular, its impact on imitation even after patents had expired. Until the Waxman-Hatch Act was passed in 1984, generic versions of drugs that had gone off patent still had to undergo extensive human clinical trials before they could be sold in the U.S. market. Even once patents had expired, it might be years before a generic version appeared. In 1980 generics held only 2 percent of the U.S. drug market.

Pharmaceutical companies' rents from product innovation were further protected by the fragmented structure of health care markets and the low bargaining power of buyers. Until the mid-1980s, the overwhelming majority of drugs were sold through retail pharmacies or administered to patients in hospitals but marketed directly to physicians (who essentially made the purchasing decisions by deciding which drug to prescribe). Buyers—the patients—had little bargaining power, even in those instances in which multiple drugs were available for the same condition. Because insurance companies generally did not cover prescription drugs (in 1960, only 4 percent of prescription drug expenditures were funded by third-party payers), they did not provide a major source of pricing leverage. Pharmaceutical companies were afforded a relatively high degree of pricing flexibility.

The New Economics of the Pharmaceutical Business

At the outset of the 1990s, pharmaceutical companies found themselves in a rapidly changing competitive environment, and the strategies and competences that had served them well for almost forty years began to show signs of strain. Growth of sales and earnings began to slow dramatically, and pharmaceutical companies saw their stock market valuations drop by 35 percent between 1991 and 1993. The industry, once an engine of job growth, witnessed its first major layoffs; Merck, for instance, announced it would cut over 38,000 jobs during the 1990s; Syntex, with patents expiring on two key products, announced it would reduce its workforce by 20 percent (and was later acquired by Hoffman LaRoche); Pfizer announced workforce cuts of 11 to 13 percent; and Eli Lilly experienced the first quarterly loss in its history.

For many within the industry, it was tempting to view these problems as a symptom of the uncertainty surrounding the Clinton administration's plans for health care reform. Although concerns about price controls were an important factor in the decline of stock market valuations, it is also necessary to examine the implications of deeper and more permanent institutional and technological changes.

Declining pricing flexibility is one clear indicator of the impact of these forces. Although pharmaceutical pricing and price trends are a subject of controversy, there are relatively consistent data demonstrating that pricing flexibility has declined markedly in recent years. As shown in figure 3.1, the growth rate of the consumer and producer price indexes for pharmaceuticals, after outpacing general rates of inflation during the mid-1980s, began to level off during the early 1990s. A detailed examination of the average list price of seventy-one pharmaceuticals by Kolassa (1993) suggests that the rate of price growth in drugs has declined from 8.32 percent in 1989 to 5.19 percent in 1992. However, average list price tends to overstate price increases because it applies only to the portion of a manufacturer's business not covered by long-

FIGURE 3.1 Consumer and Producer Price Indexes, 1984–1994

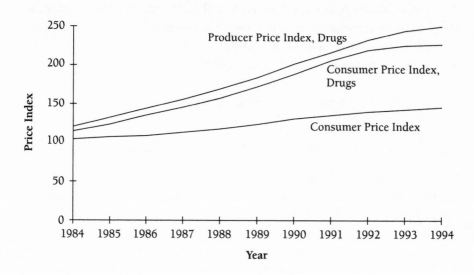

Source: Bureau of Labor Statistics.

term contracts. Historically, such contracts comprise a small portion of pharmaceutical companies' sales and thus do not distort aggregate pricing indices. According to Kolassa, these contracts can result in a gap between list and manufacturer-realized prices of up to 20 percent. As the volume of sales covered under such contracts has grown, pharmaceutical manufacturers have less flexibility to increase price. One study found that the weighted average discount from list price quadrupled from 4 percent in 1987 to 16 percent in 1992 (Boston Consulting Group 1993, p. 9).

Further evidence of declining price flexibility is revealed by trends in newly launched branded (as opposed to generic) products (Kolassa and Banahan 1995). Historically, new drugs (which presumably had performance advantages) were priced at premiums above existing market leaders. But, as shown in figure 3.2, pricing strategies for newly launched products appear to have changed markedly in the last few years: 57 percent of the new drugs introduced between 1979 and 1988 were priced above the market leaders in their therapeutic categories. Since 1989, this percentage has dropped to about 20 percent. Notably, in 1993 and for the first nine months of 1994, not a single new drug was priced above the existing market leader. There is no evidence to suggest that this decline in premium pricing for new products is the result of poor quality or lower performance differentiation than in the past; rather, a study conducted by the Boston Consulting Group (1993) suggests that it may be the result of intensifying competition. Indeed, according to the study, the average price for a new drug was *discounted* by 14 percent relative to the market leader in 1991 and 1992; in the chronic therapeutic areas with the most new product entries, discounts reached 36 percent.

Reduced pricing flexibility is a symptom of more profound institutional and technological changes in the competitive dynamics of the pharmaceutical industry. Understanding these forces is critical for firms that must develop pricing strategies. Moreover, the changes will have implications for the type of development capabilities required to compete in this industry over the longer term.

FIGURE 3.2 Pricing Strategies for Newly Launched Drugs

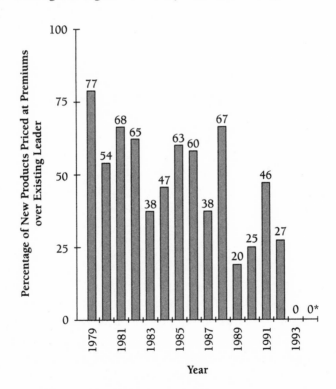

Source: E. M. Kolassa and B. F. Banahan III, "Growing Competition in the Pharmaceutical Industry: A Response to the PRIME Institute Report," Technical Report PMM 95-001, Research Institute of Pharmaceutical Sciences, University of Mississippi (January 1995). Reprinted by permission.

*First nine months of 1994.

Institutional Forces: Managed Care Networks and Generic Competition

During the 1980s, two institutional forces—rapid penetration by managed care networks and lower barriers to generic entry—began to alter the competitive landscape of the U.S. market for pharmaceuticals. By concentrating distribution channels, managed care networks created buyer bargaining power. Longer product development lead times shortened the effective patent life of new drugs, thus exposing firms earlier to generic competition. Additionally, legislative changes lowered the barriers to generic entry once those patents had expired. These forces have begun to limit the degree of pricing latitude once enjoyed by pharmaceutical companies in the U.S. market.

The Emerging Bargaining Power of Managed Care Networks. Traditionally, with most drugs prescribed by independent practitioners and dispensed through independent retail pharmacies and hospitals, buyer concentration in the U.S. pharmaceutical market was quite low. This began to change during the 1980s as health maintenance organizations (HMOs) and other forms of managed care networks emerged as institutional mechanisms for containing soaring medical costs (including the costs of prescription drugs). Managed care networks attempt to provide incentives for control by integrating (either through ownership or contracts) the functions of the insurance company with those of the health care provider. Unlike traditional insurance companies, which had little direct influence on costs, managed care networks actively seek to use their buyer power to negotiate lower prices for a whole range of medical services and supplies, including drugs. In 1980 only 5 percent of the insured U.S. population was covered by a managed care organization; by 1993 this figure had grown to 80 percent (Boston Consulting Group 1993, p. 18). With their increasing control over the pool of the insured, these organizations began to influence the pharmaceuticals market. Whereas in 1960 only 4 percent of prescription drug sales were funded by third-party payers, by 1995 managed care networks alone accounted for 75 percent of pharmaceutical purchases.[8]

Thus pharmaceutical companies in the U.S. market found themselves for the first time engaged in serious price negotiations with large-volume buyers. Large managed care providers, such as Kaiser Permanente in California, used their enormous bargaining power to press for deep price discounts on branded products—discounts as high as 60 percent (which would essentially put a branded drug at generic pricing levels). One tactic was to restrict the number of drugs per therapeutic category through what is known as a "formulary list." For example, a managed care network might specify only two brands of ulcer drugs on its formulary list. If a doctor prescribed a drug on the formulary list, it would be covered (with perhaps a small copayment); if the drug were not on the formulary list, the patient would pay the full cost. Another large (and increasingly powerful) volume buyer, representing the growing number of patients covered under Medicare, was the U.S. government. Government procurement today represents approximately 15 percent of U.S. pharmaceutical sales, and recent legislation mandates substantial rebates on drugs procured through Medicaid and Medicare programs.[9]

Related to the rise of managed care networks has been a change in the payment schemes for health care services in general, including supplies such as drugs. In recent years, managed care organizations have increasingly entered into "capitated" contracts with health care providers. Under such an agreement, the provider—a hospital or doctor, for example—receives a fixed monthly payment for each patient enrolled in the managed care organization's plan. Capitated contracts shift any risks to the provider and have both direct and indirect effects on drug prices. Under capitation, providers are motivated to choose and prescribe drugs judiciously, because all costs of drug treatment come out of the provider's budget.

Pharmaceutical companies have begun to explore the possibility of negotiating capitated contracts directly with providers and health care plans, as part of a strategic focus on disease management. For instance, Eli Lilly—the world's largest supplier of insulin for the treatment of diabetes—might enter into a capitated contract with a health plan so that Lilly would supply all diabetic treatment products and in return be paid a fixed fee per member. Under this arrangement, Lilly would make or lose money depending on whether it could keep total drug costs below the capitated rates.[10]

As drug companies begin to share in the risks of health care through capitated arrangements, they face a fundamentally different calculus for drug costs. In the new scenario, a huge seller—a "blockbuster" in industry jargon—is not necessarily good news. If the company underestimated demand for the drug in negotiating its capitated rate, it could ultimately lose money. Similarly, a drug that cost more to manufacture than expected, or that required significant additional capital expenditure because of unanticipated growth, would become a drain on profits. It is too early to tell what impact capitation will have on pharmaceuticals because the trend is still in its infancy. However, it is almost certain that companies will find themselves under increasing pressure to reduce prices.

Intensifying Generic Competition. Although U.S. patent protection lasts seventeen years, some portion of this period in pharmaceuticals has always

FIGURE 3.3 Declining Effective Patent Lives

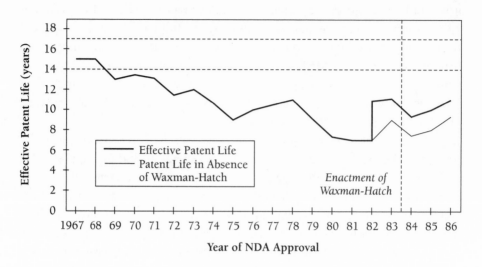

Source: Boston Consulting Group, *The Changing Environment for U.S. Pharmaceuticals* (Boston: Boston Consulting Group, 1993). Reprinted with permission from *The Changing Environment,* The Boston Consulting Group, Inc., April 1993.

been lost because of the time required to conduct clinical trials and secure regulatory approval. As the mean development time required to launch a new drug has drifted, from seven years in 1970 to twelve years today, the lag between FDA approval and patent expiration has shrunk correspondingly (see figure 3.3). The Waxman-Hatch Act of 1984, which also reduced barriers to generic entry, was designed to redress this trend by providing for an additional exclusivity period to attach to new drug approvals.[11] However, on average, the incremental gain in effective patent protection has been relatively modest (about 1.5 years on average during the 1980s), and effective patent life during the 1980s remained well below the levels of the late 1960s (Boston Consulting Group 1993, p. 16).

The Waxman-Hatch Act helped ensure that generic competition was more swift once patents expired, by accelerating the approval process for generic drugs. Instead of having to conduct its own lengthy and costly clinical trials, the maker of a generic (off-patent) product needed only show that its version of the product was chemically and biologically equivalent to the original patented version. Whereas before Waxman-Hatch it might take a few years for a generic version of a pioneer drug to appear on the market, after 1984 generics appeared literally within months of patent expiration. In the first six months after its passage, the FDA received over 800 applications for generic drug approvals. The impact of this legislation has escalated as patents have expired on a growing number of drugs. As noted earlier, generics in 1980 held only 2 percent of the U.S. drug market. By 1989 this figure had risen to 30 percent, and by 1993, to approximately 50 percent.[12] Between 1993 and 2000, patents will expire on branded products with annual sales of $20 billion, and sales of generics are expected to reach $12 billion (versus $4 billion in 1992).

Because generics are typically priced between 30 percent and 60 percent below brand-name drugs, their impact on competition can be severe. After SmithKline Beecham's antiulcer drug Tagamet went off patent in May 1994, new prescription rates fell by 79 percent.[13] Generics captured 88 percent of the market when Syntex's anti-inflammatory Naproysyn lost its patent protection in December 1993. This surge of patent expirations is catching many pharmaceuticals at a particularly vulnerable juncture. Declining rates of new drug innovation have left many companies with aging product portfolios and fewer new drugs to offset declining revenues. Since 1989 sales growth of generics has exceeded the growth of novel compounds by 40 percent (Boston Consulting Group 1993, p. 14). Table 3.1 shows a list of major pharmaceutical companies and the percentage of their sales from drugs that were coming off patent between 1993 and 1995.

Table 3.1   Company Exposure to Patent Expirations, 1993–1995 (versus 1992 sales)

Company	Percentage of 1992 Sales
Glaxo	72
UpJohn	66
Syntex	63
Schering-Plough	48
Warner-Lambert	35
CIBA-Geigy	35
Marion Merrell Dow	34
American Home Products	33
Sandoz	32
Eli Lilly	30
SmithKline Beecham	27
Lederle	14
Pfizer	8
Johnson & Johnson	4
Hoffman La Roche	0
Merck	0

Source: SCRIP's Yearbook 1994 (London: PJB Publications Ltd., 1994), 69, Table 25.

Technological Forces

At the same time that pharmaceutical companies have had to reckon with changes in their marketplace and customers, they have also witnessed dramatic changes in the constellation of scientific disciplines underpinning drug R&D. Scientific advances in genetics and genetic engineering, physiology, pharmacology, protein chemistry, molecular biology, and biochemistry, as well as deepening knowledge of the biochemistry of specific diseases—what might be referred to as the molecular biology revolution—have begun to fundamentally alter the technology of drug R&D and the capabilities required for successful product and process development. The molecular biology revolution has had two primary effects on drug R&D. One is to create new techniques for more rationally seeking and designing chemical structures with specific therapeutic effects. The other—generally referred to as biotechnology—has been to permit the development of an entirely new class of therapeutics based on protein molecules synthesized through genetic engineering. While these techniques clearly create opportunities for product and process innovation, they have also generated opportunities for entry and intensified competition between incumbents.

Rational Drug Design Methods. Rational drug design is an approach to drug discovery whereby researchers begin with detailed knowledge of the biochemistry of a disease and work backward to find or design a chemical compound that will effectively inhibit a chemical reaction involved in that disease. The most common analogy is that of the lock and key. Diseases are essentially nothing more than a series of biochemical reactions inside the body. Receptors—molecules sitting on the surface of cells—play a key role in all reactions inside the body, including those associated with diseases. Rational drug design involves finding or designing a chemical key that fits a particular receptor (the lock) and either inhibits or catalyzes a crucial reaction. More rational approaches to drug design have been made possible by advances in the details of how specific diseases work—right down to the molecular structure of the receptors that catalyze key reactions.

Rational drug design is in its infancy; to date, very few drugs have been designed completely by working backward. However, better knowledge of the biochemical roots of specific diseases and the molecular action of certain classes of drugs makes it possible for researchers to more quickly hone in on promising compounds. This approach, known as "guided search," has led to the development of many important drugs during the last two decades, including propranolol and captotril (for hypertension) and Prozac (for depression), and is still central to most established pharmaceutical firms' research strategies (Henderson 1994). While better knowledge of diseases and of the action of specific compounds is expected to improve research productivity (although, to date, there is little evidence of this happening), it also has implications for competitive dynamics and interactions. A number of characteristics of more rational approaches to drug development suggest that it may undermine the rents and isolating mechanisms associated with random screening.

First, successful rational drug design appears to require a much higher degree of cross-disciplinary integration than random screening methods. Whereas random screening drew on the capability to manage the mass screening of compounds and required relatively little communication of knowledge, either across firm boundaries or disciplines or within therapeutic areas, rational drug design requires that firms keep current across a wide range of disciplinary bases and manage the integration of those knowledge bases internally (Henderson 1994). To the extent that this integration requires new, specialized organizational capabilities, rents from random screening capabilities may be eroded. Second, because these new methods draw from basic biomedical knowledge (much of which is generated by universities and academic medical centers and diffused through conferences and publications[14]), knowledge interactions and spillovers across firms should intensify. To utilize this basic know-how, firms need strong internal scientific capabilities (Gambardella 1995). But these capabilities are a two-edged sword: while they allow firms to exploit publicly generated scientific knowledge, they also allow firms to learn from one another. As pharmaceutical companies begin to draw from the same knowledge base and develop the internal scientific capabilities needed to use this knowledge, they become better able to introduce competing versions of products without infringing on patents.

Already there are signs of this occurring in certain segments of the pharmaceuticals market. For instance, knowledge of the role of serotonin in depression helped Eli Lilly develop and introduce Prozac (a serotonin inhibitor) in 1988. But this knowledge also allowed other companies to introduce their own serotonin inhibitors; within four years, Glaxo introduced a competing serotonin inhibitor, Zoloft, and less than one year later, SmithKline Beecham introduced Paxil. There currently are five serotonin inhibitors battling in the antidepression market. A similar pattern can be found in cholesterol reduction drugs: Mevacor, launched in September 1987, was followed by Pravacol just over four years later. Retrovir, the first antiviral to slow the progression of AIDS, was followed by Vidax less than three and half years after its market introduction in April 1987.

FIGURE 3.4 Competition in Therapeutic Segments

(a) Herfindahl Indices for Five Largest Therapeutic Categories

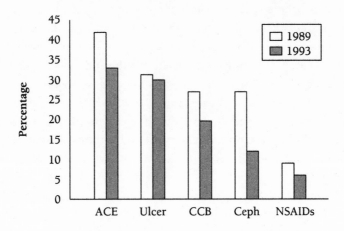

(b) Number of Brand-Name Competitors in Five Largest Therapeutic Categories

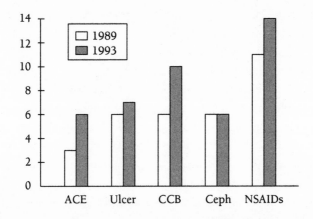

Source: E. M. Kolassa and B. F. Banahan III, "Growing Competition in the Pharmaceutical Industry: A Response to the PRIME Institute Report," Technical Report PMM 95-001, Research Institute of Pharmaceutical Sciences, University of Mississippi (January 1995). Reprinted by permission.

Note: ACE = ACE inhibitors; Ulcer = antiulcer medications; CCB = calcium channel blockers; Ceph = cephalosporins; NSAIDs = nonsteroidal anti-inflammatory agents.

There is already some evidence of new entry into specific therapeutic categories over the past several years. Figure 3.4 compares competitive intensity, as measured by the Herfindahl Index,[15] and the number of brand-name competitors between 1989 and 1993 across five major therapeutic categories (which together account for approximately 30 percent of ethical drug sales in the United States). In all segments, the Herfindahl Index dropped between 1989 and 1993 (indicating greater competition), and in all segments but one, the number of brand-name competitors increased. A glimpse of future competition in product introduction is provided in Table 3.2, which shows the number of compounds under development as of December 1993 in the top twenty pharmacological/biological modes of action. Although data are not available for the past, discussions with managers in the industry suggest that

Table 3.2   Compounds under Development by Therapeutic Segment, December 1993

Ranking[1]	Mode of Action	Ranking Number of Compounds
1	Protein synthesis antagonist	83
2	Platelet aggregation antagonist	72
3	Calcium channel antagonist	70
4	Cell wall synthesis inhibitor	67
5	DNA antagonist	59
6	RNA-directed DNA polymerase inhibitor	54
7	DNA topoisomerase ATP-hydrolyzing inhibitor	52
8	Cyclo-oxygenase inhibitor	49
9	Prostaglandin synthase inhibitor	46
10	Bone formation stimulant	39
11	Angiotensin II antagonist	38
12	5-lipoxygenase inhibitor	36
13	DNA synthesis inhibitor	35
14	Sodium channel antagonist	31
15	RNA synthesis inhibitor	31
16	PAF antagonist	30
17	Plasminogen activator stimulant	27
18	Phosphodiesterase inhibitor	27
19	Thrombin inhibitor	26
20	HIV protease inhibitor	24

Source: SCRIP's Yearbook 1994 (London: PJB Publications Ltd., 1994), 106.

[1]Four general coding categories have not been incorporated in the list. These are UN (unidentified pharmacological activity, 488 compounds), IM+ (immunostimulant, 217 compounds), NA (not applicable, 193 compounds), and IM- (immunosuppressant, 141 compounds).

the technology strategies of pharmaceutical firms have been converging over time. As one manager put it, "We're all playing in the same sandbox now."

Intensifying product development competition has contributed to downward pressure on prices. According to one recent study, therapeutic areas with the most new product introductions also tend to have lower rates of price increases. In therapeutic areas in which no new products had been introduced, prices rose an average of 5 percent, but in segments with one or more new product introductions, price increases averaged only 1 percent. As noted earlier, additional entrants into a therapeutic category discounted their price at launch by an average of 14 percent. However, in some of the most competitive therapeutic classes, price discounts on second, third, and subsequent entrants averaged 36 percent (Boston Consulting Group 1993, p. 9).

Biotechnology. Rational drug design affects the process of developing drugs, but the drugs themselves are still chemically synthesized organic molecules (sometimes referred to as "small molecules"). The molecular biology revolution has also led to the development of techniques for synthesizing protein molecules. Proteins, by their nature, are large and complex molecules that cannot feasibly be synthesized through chemical means. Until the invention of genetic engineering techniques in the mid-1970s, the only way to produce commercial quantities of proteins was to extract and purify them from natural sources. For example, insulin, a protein used in the body to metabolize sugars and lacking in diabetics, was produced by culturing pig pancreases. Factor VIII, a blood clotting protein needed by hemophiliacs, was extracted and purified from blood. Because proteins are centrally involved in most biological processes inside the body, biomedical researchers had suspected for years that they had potential as drugs.

Unfortunately, with the exception of a few proteins (such as insulin, Factor VIII, and human growth hormone), most naturally occurring proteins were simply too difficult and costly to extract from natural sources. Naturally occurring interferon, for instance, was so scarce that it cost over $1 million per gram. Then, in 1973, Herbert Cohen and Stanley Boyer of the University of California invented a technique for manipulating the genetic structure of cells in order to synthesize specific proteins. Genetic engineering opened up the possibility of developing a wide range of proteins into therapeutic drugs. Within months of Cohen and Boyer's invention, the first biotechnology firm, Genentech, was formed (with Boyer a cofounder). Within a few years, several hundred specialized biotechnology firms had been formed to undertake commercial R&D in biotechnology.

Like rational drug design, biotechnology is a relatively new field, and thus it is too early to judge its long-term competitive impact. Certainly, predictions made in the early years about biotechnology leading to the downfall of drug giants have not panned out. Today some view the biotechnology revolution as a disappointment, even a failure. Yet as a technology for R&D, biotechnology does appear to be having an effect. As of 1995 there were twenty-five therapeutics on the market based on genetic engineering. Some of these, such as Amgen's Neupon (G-CSF) and Epogen (erythropoetin), Intron A (developed by Biogen and marketed by Schering-Plough), genetically engineered insulin (developed by Genentech and marketed by Eli Lilly), and Genentech's Activase (tissue plasminogen activase), have become major sellers. As of 1994 seventeen other biotechnology-based drugs were under review at the FDA. Total sales of biotechnology drugs in 1994 came to $7.7 billion (about 9 percent of total pharmaceutical industry sales). Although biotechnology is still a relatively small segment of pharmaceuticals in terms of sales and products under development, biotechnology R&D (at $7 billion per year) now accounts for about one-third of the pharmaceutical industry's R&D investment (Lee and Burrill 1994, p. 8).

Like rational drug design, biotechnology has the potential to erode the sources of R&D rents of established pharmaceuticals firms. Creating a genetically engineered cell capable of synthesizing a specific protein requires skills in molecular biology, protein chemistry, and genetics, whereas traditional methods draw from organic chemistry. Thus, in one sense, biotechnology can be viewed as competence destroying (Tushman and Anderson 1986). However, because biotechnology-based drugs must go through clinical testing and evaluation procedures and are sold largely through the same distribution channels as traditionally discovered drugs, biotechnology complements existing downstream competencies of pharmaceutical firms. This may help explain why biotechnology innovation has been pursued largely through collaborative arrangements between new biotechnology firms (who do the R&D) and established pharmaceutical companies (who typically undertake clinical trials and marketing) (Pisano 1990). Although vertical integration exists to varying degrees, the emergence of biotechnology has created a market-for-know in which biotechnology firms act as sellers of technology and of technical competencies and established pharmaceutical companies act as buyers (Pisano and Mang 1992). While this market allows established pharmaceutical firms to capture rents on their specialized downstream clinical development and marketing competences, it also allows enough entry to potentially dissipate rents from R&D.

Biotechnology, like more modern methods of discovering new chemical

Table 3.3 Multiple Entries for Biotechnology Drugs

Drug	First Entrant—Year	Second Entrant—Year	Lag (years)
Insulin (recombinant)	Genentech/Lilly—1982	Novo—1991	9
Human growth hormone	Genentech—1985	Lilly—1987	2
Alpha interferon	Biogen/Schering—1986	Genentech/Roche—1986	0
Hepatitis B vaccine	Chiron/Merck—1986	Biogen/SmithKline—1989	3
Factor VIII (recombinant)	Genetics Institute/Baxter—1992	Genentech/Roche—1993	1
Beta interferon	Chiron—1992	Biogen—expected 1996	4

Source: Compiled from K. Lee and G. S. Burrill, *Biotech 95: Reform, Restructure, Renewal* (Palo Alto: Ernst & Young, 1994).

entities, also appears to be having an impact on the competitive dynamics of product development. While most newly introduced biotechnology drugs (such as Amgen's Epogen or Genzyme's Ceradase) have exclusive positions, several classes of biotechnology have witnessed multiple entry (see table 3.3). In some cases, the lag has been extremely short.

Upward Pressure on Costs

While pharmaceutical companies have been forced to cope with a less permissive pricing environment, regulatory and technological forces have put increasing pressure on their R&D and manufacturing costs (which together account for approximately 40 percent of a typical company's cost structure). A number of studies have documented a substantial rise in the costs of discovering, developing, and gaining regulatory approval for new drugs over the past twenty years.[16] Less well studied are the increasing fixed and variable costs of manufacturing. Until recently, manufacturing costs were not a major managerial issue. A Coopers and Lybrand study of seventeen pharmaceutical firms found that, between 1980 and 1990, manufacturing costs as a percentage of sales doubled from 10 percent to 20 percent.[17] (Because Merck is often used as a bellwether for the industry, it is worth noting that in 1993 Merck's cost of goods

Table 3.4 R&D and Capital Expenditures for Pharmaceutical Products, 1992 ($ millions)

Company	R&D Expenditures	Capital Expenditures
Merck	1,112	1,067
American Home Products	552	474
Bristol Myers*	1,083	426
Glaxo	739	533
Johnson & Johnson	643	317
Eli Lilly	925	913
Pfizer	863	674
Schering-Plough*	521	384
SmithKline Beecham	412	150

Source: Compiled from *SCRIP's Yearbook,* 1994 (London: PJB Publications Ltd., 1994).

* R&D figure for total R&D; capital expenditure for pharmaceuticals only.

FIGURE 3.5 R&D and Capital Expenditures Compared to NCEs, 1984–1993

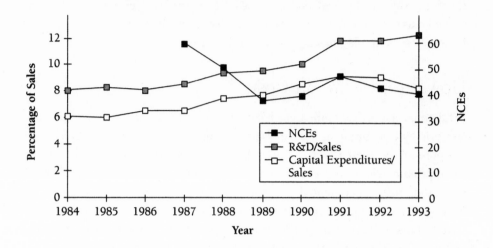

Source: Compiled from "Reshaping Things to Come," *The Economist,* 6 August 1994; *PhRMA Annual Survey;* and *Standard and Poor's Industry Survey on Health Care.*

sold represented 21 percent of its revenues.) At 21 percent, cost of goods sold represents a larger fraction of revenues than R&D spending, which averages approximately 15 percent across the industry. As will be discussed later, these averages can be deceiving; because of learning curve effects, new products generally have much higher manufacturing costs than do older products. Thus, margins on newly launched products are typically much smaller and, in some companies, may be negative during the first few years of commercial sales (when manufacturing costs exceed sales prices).

Growing capital expenditures on plant and equipment have become an important component of pharmaceutical companies' cost structures. Table 3.4 compares R&D and capital expenditures associated with pharmaceutical products for a cross-section of companies for which these data are available. It is noteworthy that capital expenditures at both Merck and Eli Lilly have approached (and in some recent years exceeded) R&D spending. Figure 3.5 shows that, throughout the second half of the 1980s, capital expenditures grew at approximately the same rate as R&D. Both growth rates exceeded the rate of NCE introductions. Part of the decline in 1992 may be related to financial pressures put on firms by plummeting stock market values. In addition, because capital expenditures are driven by new product launches and capacity expansions for products in early (growth) years of their life cycles, aging product portfolios at some larger companies have contributed to a decrease in capital spending. Drugs introduced in the years 1987 through 1989 would be at their peak in terms of capital expenditures in 1991 through 1993.

Given the sharp decrease in new chemical entities introduced between 1987 and 1989, it is surprising that capital expenditures did not fall accordingly between 1991 and 1993. These aggregate data suggest that capital expenditures per new product introduction have actually increased over the past several years. This is consistent with estimates obtained from a company involved in this study, indicating that the capital costs of a standard new manufacturing facility (for production of active chemical ingredients) doubled between 1980 and 1990. The actual amount of capital expenditures per new plant varies across companies, depending on the nature of their products. For example, one company that produces very high-volume products estimated its new facility costs at approximately $400 million. Another company, whose portfolio emphasizes lower-volume, high-potency drugs, estimated the costs of a new plant closer to $150 million.

In the biotechnology segment, out-of-pocket facility costs associated with the launch of a new product have been estimated at approximately $100 million (Bader 1992). In general, as demand for a new product increases, companies can count on making substantial investments in additional capacity. In 1993 alone, Chiron's annual report reveals that it invested $115 million in capital expenditures, largely on new manufacturing capacity for its recently approved treatment for multiple sclerosis.

These figures are noteworthy for their magnitude. At $100 million to $400 million, capital expenditures on the manufacturing required to bring a new drug to market are on a par with or higher than R&D costs (figure 3.6). Additionally, because firms are trying to get new products to market more quickly, they have been forced to invest in new facilities for new drugs relatively early in the product development cycle, when the likelihood of a product's reaching the market is still highly uncertain. In biotechnology, companies such as Centocor and Synergen were saddled with expensive idle plants when their lead drugs failed to win regulatory approval. This situation also occurs in established pharmaceutical companies, but because they can better absorb the risks, the incident is less visible. Manufacturing capital expenditures have begun to take on the risk characteristics of R&D in pharmaceuticals. Capital expenditures per new drug, including costs to retrofit facilities for drugs never approved, may be substantially higher than the out-of-pocket costs indicated above.

Discussions with managers in the industry suggest that both regulatory and

FIGURE 3.6 R&D and Facility Costs for Bringing a New Drug to Market, 1993 ($ millions)

(a) New Chemical Entity

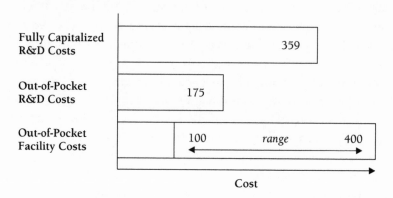

Fully Capitalized R&D Costs: R&D costs of all drug candidates (including those that did not reach the market); this figure takes into account the opportunity cost of R&D expended over the time period of development. *Source:* Estimate obtained from Pharmaceutical Research Manufacturing Association (PhRMA), *Parexel's Pharmaceutical R&D Statistical Sourcebook* (1995).

Out-of-Pocket R&D Costs: Cash outlays on molecules that reached the market. *Source:* PhRMA and *Parexel* (1995).

Out-of-Pocket Facility Costs: Cash outlays on new plant and equipment required to manufacture a new chemical entity. *Source:* Estimates obtained from pharmaceutical companies involved in the study.

(b) Biotechnology-based Drug

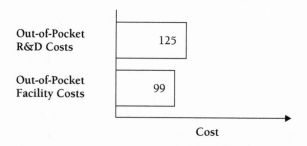

Out-of-Pocket R&D Costs: *Source:* G. Steven Burill and Kenneth B. Lee, *Biotech 94: Long-Term Value, Short-Term Hurdles* (San Francisco: Ernst & Young, 1993).
Out-of-Pocket Facility Costs: *Source:* F. Bader, "Manufacturing Costs of Biotechnology Derived Pharmaceuticals," *Proceedings of Workshop on Biotechnology,* Center for the Study of Drug Development, Tufts University, 1992.

technological factors may underlie this increase in manufacturing costs. From a regulatory standpoint, stricter FDA standards and oversight of manufacturing processes have forced companies to upgrade facilities and processing equipment. In the last few years, there have been several notable examples of FDA investigations' resulting in temporary plant shutdowns or major facilities upgrades. For example, in 1989, after inspecting Eli Lilly's tablet and capsule manufacturing facilities in Indianapolis, the FDA mandated a substantial overhaul of the plant's operating procedures and documentation systems. In response, Lilly invested over $70 million in capital to ensure that the new requirements were met throughout the company's plants. Environmental regulations have also apparently played a role. In the United States, manufacturing an active chemical or biochemical ingredient used in a drug is subject to strict regulation by the Environmental Protection Agency (EPA), requiring companies to invest in new equipment for rescuing effluents and for handling potentially hazardous wastes. In addition, more companies are introducing highly potent compounds (such as anticancer agents) which require costly containment facilities to protect both workers and the environment from possible leakage and spills.

A second major force driving up the costs of manufacturing in pharmaceuticals is growing product complexity. The emergence of biotechnology drugs based on recombinant methods of synthesis is an excellent example of this trend. The therapeutic proteins derived from biotechnology are large, complex molecules historically produced in quantities no greater than a few picograms. Manufacturing costs for these proteins, even in large quantities, are known to have been high relative to those for traditional synthetic chemical compounds. Although pharmaceutical companies are extremely secretive about manufacturing costs, their magnitude can be deduced by examining the selling prices for some of the first commercially approved biotechnology drugs. Tissue plasminogen activase (tPA), for example, sells for approximately $23,000 per gram; genetically engineered human growth hormone, for $35,000 per gram; GM-CSF, for $384,000 per gram; G-CSF, for $450,000 per gram; and erythropoetin (EPO), for $840,000 per gram.[18] Assuming a gross margin of 85 percent (some industry observers have put the figure closer to 75 percent), manufacturing costs range from $3,500 to $126,000 per gram. In contrast, manufacturing costs for chemically synthesized molecules range from less than $1 per gram to $100 per gram. Thus, with biotechnology, manufacturing costs are orders of magnitude greater.

There appears to be a parallel trend even within traditional chemical pharmaceuticals. As pharmaceutical discovery has shifted away from random

FIGURE 3.7 Number of Chemical Reactions Required to
Synthesize a Molecule

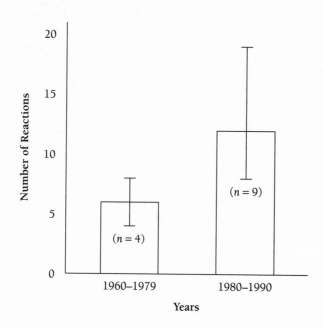

screening toward approaches based on deep knowledge of the biochemistry of specific diseases, and as the tools of chemical synthesis have become more sophisticated, drug researchers have become better able to design molecules with desired therapeutic effects. As discussed earlier, rational drug design clearly has potential benefits for the productivity and quality of R&D. At the same time, however, it can lead to very complex molecules. Under the random screening approach, in which researchers generally started with known chemicals and looked for potential therapeutic applications, manufacturability was almost a given. With rational drug design, researchers start with a disease and work backwards to the structure of the therapeutic molecules. Very complex compounds, which are costly to manufacture, may result.

Some of this trend is reflected in the data collected as part of this study (figure 3.7). One metric of manufacturing complexity for a chemical compound is the number of chemical reactions required to synthesize the molecule: structurally complex molecules require more synthetic steps. Of the twenty-three sample projects, thirteen were chemical compounds. The four chemical compounds discovered before 1980 required an average of approximately 6 chemical reactions (with a range of 4 to 7). Notably, the oldest compound in the study—originally discovered in the 1960s—also required the fewest syn-

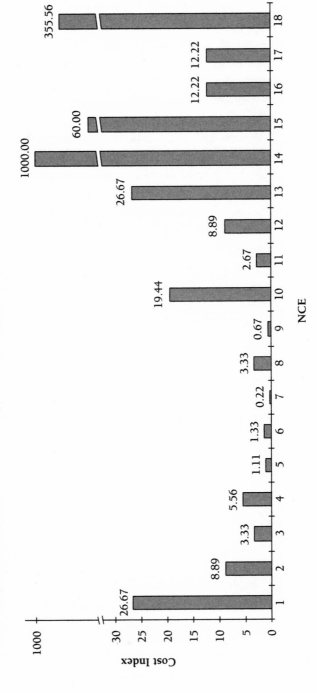

FIGURE 3.8 Estimated Initial Manufacturing Costs for Eighteen NCEs

thetic steps (4). In contrast, the nine compounds in the sample that were discovered after 1980 required an average of 12 reactions, with a range of 7 to 19. One should be careful about interpreting trends in such a small sample. However, these limited data are consistent with the perceptions of the process development scientists involved in the study. One scientist commented that, in the past, many blockbuster drugs could almost "be manufactured in a bathtub. Now, all the simple molecules are gone."

Further evidence of the growing complexity of new molecules can be found in detailed longitudinal data collected from one company in the study. Figure 3.8 displays an index of estimated initial manufacturing costs for eighteen chemical entities developed by this company over the past fifteen years, generated as part of routine economic analyses performed during process research and development. The data are presented chronologically, with the more recently developed molecules on the right. Because manufacturing costs realized in production are the result of process development effort, the metric used here is based on an estimate of the manufacturing costs that would have been incurred had the synthetic route, initially used to make the molecule in the laboratory, been followed. Thus, this metric provides a good picture of the "raw" complexity of the process before any further development. There appears to be a slightly upward trend, but the most noticeable feature is the increasing variance. The most difficult molecules to manufacture appeared most recently. Molecule 14 was an order of magnitude more costly than most of the rest of the sample. The most recent molecule, 18, was several times more expensive than the next-most-difficult molecule. Thus, whereas cost was almost never an issue in the past, these data suggest that, in a growing number of cases, extremely high production costs might become an issue in product commercialization.

Conclusion

The competitive environment described above—less pricing flexibility, more competition, increasingly complex drug technologies, and shorter periods of exclusivity—has created a new set of strategic challenges and dilemmas for pharmaceutical companies. The impact of these changes on financial performance is captured in figure 3.9. As shown, the new competitive environment squeezes firms from three directions. First, the greater complexity of new drugs and increasing regulatory pressures are increasing the fixed R&D and capital costs of launching new drugs. At the same time, intensifying competition and changes in the institutional environment are drastically reducing companies'

FIGURE 3.9 The Margin Squeeze in the Pharmaceutical Industry

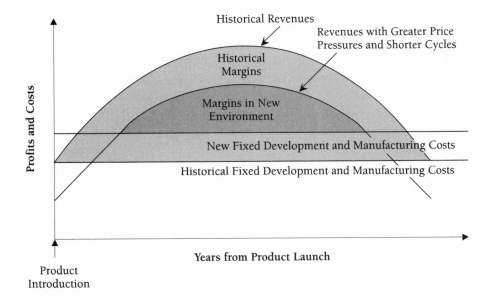

Source: Gary P. Pisano and Steven C. Wheelwright, "The New Logic of High-Tech R&D,"
Harvard Business Review 73 (September–October 1995): 99. Reprinted by permission
of *Harvard Business Review.* Copyright © 1995 by the President and Fellows of Harvard
College; all rights reserved.

latitude to recoup these higher costs through higher prices—indeed, the evidence suggests that firms are often being forced to reduce their prices. Finally, the rapid introduction of competing drugs and generic products is shrinking the economic life cycles of drugs, eroding margins earlier, and creating intense pressure to accelerate the cycle time of new product introductions.

This shift in the environment represents much more than the "natural" life cycle evolution of a high-tech industry to a more mature, cost-driven position. Costs are becoming a critical issue, and reducing development and manufacturing costs is high on the agenda of many a senior manager. But to maintain historical rates of growth, the introduction of new products with significant therapeutic improvements is even more critical to competitive advantage than in the past. By all accounts, pharmaceutical companies continue to invest heavily in R&D in pursuit of unconquered therapeutic terrain—including cancer, heart disease, AIDS, and infectious diseases. Thus companies find themselves utilizing ever-more-sophisticated R&D technologies—such as rational drug design, combinatorial chemistry, and genetic engineering—in search of increasingly complex, but potentially more effective, molecules. But this pursuit of more innovative drugs can conflict with the need to reduce development and manufacturing costs and to accelerate the product development process. Ultimately, the challenge facing pharmaceutical companies today is to pursue two seemingly incompatible goals: maintain or increase product differentiation while dramatically reducing costs and development lead times. The next chapter explores the increasingly important and often misunderstood role of process development in achieving and reconciling these goals.

CHAPTER 4

The Strategic Leverage of Process Development Capabilities

TURN TO MOST business press articles on the pharmaceuticals industry, and you will find discussions of exciting new areas of product research, promising clinical results for a new molecule, multibillion-dollar acquisitions of competitors and drug distributors, and new strategies for pricing and marketing in a managed care environment. Ask senior managers what they are doing to cope with changes in their environment, and many will undoubtedly talk about these same strategic levers. Pharmaceutical companies are investing in rational drug design, genetic engineering, and combinatorial chemistry to boost their innovative performance. They are forming strategic alliances with new biotechnology companies and universities to tap the leading edge of biomedical science. They are adopting new approaches for designing and managing clinical trials to reduce development costs and times.

All of these actions are warranted given the evolving environment, and all will undoubtedly help pharmaceutical firms compete in the future. However, as I studied a number of pharmaceutical companies grappling with changing demands and pressures, it became clear that process development—a capability long ignored by many companies—had quietly become an important part of competing in the new environment. Process development capabilities are becoming a necessary ingredient in the pursuit of, not only lower costs, but also faster development and enhanced product innovation. This chapter discusses how process development capabilities influence cost, development speed, and product innovation in pharmaceuticals.

The Traditional Approach to Process Development in Pharmaceuticals

Because gaps between existing and required capabilities are a focal point of competition, it is useful to consider the traditional approach to process development in pharmaceuticals against the backdrop of the competitive environment discussed in chapter 3. Interviews with personnel at several firms participating in this study revealed a pattern of behavior evident during the 1960s, 1970s, and, for some, as late as the 1980s. This pattern was characterized by three interrelated basic practices (see figure 4.1).

First, when developing a new chemical entity, companies delayed significant process R&D expenditures until there was reasonable certainty that the drug would be approved; in other words, companies hoped to avoid spending resources on drugs that would never make it through clinical trials. In practice, this meant investing heavily in process development only when Phase III trials were well under way.

Second, the role of process development was to stay off the critical path for the launch of the new product. In other words, process development was considered a success when it did not get in the way of new product launches. Providing a capability that would allow the company to develop more sophisticated molecules more quickly or creating a process that gave a drug a competitive advantage in the marketplace were off the radar screen. Indeed, if anything, these goals were considered a threat to the job of staying off the critical path. As one manager (who apparently still believed this philosophy) noted, "If you try to do too much process development, you'll delay the launch. That's never worth it." In practice, this philosophy translated into a very conservative approach in which major technical (or regulatory) risks were to be avoided at all costs. Most pharmaceutical firms spent relatively little effort exploring fundamentally different chemical processes for a specific molecule. Instead, the basic challenge was framed in terms of optimizing the original process developed by discovery research scientists, scaling it up, and adapting it to the production environment. This would normally translate into a relatively high initial manufacturing cost, but additional improvements in the efficiency of the process were expected as a result of increasing both scale and learning economies.

FIGURE 4.I Traditional Cost Behavior and Approach to Process R&D in Pharmaceuticals

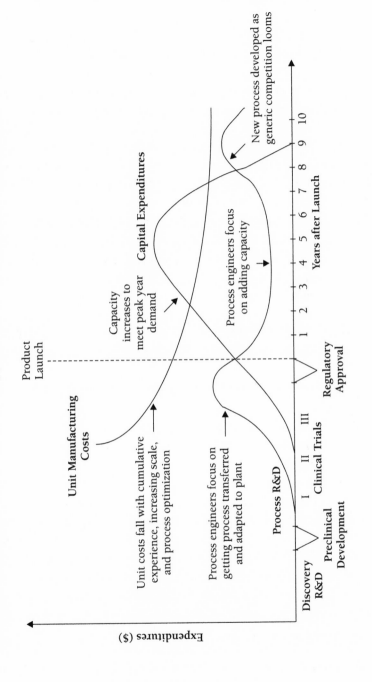

Finally, once a product was approved and on the market, the focus of manufacturing and process engineering shifted to bringing more physical capacity on line to meet growing demand, rather than attempting to stretch capacity through major process improvements. Although troubleshooting and minor process improvements were routinely undertaken, major changes to the process technology were generally avoided. There were two reasons for this. First, simply replicating an existing process through additional physical capacity did not require new regulatory approval. Second, adding physical capacity was unlikely to interrupt supply—a real risk in the development of a new process. Should a project encounter difficulties or delays, existing capacity might be insufficient to meet demand. Investing in additional plant and equipment was the safest way to increase capacity. By locating plants in tax havens (such as Puerto Rico), expanding capacity in this way could also create significant tax advantages. Generally, companies invested in major new process technologies only late in a product's patent life, when the threat of low-cost generic competition loomed.

This approach to process development appears based on sound logic and irrefutable principles: don't waste resources on products that will never make it to market; don't delay new product launches; don't stock out of high-margin products; do minimize taxes and maximize after-tax earnings; and do extend product life where possible. In the traditional competitive environment, it made perfect sense to approach process development in this way. The vast majority of drugs were relatively simple to manufacture; process development in turn involved few major technical challenges. In addition, process development could be completed quickly, and companies could afford to wait until relatively late in the development cycle to start it. Moreover, FDA regulations (and their overseas equivalents) were such that the process need not be finalized until the very end of the development cycle. Furthermore, with manufacturing costs amounting to less than 10 percent of revenues and capital expenditures being a small share of total investment costs, even grossly inefficient processes had little impact on a company's competitive position or financial results.

Today's Requirements

Today, however, pharmaceutical firms find themselves in an environment characterized by downward pressure on revenues (driven by greater competition and institutional changes), upward pressure on development and manufacturing costs (driven by technological complexity and regulatory forces), and

FIGURE 4.2 Financial Impact of Superior Process Development over Product Life

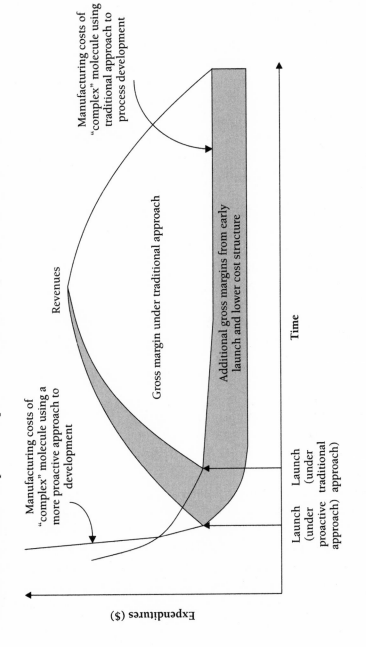

shorter product life cycles over which to recoup fixed R&D and capital investments. Given the complexity of new molecules and stricter regulatory requirements regarding process validation,[1] waiting until late in the development cycle to start process R&D will almost certainly lead to a delay in product launch. Additionally, shorter product lives mean that firms have less time to drive down costs to profitable levels before substitute or generic products reach the market. In such an environment, the job of process development is much more complex. Figure 4.2 depicts the interaction of three dimensions of leverage that superior process development capabilities might create. First, the figure assumes that sophisticated process research skills permit the development of structurally complex molecules, a capability complementary to product innovation. Second, rapid process development supports a company's ability to launch new products sooner. This enables firms to start earning revenues sooner than under the traditional approach. Finally, the ability to develop processes with a fundamentally lower cost structure generates extra margins over the life of the product. These three interacting benefits—reduced manufacturing costs, faster product development, and enhanced product innovation capabilities—are the focus of this chapter.

The Impact of Process Development on Costs

As pharmaceutical companies faced the competitive environment of the early 1990s, many recognized that years of growth and high margins had saddled them with uncompetitive cost structures—particularly in manufacturing. Historically, manufacturing strategies were driven by three basic objectives. First, to minimize economic liabilities, plants were located in tax havens such as Puerto Rico and Ireland. Such plants were generally far from the R&D site, thus increasing the costs of technology transfer. Second, to gain favor with local regulatory and government agencies responsible for drug approval, pricing, or even distribution, or to overcome protectionist barriers to entry, companies often built manufacturing plants in numerous local markets. This practice led to a proliferation of small, relatively inefficient, unfocused plants scattered around the world. Finally, given traditionally high margins and the high costs of stocking out, plants were generally sized with a significant capacity buffer.

It is not surprising, then, that pharmaceutical companies have embarked on a wide range of improvement efforts. Plants are being closed and networks restructured around fewer, more focused facilities. As companies seek ways to reduce fixed costs, outsourcing intermediate stages of production is being

FIGURE 4.3 Unit Costs for Three Molecules, 1982–1993

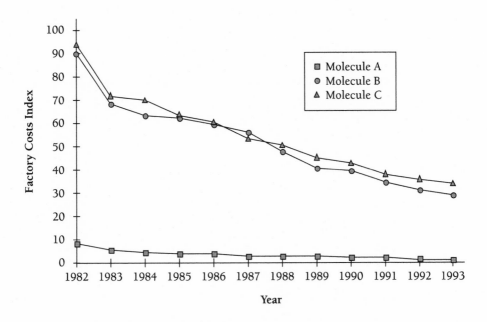

pursued with renewed vigor. Although the recent flurry of mergers and acquisitions is being driven largely by the pursuit of scale economies in R&D and distribution, the results include a consolidation of manufacturing networks. Eliminating redundant plants, streamlining networks, and outsourcing production will almost certainly help reduce manufacturing costs. The question is whether these actions alone will make any individual company more competitive. Restructuring may be necessary, but as a weapon of competitive advantage it fails a critical test: it can be easily imitated. In fact, restructuring in the pharmaceutical industry, as in other contexts, is largely about "picking the low-hanging fruit"—everyone can do it, and eventually cost structures will again converge around a new (albeit lower) level. How, then, do companies achieve a cost structure that provides a sustainable competitive advantage?

The answer lies not so much in the physical structure of their operations, but in the intellectual capital that underlies it. Here is where process technology and development capabilities play a critical role. To identify the potential impact of process development on manufacturing cost structures, an in-depth analysis was conducted of the cost histories of three molecules developed and manufactured at a major pharmaceutical company.[2] Figure 4.3 shows an index of factory cost per kilogram in constant dollars over the period 1982 through 1993 for each of the three molecules. As shown, unit costs fell dramatically.

FIGURE 4.4 Process Development Investment and Cost for
Three Molecules

(a) Molecule A

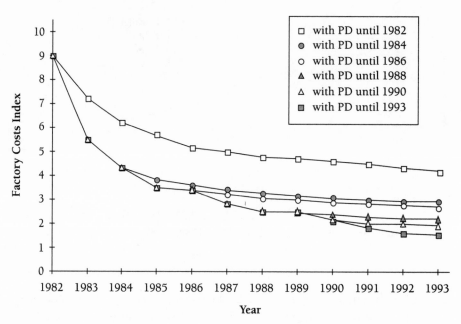

(b) Molecule B

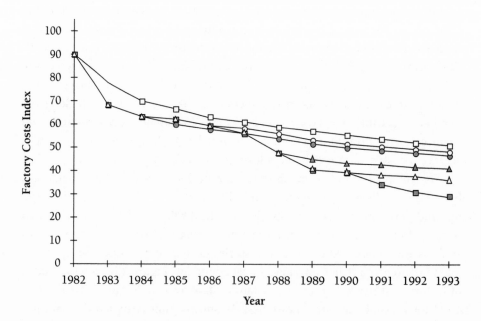

(c) Molecule C

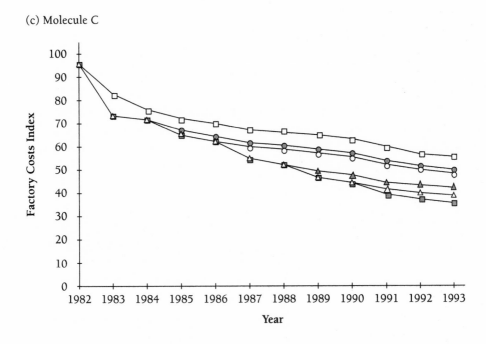

One possible explanation for this drop is the effect of cumulative production experience—the learning curve. During this period, cumulative production volume of all three molecules grew significantly. Thus costs might be expected to fall as a result of increases in static scale economies, improvements in operating effectiveness (reduced downtime because of better scheduling), and higher labor productivity (as workers become more familiar with the specifics of the process). However, the company also conducted a number of development projects on each of the processes associated with these products, with the aim of improving yields, accelerating throughput, and reducing manufacturing cycle times. Data were not available to isolate the specific impact of a given project on the manufacturing costs of each molecule (the company did not collect data at this level of detail). However, using historical data on pure volume effects, it is possible to isolate the residual impacts that might be attributed to process improvements.

Historically, pure volume-driven learning curve effects in pharmaceutical production are relatively low for two reasons. First, because of the regulated nature of the production process, incremental tweaking of production is not as easy to implement as in nonregulated contexts. Workers are actively discouraged (if not outright prohibited) from changing production routines in any significant way. Second, the capital-intensive nature of the process does not lend itself to the type of online worker learning that one normally finds in an assembly plant. Based on its historical experience with products that received relatively little process development expenditures, the company believed that an 11 percent reduction in costs with each cumulative doubling of volume was a reasonable benchmark, if somewhat aggressive.[3]

Figure 4.4 traces out a series of learning curves based on different assumptions about the year in which process development investments ceased. It assumes that, once process development ended, costs could have continued to fall cumulatively by 11 percent. For example, the top curve in each graph shows what the actual cost behavior would have looked like had process development ceased after the first year of commercial production and costs continued to fall at the 11 percent rate. The difference between the bottom curve (which assumes that process development stopped in 1993) and the top curve (which assumes that process development ceased in 1982) provides some idea of the total impact of process development over this period. The present value of cumulative savings was quite large. For example, the additional process development expenditures between 1983 and 1993 for molecule A generated a present value of savings (in 1983) of approximately $600 million (discounted at 10 percent, using constant dollars).

To gain additional insight into the impact of process development on manufacturing performance, the pattern of yield improvement over a fourteen-year period (1980 through 1994) was examined.[4] A primary advantage of using yields as a measure of performance is that a significant amount of improvement can be traced to specific process technology changes (such as in the basic chemistry of the process or the purification schemes). Figure 4.5 shows the history of yield improvement for molecule A. By essentially reducing the amount of production broth required to produce a kilogram of product within a given time period, yield improvement can have a significant impact on capital expenditures: less physical capital needs to be deployed to produce a given volume of output. Figure 4.6 shows how many production vessels (reactors) would have been required if 1994 production requirements had to have been met at the yield levels of different years. Take the extreme case as an example. If 1994 demand had to have been met in 1980, when the process was first introduced, this company would have needed 118 fermenters. Instead, given the yield improvements in the process, only about 12 vessels were actually required in 1994. In this context, the company was able to keep total physical capacity (in terms of number of reactors) relatively constant despite rapidly escalating demand. Through process development improvement, the company essentially bought itself capacity without significant capital expenditures.

FIGURE 4.5 Yield Improvement for Molecule A

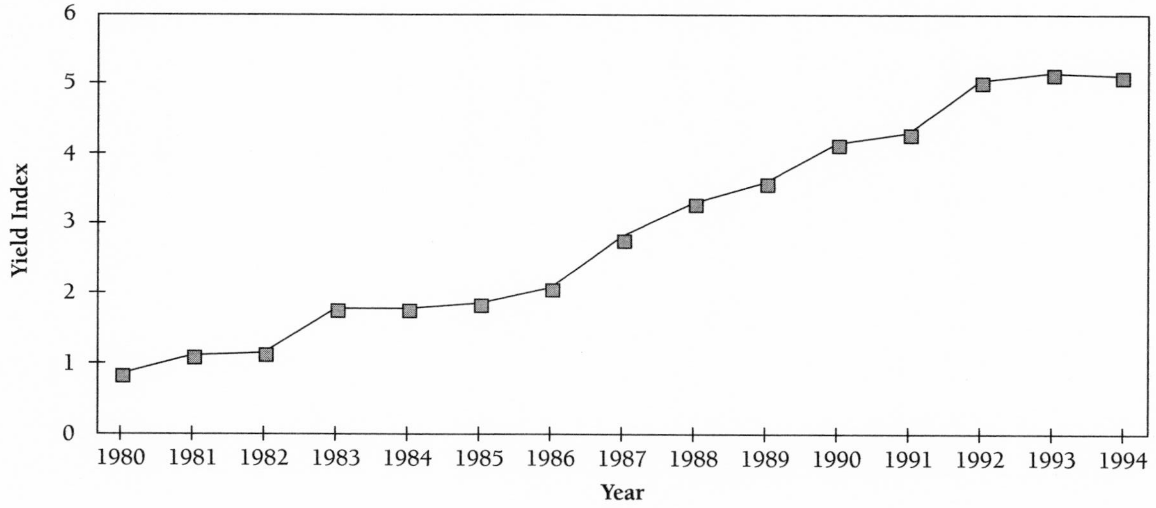

FIGURE 4.6 Reactors Required to Meet 1994 Demand for Molecule A

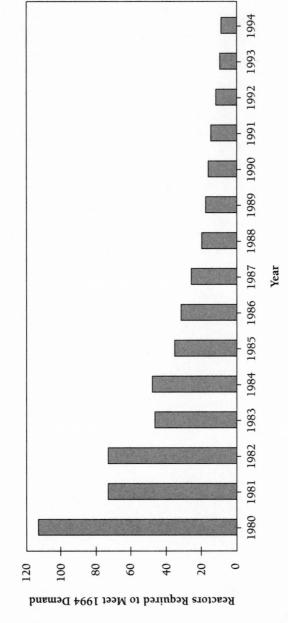

Note: Bars refer to the number of reactors required to meet 1994 demand had yields stopped improving in the year indicated.

The timing of process improvements appears critical to their economic impact, and early is better than late. If process improvements are concentrated toward the end of the product life cycle, the company misses the opportunity to reap unit savings on production up to that point. In addition, investments in physical plant and equipment needed to meet demand are sunk and cannot be recovered. The capital avoidance benefits of process development can be reaped only if there are investments left to avoid. With peak annual demand occurring in the fourth or fifth year after launch, there are significant financial benefits of having high-productivity process technologies in place very early in the product's life. Interestingly, the typical pattern of behavior observed in most companies in the study was for process development investments to be made as a reaction to volume changes. That is, rather than trying to influence cost structure and capital requirements in anticipation of demand, investments in process development were held back until demand materialized. Molecule A (discussed above) is a typical example. Cumulative volume and cumulative process development expenditures tracked each other closely over the life of the product, with a correlation of 0.99. Although process development had a significant impact on the product's cost structure, still further savings were missed by failure to invest more resources in process development early in the product life cycle.

This failure could be attributed to three factors. One possibility is that management simply undervalued the potential financial impact of process development. A second possibility is that not all opportunities for process improvement (and thus for process development projects) were apparent early in the life of the product. Cumulative production experience may be necessary to generate sufficient data, which in turn are needed to systematically identify opportunities for process improvement. Adler and Clark (1991) empirically demonstrated that such "second-order" learning effects were a significant contributor to reduced costs over cumulative volume. A third possibility is that management simply did not anticipate subsequent increases in volume and thus invested in process development only to relieve capacity bottlenecks.

To understand how cumulative volume affected opportunities for process improvement, and what early opportunities the company may have had to undertake process development projects, the distribution of process development projects for molecule A over time was analyzed. Two types of projects took place. One category comprised minor process changes (fine-tuning) to eliminate a specific problem. These were essentially troubleshooting projects carried out in response to a specific problem (such as a compound caking up in the dryers) that arose during production. A second category included larger-scale

FIGURE 4.7 Troubleshooting and Major Development Projects for Molecule A

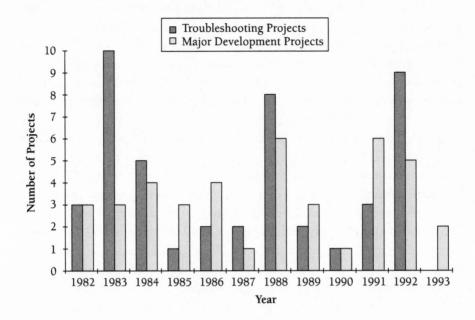

development projects aimed at improving the cost, yield, or throughput performance of the existing process. Whereas the first type of project was designed to return the process to standard levels of performance, the second type focused on improving the standard of performance. These projects typically involved changes to equipment design, process flow, or the basic biochemistry of the process.

Figure 4.7 shows the pattern of the two types of projects over time. Troubleshooting projects follow an interesting pattern: there is a clear surge early on, which suggests that some problems left unresolved during development needed to be addressed during the early phases of commercial production. This is not surprising; the same pattern would likely be found in other industries. The number of troubleshooting projects varies over time, but in later years there is a significant amount of troubleshooting still going on. This pattern is consistent with second-order learning by doing. Because troubleshooting projects are a response to actual problems arising in production, we might expect their occurrence to be correlated with production experience: it is hard to troubleshoot before you have had an opportunity to observe the problem. Over enough batches, it becomes clearer which problems are systematic flaws in the process and which are random.

The pattern of major development projects is somewhat more surprising. They seem to hold fairly steady throughout the life of a project, with a slight bulge toward the end. Since larger-scale development projects focus on making significant changes in process technology and performance, it is unlikely that cumulative experience with this specific product is a major driver. The company's process development scientists and production engineers have some ideas about the performance envelope they can expect with certain types of chemistry and process configurations at the outset of production. Thus, if there were opportunities to significantly improve the process, they could have been exploited early in the development cycle. The fact that major development projects were still being initiated late in the life cycle of the product indicates that potential opportunities for improvement were not being exploited. In fact, managers at this company conceded that, as the product aged and the threat of generic competition loomed, major concerns about cost arose, which triggered additional major development projects. This pattern is consistent with using process development to relieve capacity bottlenecks that arise as demand increases.[5]

Process Development as a Source of Speed

It is not surprising that process development helps reduce costs—most process development projects are aimed specifically at cost reduction. If there is a surprise, it is the magnitude of potential savings (and the opportunity for achieving them much earlier in the product life cycle) and the fact that management decisions regarding investments in process development are the key driver. However, the story does not end here. Because process development is a critical activity in the development phase of new drugs, it can have a powerful influence on lead time (from concept discovery to market launch). This may appear unusual, particularly in an industry where product testing (clinical trials) may take up to ten years. It is hard to imagine process development winding up on the critical path with such a large time window before launch. A closer look at the drug development cycle, however, suggests that the window for process development is much shorter than what might be expected.

Figure 4.8 shows the product development cycles for a typical new chemical entity and a typical new biotechnology-based drug, starting when the entity is discovered or the genes for a specific protein molecule are cloned (note that the discovery process leading up to this point can itself take a number of years). Once a molecule is discovered or synthesized, the preclinical research phase

FIGURE 4.8 The Product Development Cycle

(a) New Chemical Entity

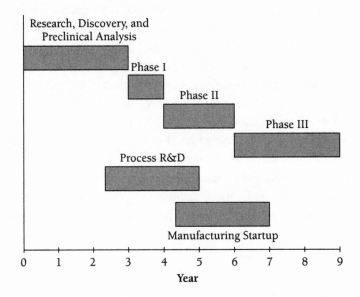

(b) New Biotechnology-based Drug

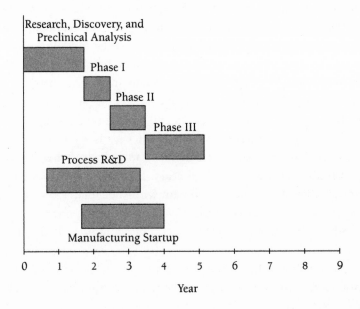

begins, with the goal of gaining information about the molecule's safety and therapeutic properties. As discussed in chapter 3, this typically involves subjecting it to a series of screens or tests in both test tubes and laboratory animals. Are there toxic side effects? Does it reduce blood pressure in hypertensive rats? Does it bind to the appropriate receptor? How quickly is the compound metabolized in the body? What improvements in safety or efficacy might be achieved with slightly modified versions of the molecule?

The next major stage of drug development is human clinical trials. Once a company has reasonable confidence in a compound's safety and therapeutic benefits, it can begin tests on human patients. Phase I clinical trials, in which the drug is administered to a small sample of healthy volunteers, are designed to determine the drug's safety. Phase II trials are designed to determine the appropriate dosage regime (such as 5 mg twice per day, 10 mg once per day) and form (tablet, capsule, liquid) for the drug. In general, the end of Phase II trials marks an important project milestone. At this time, the company should be relatively confident that the drug has no serious side effects and know which doses are most effective. In most companies, a senior management committee will review the results of Phase I and II trials to make a "go or no-go" decision on Phase III. Phase III trials, which involve head-to-head comparisons of the drug against placebos or existing drugs in a large sample of patients, are by far the most costly phase of human clinical trials, with an average cost (across all drug classes) of approximately $20 million (1987 dollars) (DiMasi et al. 1991, table 4). However, for some types of drugs requiring very long or complex testing, Phase III trials can cost upwards of $40 million. Thus, before committing to this phase of development, management should be reasonably sure that it has a compound with a high probability of success. It is important to note that ultimate commercialization is by no means assured simply because a company reaches Phase III clinical trials: approximately 13 percent of new chemical entities are abandoned after the start of Phase III trials. After Phase III trials are completed, the company must submit its clinical data for review to the FDA in the United States or to the analogous international regulatory body.

Several features of the product development cycle in pharmaceuticals bear directly on process development and the influence of process development on timing. First, the lead times shown in figure 4.8 are averages around which there is considerable variation: some drugs have made it all the way from discovery through regulatory approval in just 4 years (Bienz-Tadmor and Brown 1994). For certain acute conditions, efficacy can be determined relatively quickly, and trials for these drugs can be as short as 2 years. For conditions where no known treatments exist, such as AIDS, multiple sclerosis, and cystic fibrosis, the FDA will assign candidate drugs a high priority or permit relatively compacted clinical trials. For example, the average AIDS drug candidate has spent only 3 years in clinical testing, compared to 5.8 years for all other conventional drugs (Bienz-Tadmor and Brown 1994). Thus, in some instances, the window during which companies may develop, transfer, and validate their process technologies for new drugs is relatively narrow. Over the last several years, recognizing the huge financial impact and strategic value of bringing drugs through development faster, many companies have embarked on programs to accelerate their clinical trials. As overall development lead times shorten, the window for process development shrinks accordingly.

Second, the relevant window for process development is not the entire development cycle. At the front end, process development cannot begin until a molecule has been specified; this generally occurs less than a year before the start of Phase I clinical trials. At the back end of the cycle, FDA regulations require that Phase III trials be conducted with materials produced using essentially the same technology that will be used to manufacture the product commercially.[6] Further shrinking the window for process development are the lead times required for ordering, installing, and validating new production equipment or entire facilities. Some equipment may have procurement lead times of up to a year. Thus, decisions about certain critical process parameters must be made shortly after the start of Phase II trials. Essentially, for both new chemical entities and biotechnology-based products, the start of Phase III trials is the point at which most companies want to have the process locked down. After this time, minor refinements and changes are permitted, but anything greater will require costly additional trials and may delay launch. Thus, although the clinical testing period averages six years, the window for process development is only about three years—much shorter for products going through clinical trials more quickly.

In several industries, companies have succeeded in keeping process development off the critical path through simultaneous product and process development. This is already being done to some extent in pharmaceuticals. Indeed, many companies involved in the study reported that they routinely need to start breaking ground on new facilities as early as the start of Phase I trials in order to avoid delaying the total development cycle, and they may start construction of some facilities during the preclinical research phase. To fully appreciate the challenge of starting process development this early, bear in mind the extreme uncertainty facing process developers. From the outset, there is a very high probability that the product for which the process is being developed will not make it to market. DiMasi et al. (1995) found that the probability of a drug making it from the start of Phase I trials to the FDA review phase was only 23 percent. The odds of reaching FDA review increase to only 31 percent for drugs entering Phase II trials. Even for drugs reaching Phase III trials, the chances of success increase to only 63.5 percent.[7]

To hedge this uncertainty, larger companies generally have multiple projects entering clinical trials simultaneously. Because some process development must be completed in order to launch clinical trials, process development groups typically work on multiple compounds concurrently and face severe time pressures. The director of chemical process research at one pharmaceutical company described the dilemma this way:

> My group needs to work on twenty compounds; for each one, we are on the critical path for starting clinical trials. But I only have so many resources. I can speed one project up by putting more people on it, but that means another one will have to wait. The reality is that most of these compounds are never going to make it to market—we just don't know which ones.

It is useful to put this uncertainty in perspective. There is almost no possibility, for example, that an entire automobile development project will be terminated. Even in high-tech contexts such as that for semiconductors, process developers generally work on projects for which ultimate commercialization is reasonably certain. Thus methods like simultaneous engineering are economically far more practical in these environments. In pharmaceuticals, there is real value in being able to start process development as late as possible, but this requires the capability of completing it quickly.

A second element of uncertainty confronting process development in the pharmaceutical context is uncertainty over the project's commercial requirements. Capacity needs, for example, are an essential starting point of process development in virtually any context. Demand for any product is uncertain, however, and thus process developers never have the luxury of knowing precise capacity targets. The even greater magnitude of uncertainty in pharmaceuticals, as well as the timing of relevant information's becoming available, creates challenges and pressures unlike those found in virtually any other context.

The capacity requirements for any drug are determined by two factors: the number of patients who will use the drug (the size of the market) and the dosage (how much of the drug a patient must consume). Market size is always difficult to predict, but information about the population with the specific condition and the efficacy of other treatments does provide some guidance.

For example, a drug to treat a condition afflicting 100,000 people worldwide will not unexpectedly reach a market of 2 million people. Dosage, however, presents a different picture. At the outset of most projects, little information is available; dosage is typically determined during Phase II trials, after experimentation with a wide range of options (sometimes as much as a factor of 100 between the minimum and maximum dosage). Even a conservative change in dosage—from, for example, 5 mg to 10 mg per day—would double the required capacity. Among the twenty-three projects observed in this study, particularly in the biotechnology arena, initial estimates of potency were often very inaccurate (in both directions).

To put this in perspective, consider the development of a 16-megabyte DRAM chip. Process developers in this context do not have to worry that product designers will one day rush into their laboratories and proclaim that they accidentally came up with a 1-gigabyte chip (which would dramatically reduce the capacity requirements for chips per year). Similarly, they need not figure out how to quadruple capacity if product designers come up with only a 4-megabyte design. In the pharmaceutical context, process development must be extremely responsive to capacity requirements that can change drastically. Given that this information becomes available only late in the game (relative to when process development needs to be finished), fast response is absolutely critical to keeping the project on time.

Process development can influence overall lead time in various ways. Its most visible impact occurs when a major unanticipated problem with the process technology emerges very late in the development cycle (for instance, the technology cannot be brought up to full scale), and regulatory filing or launch must be delayed until it is resolved. Although this situation occurs relatively infrequently (in the twenty-three projects in this sample, it occurred only twice), it can be very expensive. Virtually anyone associated with process development dreads this situation because the financial impact is so visible. After years and millions of dollars of development work, the launch must wait for process development to finish its work; with each passing month, the company may be forgoing tens of millions of dollars of profits. One organization involved in the study found a glitch in its process technology shortly before the scheduled launch of a major new product in the U.S. market. With a massive technical effort, the company was able to get the problem resolved relatively quickly but still could not avoid delaying the product launch by one month—with a loss of approximately $45 million in revenues.

Although this type of situation is quite visible, process development also frequently affects product development lead times in more subtle, but no less important, ways. In virtually all the biotechnology projects and most of the chemical projects in the sample, process development was on the critical path during some portion of the project. Typically, developing a process technology suitable to meet quantity and quality requirements for toxicology tests and for Phase I clinical trials is on the critical path for biotechnology and chemical projects. In addition, process development is often on the critical path during the transition from Phase II to Phase III trials if there are problems during technology transfer or scale-up. When process development is on the critical path at various points during a multiyear project, the impact tends to be less visible than when a major technical problem arises at the end; however, the impact on overall lead times and financial returns can be equally large.

Process development performance may also influence overall lead times by determining the amount of material available for clinical testing. As clinical trials progress and expand to include more patients, the amount of product needed for testing grows accordingly. For some very complex products, a critical challenge for process development is to develop a process technology with high enough yields and fast enough throughput to produce required amounts of clinical trial materials with available capacity. This was a very common situation in the biotechnology projects, in which extremely novel and complex process technologies initially resulted in very low yields and commensurably low levels of output. It also occurred in chemical pharmaceutical projects in which the molecule was very complex and a large number of synthetic steps resulted in low yields. Interestingly, in many of these situations process development was not perceived internally as on the critical path because the clinical trials were rescheduled (in other words, slowed down) to accommodate the material shortage.

An interesting example at one company in the study was revealed when a group of project managers was asked whether process development had delayed clinical trials. Simultaneously, the director of process development asserted, "No," while the medical director overseeing clinical development contended, with equal emphasis, "Yes." Ultimately, both were correct. The process development group, responsible for making clinical trial materials, had supplied enough of the drug for trials for one specific therapeutic application. However, as is true for many drugs in development, many applications were possible. The company's original development strategy was to run parallel clinical trials for multiple indications. Because the process yields were so low, however, insufficient materials were available to run all trials in parallel (with existing pilot capacity), and the additional trials had to be rescheduled for a later date.

Although rare, there were three documented cases in the study in which problems with the process led to inconsistent test batches; this led in turn to confusing and distorted results during preclinical and clinical trials. For example, certain types of impurities might cause adverse reactions in animal tests or human clinical trials. Trials are then delayed until the causes of the problem are fully identified and resolved. Here again, such problems are subtle, but they have a significant impact on the costs and timing of clinical trials.

An excellent illustration of how process development can accelerate overall development lead time can be found in publicly available information on Genentech's Pulmozyme project.[8] In December 1994, just five and a half years after it was cloned in the laboratory, Pulmozyme became the first FDA-approved drug to treat cystic fibrosis. A critical factor behind this short discovery-to-market lead time was a compressed clinical trial design, which Genentech scientists developed in consultation with cystic fibrosis experts and the FDA. The compressed lead time also hinged on supplying clinical trials with materials produced using the final manufacturing process in the actual production plant. As noted earlier, Phase III trials must be supplied with the commercial manufacturing process, or the company risks having to perform additional clinical studies and analytical tests to demonstrate the therapeutic equivalency of products produced using the earlier process. By having its commercial manufacturing process developed and running early, Genentech was able to supply its clinical trials using its final manufacturing process and to avoid regulatory delays associated with gaining approval for process changes.

Clearly this strategy entailed risk. Genentech, for instance, had to invest $40 million in its commercial manufacturing plant early in the development cycle; had Pulmozyme failed in clinical trials, this money would have been lost. However, superior process development helped limit the capital risk. Genentech has publicly reported a tenfold increase in the manufacturing productivity of the Pulmozyme process over its previous-generation process, which allowed the firm to invest in a smaller manufacturing facility to meet initial commercial demand. Although $40 million was a significant outlay, a process that achieved only equal productivity levels with the previous generation would have required a much higher level of capital investment and made the early commitment a much riskier proposition. Thus developing a high-productivity process actually reduced the company's financial risk, in turn shortening the product's overall development lead time.

Process Development as an Enabler of Product Innovation

In helping to reduce costs and accelerate lead times, process development can play an important supporting role in product development performance. What is not commonly recognized, however, is that process development in an industry like pharmaceuticals can be a critical enabler of product innovation. In pharmaceuticals and other industries where process technologies directly influence a product's characteristics, product innovation often cannot occur without a significant degree of process innovation. Indeed, one need only refer back to the discussion in chapter 3 about the early commercial development of penicillin. Without new process technologies for fermentation, penicillin would have been no more than a research material.

The role of process innovation early in the life cycle of new drug product technologies is depicted in figure 4.9. The intertemporal distribution of both product and process patents is shown for two classes of antibiotics, beta lactam inhibitors and cephalosporins, both initially developed in the early 1970s.[9] As shown, the relationship between product and process innovation for both antibiotics appears to be highly complementary. Notably, both appear to contradict Abernathy and Utterback's (1978) product life cycle model, which would predict a dominance of product innovation early on and a surge of process innovation once product innovation began to decline.

These patent statistics are consistent with interviews with scientists in the companies studied. Novel classes of drugs often require the invention of novel process technologies. Biotechnology is an excellent example of the intersection of product and process innovation. At its roots, biotechnology is essentially a process technology: it is a method of producing proteins far too complex to be manufactured through chemical synthesis. However, as will be discussed in the next chapter, manufacturing a biotechnology-based product requires far more than genetically altering a cell. As pioneering biotechnology companies quickly learned, inducing bacteria or mammalian cells to produce a specific protein on a large scale represents a major technical hurdle and is a very different issue than getting synthesis in a laboratory. Because the basic inventions of genetic engineering were made in the early and mid-1970s and no products had been manufactured using these methods before, little was actually known about how to manufacture these proteins on a larger scale. Thus, like the emergence of antibiotics nearly forty years earlier, biotechnology required a significant investment in process innovation. Companies on the lead-

FIGURE 4.9 Product and Process Patents

(a) Beta Lactam Inhibitors

(b) Cephalosporin Antibiotics

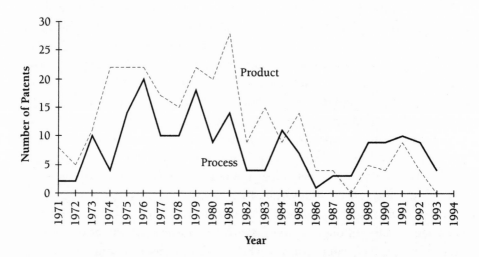

Source: Data compiled from patent records, U.S. Department of Commerce, Patent and Trademark Office.

ing edge of biotechnology product innovation found themselves needing to solve process technology problems that had never before been encountered.

In chemically synthesized drugs, process innovation has become more important as drug molecules have become more complex. Protease inhibitors, believed to be potentially effective against the virus that causes AIDS, are an excellent example. Recently, both Merck and Hoffman La Roche—two companies developing a protease inhibitor for AIDS—announced that their supplies of this drug were severely limited because of the extraordinary difficulty of the manufacturing process. Because of this shortage, the drug was made available (by lottery) only to patients with very weak immune systems, and patients on a waiting list would get the drug when more supplies were available.[10] The ability to develop commercially feasible processes for potentially effective but very complex products clearly provides a source of competitive advantage. Bristol-Myers Squibb's development of a synthetic process for Taxol, a treatment for ovarian cancer, is a good example. Taxol was originally extracted from the bark of the relatively rare Pacific yew tree. Although Taxol was relatively effective in clinical trials, the drug caused a major controversy because of its environmental impact. By developing a semisynthetic process that uses raw material from a far more common tree species, Bristol-Myers Squibb freed itself from the controversy. More important, by creating plentiful supplies, the company is now able to expand clinical testing of the drug for several other types of cancer.

A contemporary example of how advances in process science can unlock the potential for product innovation can be seen in the development of chiral synthetic processes. Some organic molecules, known as optical isomers, come in two versions—each a mirror image of the other—which can be thought of as right-handed or left-handed. Although optical isomers have essentially identical physical and chemical properties, they can have different biochemical effects. Inside a cell, a right-handed drug molecule will not react with a left-handed receptor or enzyme. Although Louis Pasteur discovered optical isomers more than 145 years ago, only recently—with advances in the understanding of the biochemistry of diseases—have medical scientists recognized their therapeutic implications.

The primary bottleneck to date in developing pure isomer forms of drug molecules has been processing. It is extremely difficult to differentiate left-handed and right-handed versions of an isomer, and as a result, roughly 90 percent of the 500 isomers on the market today are produced in fifty-fifty mixes of both forms.[11] This means that only about half the output of a batch contains the version of the molecule with the desired therapeutic effect.

Advances in chiral chemistry, the body of knowledge concerned with isomers, has permitted the development of chiral synthetic routes that generate the desired isomer in pure form. Most large pharmaceutical firms today have capabilities in chiral chemistry, and a number of companies have been formed that specialize in the development of process technologies to separate isomers.

For example, Sepracor has isolated and patented pure isomer versions of forty existing prescription drugs, including fluxotine (the active ingredient in Eli Lilly's blockbuster antidepressant Prozac).[12] Lilly hopes that these isomerically pure versions will have superior efficacy and fewer side effects than the mixed forms currently on the market. According to one recent estimate, roughly 80 percent of new compounds in the early stages of development are single-isomer, and by the year 2000, an equal share of prescription drugs will be based on single isomers.[13]

Strategic Leverage in Action

Throughout this chapter, data and specific examples have been presented to demonstrate how superior process development capabilities can contribute to competitive advantage by reducing manufacturing costs and capital investment, shortening overall development lead times, and enabling the development of more complex molecules. Here, two case studies are presented to illustrate how management actions and decisions determine whether a firm exploits its potential for process development capabilities to influence competitive outcomes. Both case studies involve chemically synthesized molecules that were complex to manufacture and targeted at relatively competitive therapeutic markets. Each company, however, followed a very different approach to process development, with significant results for the overall commercial success of its product. Although the names and specific products discussed have been disguised, the relevant data are not.

American Pharmaceutical Company:
A Traditional Approach in a New World

American Pharmaceutical Company, long a successful player in the world arena, had introduced a number of major therapeutic breakthroughs and had achieved strong competitive positions in a variety of key therapeutic markets. Like many of its counterparts, American enjoyed double-digit earnings growth during the 1980s; the company's senior management viewed this success as a result of the firm's drug discovery capabilities. Process development and manufacturing were seen as secondary support functions. As one senior manufacturing manager noted, "Our job traditionally has been to keep from stocking out of product, and to avoid running afoul of the FDA."

However, American also found that its R&D productivity had been slowly declining. Despite spending more on R&D each year, the company was launching fewer new chemical entities. Even more worrisome, American was dependent on a handful of patented products for a disproportionate share of its revenues and profits. Thus, when one of the company's research scientists learned at a conference that EuroLab, a small European pharmaceutical company, had discovered a new generation of anti-infective compound (SPP-1), American moved quickly. It signed an agreement with EuroLab to evaluate SPP-1, with an option to license and commercialize the compound within the next two years, in return for which it received a 1-gram sample—probably half of EuroLab's total supply. Over the next six months, the sample was subjected to a variety of analytical tests and animal experiments in American's research laboratories. The biological data from these tests were very promising: the compound had the desired anti-infective properties and also appeared to have a better pharmacological profile than existing compounds in development and on the market.

Based on these data, American licensed SPP-1 from EuroLab and immediately initiated preparations for clinical trials (see figure 4.10 for the overall project time line). It was at this stage that process research chemists first became involved in the project, forming a team to look at ways of manufacturing SPP-1. At first, the process researchers thought they might use the synthetic route discovered by EuroLab, but this option was discarded when preliminary analysis showed it was far too complicated and expensive. As they learned more about the structure and chemistry of SPP-1, the process research team realized that the molecule would be much more difficult to make—even in small quantities—than had been anticipated. Dr. Tony Rogers, a senior process chemist on the project, noted, "We made the mistake of thinking that SPP-1—because it was structurally similar to other molecules we had worked with—would behave the same way and use similar synthetic processes. We thought it would be straightforward to manufacture."

Because the company lacked sufficient SPP-1 to support preclinical tests and analyses, pressure on the process research team began to mount. Scientists at American turned to a leading chemistry professor who had worked with the company previously. After ten months of research, conducted largely in the professor's lab, a twenty-three-step synthetic route was developed (referred to as the Smith route). Dr. Mark MacLeod noted,

> From our laboratory experiments, we generated enough data to be confident that we could make enough SPP-1 to start clinical trials, but we knew the Smith route would not be a suitable process for large scale manufacturing. It was way too complicated and had too many steps. But because [the process research

FIGURE 4.10 SPP-1 Project Time Line

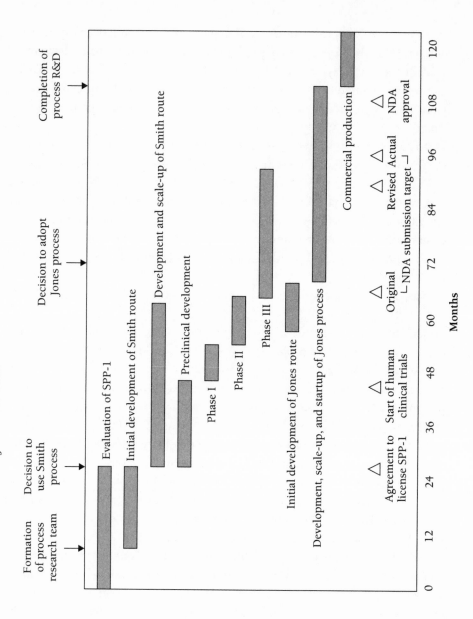

team] was holding up the project, the overriding goal at this stage was supply; no one was worried about commercial goals. We thought we could come back to them later.

The Smith route was adopted as an interim solution and transferred to a small pilot plant adjacent to the process research laboratories. Almost immediately, however, availability became a serious issue. Total process yields decline multiplicatively with the number of steps in a process, and the twenty-three-step Smith route had extremely low yields—about 2 percent. To meet growing demand from the clinical trial team and other development groups within the company (such as formulation), the first twenty steps of the Smith route were transferred to the company's larger-scale pilot facility, and the chemical engineering group assumed responsibility for improving this portion of the process. Process research maintained responsibility for the final three steps, considered the most critical. Now, however, with a growing percentage of American's process research and chemical engineering personnel assigned to SPP-1, availability of technical resources became an issue (the original development strategy for SPP-1 called for parallel development of two slightly different versions of the molecule). A decision was made to abandon work on the second version, and work on several other process development projects was put on hold as well.

The combination of larger scale and improved yield helped alleviate the supply problem. But, as the project progressed and excellent clinical results were reported, internal requirements for SPP-1 grew: the clinical development group needed more SPP-1 to expand the number and size of clinical trials, and the formulation group needed suppliers to experiment with different formulations. Dr. MacLeod noted, "Because we lacked materials, we could not do all the analytical work we wanted to do up front. As a result, we failed to generate the data needed to make sound decisions." Even more problematic was the effect of short supply on the pace of clinical trials. Throughout most of Phase II trials to determine proper dosages, the pace of testing was determined by the availability of SPP-1.

At this point, several steps of the Smith route were transferred to a commercial manufacturing site, where they could be run at much larger scale. This caused even more problems. Yields continued to be low, and a new round of development was necessary to "shoehorn" the process into existing equipment. Moreover, the Smith route was now divided among three sites, and material had to be shipped from location to location. Despite extensive communication across sites, integration was a serious challenge, because each site focused on developing and improving only those steps for which it had responsibility. Dr. Gary Mathews, a senior process development chemist, noted, "No single individual was responsible for the process in its entirety. In fact, I was the only senior scientist to stay with the project from start to finish."

As the project moved into Phase III trials (roughly three years after the project had been started), an air of crisis began to set in. Although senior management had been delighted with the clinical results to date, it was starting to become apparent that the manufacturing process had serious problems, and it was nearly too late to switch to an alternate process. Most of the technical resources for the project had been consumed attempting to optimize the Smith route. Mathews summed up the situation. "It was a vicious circle. We needed to find a completely new process, but to meet the project's supply needs, we had to pour all our resources into fixing the Smith route and making materials for clinical trials." From a regulatory standpoint, the project was reaching a critical juncture: if the Smith route were used much longer to supply clinical trials, then it would have to be used for commercial production; demonstrating equivalency on a new process would lead to unacceptable delays.

About a year earlier, some preliminary research had been started on alternative synthesis routes. One in particular looked promising, but it was discovered that its underlying economic analysis was flawed, and manufacturing costs would be too high. Another process, the nineteen-step Jones route, was also being tested. Although it had been run only at small scale (1 liter), a decision was made to adopt it. Mathews noted, "This was a huge risk, and we knew it. But we basically had no choice. We knew the Smith route would never be commercially feasible, no matter how hard we tried. And we knew the Jones route had problems, but we thought we could solve them."

Over the next three years, the Jones route was further developed, modified, and optimized. Optimization in particular caused serious problems. Mathews explained, "The last step was the Achilles heel of the process. It didn't work in the research labs, it didn't work in the pilot plant, and it didn't work in commercial manufacturing. But each time we thought we could solve the problem once we got to larger scale—that was how we had done it on other projects." Eventually, through massive commitment of technical resources (nearly 40 percent of the process R&D organizations were assigned to the project), the problems were ironed out. By this stage, however, the project was already well behind schedule. An application for a new drug approval was submitted to the FDA roughly two years later than originally planned. Although the drug received approval eighteen months later, the commercial plant—which was still waiting for critical equipment—was not ready to produce SPP-1 until three more months had passed.

The process development problems had ramifications for product design as well. For competitive purposes, American originally planned to market several dosing formulations for SPP-1 (5-mg, 10-mg, and 20-mg capsules). Unfortunately, work on formulation had been seriously constrained by lack of materials. Moreover, because changes to the process also changed the quality and character of SPP-1 in bulk form, the formulation group found itself repeating much of its work. As Mathews noted, "Every time we scaled up the process, we changed the characteristics of the final product slightly. This drove the formulation group crazy; they had to start all over again." Once the process was finalized, the formulation group was able to carry out the required analytical tests and development work on only two dosing formulations. Thus the company entered the market with fewer formulations than were initially deemed necessary to compete.

Finally, after having invested record amounts of technical resources, the final process—although meeting regulatory requirements for quality and consistency—was economically disappointing. Shortly after launching SPP-1, senior management approved the start of a new process research project aimed at finding a radically different process technology to meet the company's commercial goals.

Atlantic Research: A Proactive Approach

Like American, Atlantic had long been one of the world's most successful pharmaceutical companies; it, too, had enjoyed double-digit earnings growth during the 1980s, had pioneered several major therapeutic breakthroughs, and had seen little need to focus on process development capabilities other than scale-up and optimization. During the 1970s, the company had shifted its research strategy from an emphasis on highly random screening processes to an approach based more on the application of biomedical knowledge to the design of specific molecules. This more rational approach had yielded a major product breakthrough in the treatment of cardiovascular disease, which had gone on to become one of the industry's best-selling drugs of all time.

The company's next development project, however, encountered serious problems. The molecule was much more complex than in past projects, and Atlantic encountered significant roadblocks when it attempted to scale up the process in its commercial factory. Ultimately, the product launch was delayed because the FDA was dissatisfied with the documentation of the process. Dr. Tony Rogers, who had joined the company when the project was under way, noted,

> The project was a fiasco, but we learned an important lesson: the world had changed. The more complex molecules coming out of research necessitated more complex processes. Simultaneously, the FDA had become much stricter in its definition of a complete process description and its requirements for backup analytical work and documentation. To make sure this kind of project would never emerge again, we adopted an entirely new approach to process development.

The need for a novel approach was echoed by one of the company's senior product discovery scientists, Mike Pinella, who noted, "During the early 1970s, no one in discovery wanted to go after really complex molecules because we knew the process development group couldn't handle them. The medical chemists at Atlantic compromised their targets because of the lack of process development capabilities."

To help align the company's process development capabilities with its product development strategy, Atlantic put a new organizational structure in place. A process R&D group (which reported through the vice president of R&D) focused on the early stages of development. It was divided into two subgroups: process research and process development. Process research, which was colocated with discovery research, was charged with evaluating alternative process technologies at a very early stage in the development cycle—in some instances collaborating with discovery chemists during the discovery phase. As Tony Rogers noted, "The job of process research is to reach back into discovery and 'jump start' development." The process development group was responsible for scaling up the process to an intermediate (pilot) scale needed to supply initial phases of clinical trials. Finally, the chemical development group within manufacturing was responsible for optimizing the process for commercial manufacturing volumes and for adapting it to a specific site. Chemical development tended to become involved as the project moved into larger-scale clinical trials.

Atlantic also developed a new strategy for process R&D. Although the company recognized that each project involved unique challenges, a three-cycle approach was adopted as a basic framework. The first cycle, initiated as soon as a promising candidate molecule was identified, emphasized developing a technically feasible process that could meet the immediate supply needs of the product development and clinical groups as quickly as possible. Because this process would be used to create only a few kilograms of material in the laboratory, speed took precedence over production costs or manufacturability.

In the second cycle, which began as soon as there were promising data on the molecule's safety and efficacy, emphasis shifted to developing a process that was practical for pilot-scale manufacturing needs. Finally, as the project approached Phase III trials, the third cycle would focus attention on developing a commercially attractive process for launching the new product. To ensure that materials used for Phase III trials were highly representative of the commercial product, Atlantic transferred production to the commercial site at this time. The example of Pressidol, a treatment for high blood pressure, demonstrates this approach to process development in action.

Pressidol, which originated in research that Atlantic had been conducting over several years, was one of sixteen closely related versions of a family of molecules suspected of being able to reduce high blood pressure. As was typical in the early phases of discovery, scientists were unable to pinpoint which version of the molecule might work best or be the most suitable candidate for further development. Thus they conducted a series of experiments and derived even more versions of the molecule until, after about eighteen months, they were able to identify a version that looked particularly promising. At this stage, process research scientists were called in to begin exploring alternative ways of synthesizing this "lead" compound (see figure 4.11 for the overall project time line). To help ensure that their efforts would not be wasted if the lead compound changed, they focused on the core components that were common to all related versions of the compound. Mike Pinella noted, "The process research chemists can explore the options much more thoroughly than the medical chemists; they do things we wouldn't even imagine."

After several months of experimentation, process research chemists identified a slightly different version of the compound—Pressidol—which appeared to have more promising therapeutic effects. The project took on new urgency when Atlantic's primary competitor announced that it, too, had discovered a compound in this area and hoped to start human clinical trials within the year. Atlantic's senior management decided to move Pressidol into human clinical trials as quickly as possible and pressed for a small-scale production process that would supply sufficient quantities of the compound for the extensive laboratory and animal tests needed (until this time, less than 200 grams of Pressidol had been synthesized, through an extremely time-consuming and cumbersome laboratory process). Although much of the process research on its predecessors could be applied to Pressidol, its synthesis required a difficult carbon-to-carbon transformation that took nearly three months of work to

FIGURE 4.11 Pressidol Project Time Line

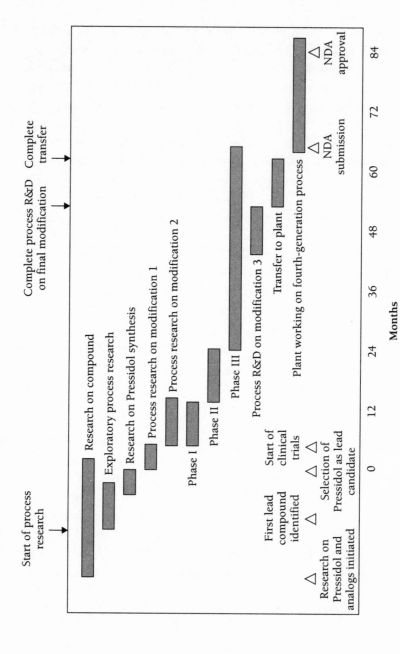

resolve—and involved collaboration among forty-five chemists from discovery research and process research. At this point, Atlantic's product development committee upgraded Pressidol from a "research" stage project to a "development" project.

Within four months, the process research group had developed a twelve-step synthetic route for Pressidol, which was used to produce the needed quantities for toxicology studies.[14] Shortly after the start of Phase I clinical trials, the process was transferred to the pilot facility under the eye of the process development group. Process research, however, did not stop its work; knowing that the modified process it had developed would be impractical at larger scale, a small team of chemists continued to seek alternative routes. Within six months, a new fifteen-step route was put in place to supply Phase II and the early stages of Phase III trials. Although it involved more steps and had lower yields, it bypassed some of the more difficult steps, which had limited the scale at which the older process could be run.

The final phase of process R&D was initiated as Pressidol progressed through trials and as the likelihood of eventual commercialization increased. The next critical milestone was one year before the process would have to be transferred to its overseas commercial manufacturing site. Larry Temon, who headed process development, noted, "At the stage where we are ready to go into the manufacturing plant, we get serious about developing a process for the launch."

Over the next several months, chemists from process research and chemical engineers from process development worked collaboratively to develop a modified version of the route that would be commercially attractive at large scale. They focused exclusively on a portion of the process that had no effect on the final step of the bulk production process—an advantage for the formulation group, which was able to work with a constant specification for material. Working on only an early portion of the process also helped minimize the additional analytical backup work and documentation that would be required for FDA approval.

The final modification to the route was made in time to allow transfer of the process to the commercial plant within the originally planned time frame. During the two and a half years in which the company waited for FDA approval, the process underwent small refinements and optimization by the chemical development group at the commercial plant. Once approval was granted and the product launched, the chemical development group initiated yet another round of work aimed at finding a fourth-generation process. Although the existing process met all the company's commercial goals (such as capital expenditures and variable costs), the group believed that significant improvements in yield and throughput could be achieved, which would be increasingly necessary as demand for Pressidol grew. The work on this fourth-generation process was completed two years after the original new drug application (NDA), at which time Atlantic filed a supplemental NDA (s-NDA). The s-NDA for the new production process was approved within weeks.

The example of Pressidol stands in stark contrast to SPP-1 and illustrates the multifaceted role of process R&D in the development process. Superior process R&D enabled Atlantic to develop a complex molecule; it was critical to moving the project into clinical trials ahead of the competition; it ensured that lack of materials never became a constraint on the progress of trials or in the timing of regulatory filings; it provided a commercially effective process with which to launch the product; and finally, by improving the process early in the product's life, it economized on future capital expenditures.

Conclusion

In the evolving world of pharmaceutical R&D and competition, the ability to develop novel process technologies rapidly, efficiently, and effectively plays an increasingly interdependent strategic role with product development in achieving and sustaining competitive advantage. High-performance process development, however, requires more than an acknowledgment of its importance by senior management. And it requires more than simply investing additional resources or taking bigger risks. Process development is rooted in specific capabilities to solve technical problems, integrate from the laboratory through the factory, and learn across projects in a way that deepens fundamental process knowledge. The chapters that follow go inside the development process to gain a better understanding of these capabilities and how management can nurture them over time.

CHAPTER 5

The Anatomy of Process Development

THE PREVIOUS TWO chapters examined changes in the competitive, institutional, and technological environments in which pharmaceutical companies operate, as well as the implications of these changes for process development. In the new environment, illustrated by the examples of American and Atlantic, it is critical that senior management pay attention to process development. Yet even this is not enough; high-performance process development—as measured by speed, efficiency, and overall quality—requires technical and organizational capabilities that may take years to build. These capabilities are in turn rooted in systems, behaviors, and organizational processes that shape how problems are framed, how options are explored and tested, and how solutions are implemented across functional domains and over multiple phases of the development cycle. Building the appropriate set of capabilities requires an understanding of the factors that contribute to effective development under a multitude of conditions. The next set of chapters is devoted to an exploration of these factors in a sample of twenty-three projects.

Before delving into empirical analysis, it may be useful to provide more in-depth background on product and process development in the pharmaceutical industry. This chapter begins with a description of the overall development cycle—a journey that begins with the discovery of a new molecular entity and ends some five to fifteen years later with an approved drug product. Even for readers familiar with the drug development process, this discussion should help illuminate how and where various process development activities fit into the broader development effort.

The second section of the chapter examines process development itself. The purpose here is not simply descriptive. The framework outlined in chapter 2 suggests that different types of learning strategies are required in different knowledge environments. This chapter depicts these learning strategies in action and provides insight into how organizations learn. By providing specific examples, it also illustrates how the knowledge environment influences the types of problems that can be solved through simulation (learning before doing) and those for which experiments must be conducted under actual operating conditions (learning by doing). Both chemically synthesized and biotechnology-based projects are examined.[1]

The Development Cycle

For all drugs, whether chemically synthesized, extracted from natural sources, or derived through biotechnology, the product R&D cycle can be divided into four stages: discovery, preclinical development, clinical trials, and regulatory approval (see figure 5.1).

Discovery

Drug discovery is akin to what other industries generally call "exploratory" or "basic" research. Whereas the mission of basic research may be unclear in many industries and the output difficult to assess, the mission and output of drug discovery is clear: identify molecules that will prove safe and effective in the treatment of disease. As discussed in chapter 3, the technology for drug discovery has evolved substantially over the past decade. Although once dependent on random screening of existing synthetic or naturally occurring compounds, most pharmaceutical companies today approach discovery much more rationally. Starting with knowledge of a disease and its biochemistry, scientists—including analytical and protein chemists, molecular biologists, biophysicists, and medical doctors—work backward to isolate classes of compounds or even a specific molecule structure that is likely to have the desired therapeutic effect (such as blocking a particular enzyme that may cause elevated blood pressure). Although much of the work at this stage is carried out using test tubes and laboratory animals, X-ray crystallography, nuclear magnetic resonance spectroscopy, and computer-aided simulation have also be-

FIGURE 5.1 Time Line for Discovery and Development of a New Chemical Entity

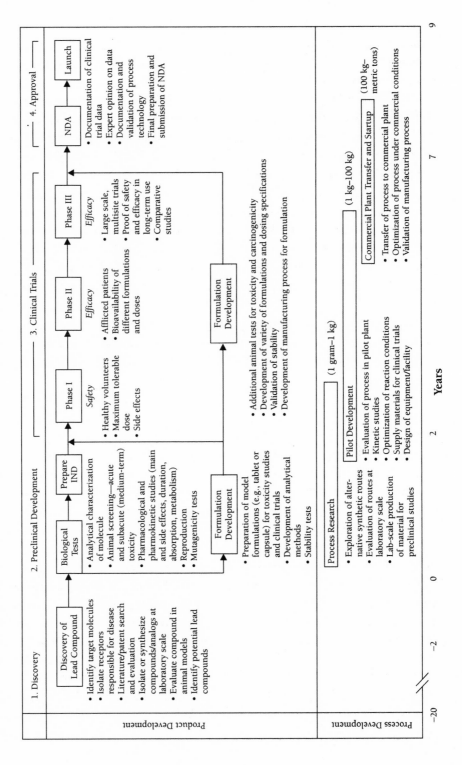

come essential tools.[2] The discovery phase is heavily dependent on trial and error. The generally accepted rule of thumb is that, of 10,000 compounds explored at this phase, only about 20 are deemed sufficiently promising to warrant further development.

One key milestone of the discovery phase is demonstrating a compound's biological activity through test tube and animal experiments. To do this, researchers must synthesize enough of the compound for testing. Thus a critical activity during discovery research is the synthesis of compounds suspected to be attractive candidates. This would be parallel, in other industries, to building first engineering prototypes. In some cases, the needed compound can be extracted from natural resources (soil, plant or body tissue, or blood and other body fluids); in others, it must be synthesized chemically. Over the past fifteen years, it also has become possible to derive compounds from living cells whose genetics have been "engineered" to produce a specific protein. These latter two techniques—chemical synthesis and genetic engineering (biotechnology)—are the focus of this study. Although the amount required is usually less than a few grams, deriving a synthetic molecule for a complex molecule can be extremely difficult. Molecular biologists, for example, may spend several years trying to find the genes responsible for a specific protein and then cloning those genes in an appropriate host cell.

Traditionally, responsibility for developing a method for synthesis in the laboratory resided with chemists or molecular biologists in the research laboratories. When faced with challenging synthesis problems, however, research scientists often call for assistance from process research scientists, who have deeper expertise in the methodologies available to resolve such issues. In the example of Atlantic Pharmaceuticals in the previous chapter, for example, process research chemists were called in during discovery to help generate a carbon-to-carbon bond.

The method of synthesis developed at this stage—typically referred to as the discovery route (in chemical synthesis) or the research process (in biotechnology)—is a world away from the process technology one might find in an actual manufacturing setting. For a chemically synthesized molecule, a typical discovery route might involve a large number of reactions carried out in a series of test tubes and beakers, using expensive raw materials or volatile solvents. Yields would likely be extremely low, and the process might produce only a few picograms (just enough to run the requisite experiments). In the discovery laboratories of a biotechnology firm, the initial cell line used to make the protein may be highly unproductive and short-lived, or may require a diet of expensive nutrients in order to grow to even minimal levels of density. Moreover, purity levels may be so low that an extensive array of purification techniques (such as liquid chromatography) would be needed to extract small quantities of protein from several liters of fermentation broth.

Like the hand-built prototype found in other industries, the initial discovery process in the pharmaceutical industry is useful for producing low volumes of product needed for further evaluation and testing, but it is not feasible for commercial manufacturing, where processes must meet an array of strict cost and quality targets. (Table 5.1 compares a typical initial discovery process with a full-scale manufacturing process.) The goal of process development is to move from a process that is complex, inefficient, and potentially unsafe to one that is practical, efficient, robust, and safe. The search for such a process usually begins after the project moves into the preclinical development phase.

The length of the drug discovery phase varies dramatically across projects, and simple "number-of-years" measurements can prove ambiguous. For instance, companies commonly support research programs targeted at specific diseases (such as high blood pressure or cholesterol) and may spend years researching the basic biochemistry of those diseases, long before attempting to identify a compound that may be an effective therapeutic. Scientists at Merck in the early 1970s, for instance, discovered an enzyme involved in the production of cholesterol. This led to research on compounds that could block the

Table 5.1 Initial Discovery versus Full-Scale Commercial Production

	Initial Discovery Process	Final Commercial Production Process
Number of Chemical Steps	25	7
Equipment	Test tubes 1-liter flasks	2,000–4,000-gallon stainless steel vessels
Batch Size (Output)	~ 1 gram	100–200 kg
Operators	PhD chemists	Technicians; semiskilled plant workers
Purity	1%–10%	99.9%
Cost per Kilogram	~ $20,000–$50,000/kg	~ $3,500/kg
Criteria for Process Design	Biological activity of molecule; patent issues	Cost; quality (purity); conformance to drug and environmental protection regulations; operability

action of this enzyme, known as HMG-CoA, which in turn led to the discovery of a compound called lovastatin. Merck went on to commercialize this compound as Mevacor, one of the industry's top-selling drugs over the past decade (Gambardella 1995). In this case, as in many others, an actual start date for the project would be difficult to identify.

Preclinical Development

During the preclinical development phase, a company's goal is to amass sufficient data on the candidate drug to warrant the much more expensive and risky step of testing in humans. The transition of a project from discovery to preclinical status is a significant milestone because it triggers much broader involvement from several parts of the organization and entails significant costs. As a result, the formal decision to upgrade a project is typically made by a committee of senior managers.

During preclinical development, several product and process development activities occur in parallel. On the product side, the compound is injected—initially as a single dose and then over multiple doses—into two animal species, to determine toxicity. In addition, pharmacologists use animal experiments to assess the pharmacological and pharmokinetic properties of the compound inside the body. How quickly is it absorbed and metabolized? Does it appear to have the desired therapeutic effect? What are the side effects, if any? Does it cause any reproductive or genetic defects? While these evaluations are being conducted, another group of scientists (usually analytical chemists, protein chemists, and pharmacists) begins to devise formulations for administering the drug (tablet, capsule, injection, or cream). This group also seeks to identify which "buffers," or inactive ingredients, will be used.[3]

During this phase, process research begins in earnest, although some companies invest more aggressively than others in process technology at this time. The chief customers of process research during preclinical development are the clinical development and formulations groups, which require small batches of the product to conduct experiments. Preclinical trials almost always necessitate the development of a process different from the one handed over from discovery. As discussed in the previous chapter, rapid development of a new process is critical because material availability can set the pace for preclinical development. Moreover, in order to start clinical trials, pharmaceutical companies need a process robust enough to make requisite volumes in the pilot plant and to achieve very high levels of product consistency.

Roughly half of all potential drug candidates are abandoned during pre-clinical development because of either lack of demonstrated efficacy, poor pharmacological properties (such as extremely low rates of absorption that necessitate huge doses), toxicity, or undesirable side effects. The end point of this phase is the preparation and filing of an Investigational New Drug (IND) application with the FDA (or its equivalent outside the United States), which officially seeks approval to begin testing the drug candidate on human patients.

Clinical Trials

The majority of time and resources in the drug development cycle are consumed by the process of evaluating safety and efficacy in human patients. As discussed earlier, clinical trials typically are divided into three phases.[4]

Phase I Trials. During Phase I trials, the drug is administered at multiple dosages to healthy volunteers to determine whether there are any intolerable side effects. Although even minor side effects, such as a rash at the site of an injection, are investigated, they usually are not enough to halt trials.[5] The drug is typically administered in a prototype formulation such as a capsule or injection.

Phase II Trials. During Phase II trials, emphasis shifts to demonstrating the drug's efficacy in controlled studies (although safety is still monitored closely). These studies are typically carried out by giving the drug to one group of patients and a placebo or alternative treatment to a control group. These trials often are double-blind: neither the persons administering the drug nor the patients know whether they are receiving the drug, the placebo, or an alternative. It is during this phase that the formulation group designs a number of dosage forms (such as pills or capsules) and attempts to determine which performs best in human patients.

During Phase II trials, process development has two primary customers: the formulation group, which needs high-quality product samples for their analytical experiments, and the clinical development team, which requires material for human testing. Internal demand for the drug escalates substantially as formulation work intensifies and the number of patients enrolled in trials increases. To meet this demand, the process development group will need to scale up the process, which may in turn require the development of an entirely new process technology. As clinical trials progress, process developers often feel squeezed between the short-term need to supply clinical trials and the impending need for a process technology that will be feasible and efficient in a commercial manufacturing setting. The cases of American and Atlantic in the previous chapter provided an illustrative contrast of the effectiveness with which different companies manage this balance.

Phase III Trials. The start of Phase III trials is perhaps the most important milestone in the drug development process. The purpose of this phase is to generate definitive data on the safety and efficacy of the drug in large-scale, long-term, multisite trials. Depending on the therapeutic indication, Phase III trials may involve thousands of patients taking the drug over years. It is during this phase that the drug is compared to competing products. By the time a drug has reached Phase III, there is an 85 percent probability that it will reach the market (DiMasi et al. 1994). However, because these trials are typically the longest and most expensive phase of the entire development process, the decision to advance a product into Phase III generally requires senior management approval.

Phase III trials are also an important milestone in the sense that the company's development options begin to narrow as it moves toward regulatory approval. It is vital to hold constant as many product and process specifications as possible to validate the drug's effect on a large sample of patients. In practice, this means that most critical product and process specifications must be set prior to the start of Phase III trials.

During Phase III trials, process development usually focuses on nailing down the final details of the process, resolving any remaining problems, and transferring the process to the commercial manufacturing site, where it is then validated and documented. Most companies consider the process development cycle finished once the plant is able to successfully run three full-scale production batches in a row. Data from these validation runs are submitted to the FDA as part of the regulatory filing. By the end of this phase the output of process development, and its customers, has again changed. One customer has become the manufacturing plant, for which the goal is to develop a process that meets commercial needs. The other customer is the FDA, which requires data and documentation on the process.

Approval

Once trials have been successfully completed and the process technology has been validated and documented, the company assembles and files an application with regulatory authorities (in the United States, the FDA), seeking permission to sell the drug.[6] The application, which can run thousands of pages long, includes all the experimental data generated during clinical trials, detailed descriptions of the clinical protocols, statistical analysis of the results, expert opinions on the data, and a thorough description of the manufacturing process (all contained in the "Drug Master File"). During this period, which can last up to two years, regulatory authorities and a panel of experts review the data and query the company. Additionally, the designated manufacturing sites for the new product are inspected to ensure that they comply with a set of guidelines known as "Good Manufacturing Practice" and that they are capable of manufacturing the process as specified. Only when the product license is granted can the company begin to manufacture the product for commercial sale.

Process R&D for Synthetic Chemical Drugs

Because the character of process R&D varies substantially between drugs synthesized chemically and those derived through recombinant biotechnology methods, they are discussed separately here, beginning with synthetic chemical drugs.

Figure 5.2 provides an overview of the flow of activities associated with process R&D in chemical pharmaceuticals. The entire cycle involves three phases: (1) *process research,* in which the basic process chemistry (the synthetic route) is explored and chosen; (2) *pilot development,* in which the process is run, evaluated, and refined in an intermediate-scale pilot plant; and (3) *technology transfer and startup,* in which the process is transferred and adapted to the commercial manufacturing site. Below, each of these phases is examined in detail. Although they are described sequentially, some degree of overlap is common (as shown in figure 5.2). As explored in later chapters, the particulars of the process in terms of the extent of overlap, the number of iterations, and the relative emphasis on different stages tend to vary across companies and projects.

Process Research

In synthetic chemistry, synthesizing a molecule involves transforming raw materials into a desired final product through a series of chemical reactions that either add or subtract atoms. The starting material and the sequence of transforming reactions defines what is called the "synthetic route," which can be thought of as the basic architecture of the process. For example, the synthetic route for many types of semisynthetic forms of penicillin (such as

FIGURE 5.2 The Process R&D Cycle for a Chemically Synthesized Drug

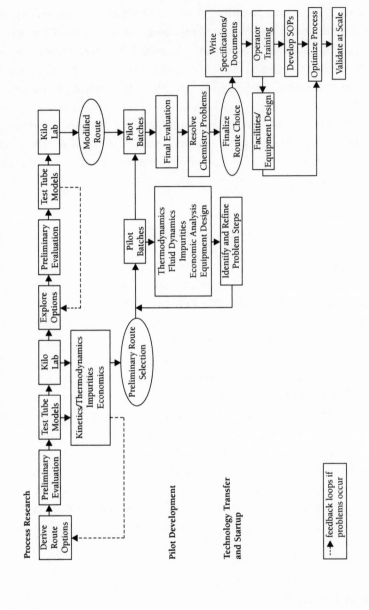

ampicillin) involves appending chains of atoms to the intermediate 6-aminopenicillanic acid (6-APA).

Any given molecule can be synthesized through a number of synthetic routes whose scope is bounded primarily by chemical and physical laws.[7] Process research chemists start their search by generating a list of theoretically feasible routes. Although research conjures up images of test tubes, instrumentation, and other laboratory apparatus, the search initially involves a set of conceptual experiments using paper, pencils, journal articles, and computers. Options are derived from chemical theory, from clues provided in published literature, or from internal databases of processes used for other molecules. In the Atlantic Pharmaceutical case discussed earlier, for example, a significant challenge in synthesizing Pressidol was a carbon-to-carbon bond-forming reaction. In facing this challenge, process research chemists had at their disposal a rich array of techniques (such as the Friedel-Crafts akylation process) available in the published literature. Chemists will sometimes talk about conducting "paper experiments," meaning that they worked out a potential route on paper. In more recent years, chemists have utilized computer simulation to aid the process. Researchers interviewed in this study described route search as a creative process in which groups of chemists brainstormed clever ways to construct a molecule. The process can be iterative. As one process research chemist noted, "As you see more routes, you get a better idea of what is possible."

The next step in route selection is to narrow down the list of alternatives. Before any physical laboratory experiments are undertaken, extensive modeling and analysis are carried out to eliminate the processes with serious shortcomings. Two bodies of knowledge interact at this stage: knowledge of the future manufacturing environment and knowledge of the chemistry. Knowing that the process ultimately must meet commercial objectives, be safe and practical to operate in an actual plant, and pass stringent quality and environmental protection requirements, researchers look for characteristics of the chemistry that make a particular route more or less attractive. This knowledge is often embodied in heuristics, such as "a good route contains as few discrete chemical reactions as possible." In one project in the study, the process research group initially identified twenty-seven theoretically possible ways to synthesize the desired molecule. Twenty-three were discarded relatively quickly because of a structural flaw. (For example, the chemistry of one route generated a hazardous by-product, which researchers knew would be costly and potentially dangerous to handle at full scale, and several others required too many reactions to be operationally or commercially viable.) In selecting routes to explore in greater depth, past experience also plays a critical role. Researchers may remember, for instance, that a particular intermediate was difficult to purify at commercial scale.

Conceptual exploration and theory can narrow the options only so far. In general, "thought experiments" are useful for identifying promising leads or, conversely, fatal flaws. But they cannot be used to select an optimal route. For example, although chemical theory gives researchers a good idea about which molecules bond well, it does not provide clues about a reaction's kinetic properties (how fast the reaction will occur). Kinetic theory is not well enough developed to predict which of two different reactions will occur faster or whether one will require a much higher temperature. Thus the next step is to evaluate the remaining candidate routes in small-scale experiments, to gather the physical data needed for thermodynamic and kinetic studies for each reaction in the process. For example, if route A requires fifteen chemical reactions, process chemists analyze each reaction separately. The advantage of this approach over one that combines multiple reactions into fewer steps is that researchers can fully characterize the process at each step and trace problems (such as the existence of impurities) to specific points in the process. Multiple iterations are conducted to examine the impact of variations in temperature, concentration, solvents, and other reaction conditions. These small-scale laboratory experiments are useful for answering such questions as: Does the route actually work as predicted by theory? How fast does it take place and how much energy is required? What solvents are needed? Are there any unanticipated side reactions?[8] What are the yields? What is the impurity profile? Are there any problem steps, and how might they be resolved?

The approach to answering these technical questions will depend on the company's development strategy and how well its process R&D is linked to the overall product development cycle. As noted earlier, the process research group often must choose between two crucial demands: providing sufficient quantities of material for preclinical trials and developing a commercially viable manufacturing process. Most companies adopt some form of Atlantic's strategy, whereby an initial route is chosen for expediency, while the search for commercially attractive routes continues as the project progresses. Thus, at the earliest stages of the project, evaluation of a potential route may focus on its ability to satisfy short-term material needs, while during later stages, issues of commercial performance move to the fore.

Beyond obvious problems (such as that the process did not work at all), the challenge confronting researchers at this stage is to predict manufacturing performance under commercial operating conditions from data generated under laboratory conditions. As discussed in chapter 2, these data may not provide accurate indications of future manufacturing performance. In moving from the laboratory to the commercial manufacturing setting, the process will be affected by variations in scale, equipment, operating procedures, and other elements of the environment; it is impossible to identify (let alone to model) the impact of these many subtle changes on process performance. Thus, at this early stage, the focus is on modeling the impact of the dimensions of the manufacturing environment that are known (based on past experience) to have a major influence on process economies. In chemical processes, perhaps the most important dimension is scale. Modeling scale effects is critical to an economic assessment of a process and thus central to the task of route selection.

Although scale-up is commonly viewed as a critical problem in chemical projects, there are no quantity or scale variables in chemistry. That is, simply scaling up does not, by definition, change a process's chemistry. Scale can, however, have important second-order effects. Scale can influence such process parameters as pressure, temperature, and sheer forces; these may in turn influence the performance of the process. For example, at larger scale, heat may not be uniformly distributed throughout a reaction vessel. Thus the chemical reactions taking place within the vessel may vary: a reaction may fail to take place in those areas where the temperature has fallen below a predetermined threshold, thereby reducing yields or increasing the number of impurities.

In trying to assess future manufacturing performance, chemical engineering models, dimensional analysis, and process simulation models play a critical role in bridging the gap between laboratory observations and commercial performance. But it is important to recognize that the fruitful application of these tools requires a detailed understanding of the process's basic chemistry (independent of scale). Thus what is learned about the process at the laboratory scale (and even in the conceptual exploration phase) lays a foundation for predicting how it will perform in a much different environment.

Before entering the pilot manufacturing facility, data are collected at a slightly larger scale in what is called the "kilo lab." The kilo lab is still a laboratory setting and uses laboratory glassware (not tanks), but is large enough to produce a few kilograms of material. Often, the reason for making material in the kilo lab is to supply the other development functions (such as toxicology) with sufficient material for their work. Kilo lab quantities also give process chemists an opportunity to uncover additional problems (such as trace impurities that are difficult to detect at laboratory scale) and to validate knowledge acquired earlier.

Honing in on promising options requires integrating two equally important types of knowledge: scientific knowledge of the chemistry and knowledge about what is feasible in a factory setting. On the one hand, failure to understand the chemistry may make it hard to resolve development problems later on. On the other, if researchers do not understand the factors affecting factory performance, they are likely to choose technically elegant but commercially impractical processes. One process researcher described the evolution of his organization's capabilities over the past ten years:

> We have gotten much better at finding good synthetic routes with fewer iterations. The [process research] organization has much more experienced people now who have a better understanding of what's practical in a factory and what's not. . . . I learned a lot from doing a plant startup. For example, I learned that, because of union rules in one of our plants, only designated people can open a [reaction] kettle. These people are not always immediately available, so parts of the process may have to wait. This taught me that the chemistry has to be very robust. You cannot have a process where a few minutes make a big difference.

It should be reemphasized that route identification and selection are not typically as linear as described here. More commonly, even as an initial set of potentially attractive candidates is being analyzed in the lab or used in the pilot plant to produce supplies for clinical trials, the search for alternatives continues. Thus process research actually takes place over a series of iterative cycles.

Pilot Development

Pilot development entails moving the process to an intermediate scale and selecting reaction parameters (such as flow rates, temperature, and pressure) that optimize efficiency. In some companies, more than one synthetic route is transferred to the pilot plant for evaluation. Pilot plants, unlike laboratories, are more representative of the final commercial environment and are larger in scale. Whereas a research laboratory might use 1- to 10-gallon glass vessels, a typical pilot plant uses 50- to 500-gallon stainless steel tanks to produce 10- to 100-kilogram batches. Pilot plants also operate more like factories. For example, in the laboratory, mixing is done by a scientist or skilled lab technician; in the factory, stirring is mechanized. By subjecting the process to a more representative production environment, it is possible to get a better read on future performance and to identify potential problems.

Two types of problems may be discovered at this stage. First, a process that had high yields and few impurities in the lab might have lower yields and more impurities when run in the pilot plant. As discussed earlier, however, these scale-up effects are the result of changes in the chemistry rather than of scale per se, and lower-than-anticipated process performance would trigger a search for how the chemistry might have been altered. The second class of problems is operational in nature. Certain processes may be easy to perform in a laboratory but virtually impossible to perform consistently in a factory. In one project in the study, process researchers were working with a synthetic route that, although attractive along many dimensions, involved a reaction that was particularly difficult to catalyze. Through a series of experiments, scientists learned that, by shining a light beam through the solution, the reaction would occur. Although a creative and scientifically elegant solution, this method was virtually impossible to implement in the pilot plant, which lacked the needed equipment and operational skills. The process was sent back to the process research chemists, and ultimately a new synthetic route that could be operated in the pilot plant was developed.

Interestingly, operational and scale-up issues can be avoided in a similar fashion. What is learned and anticipated during the process research phase appears to be critical. Through careful analysis and characterization of the process at laboratory scale, process chemists can get a good idea of potential operational problems. It is here that the organizational capabilities of the process research laboratories come into play. The better the researchers understand how plants operate, the more able they are to identify and avoid serious operational problems. In the organization that developed the light-catalyzing reaction, the researchers simply assumed that process engineers in the plant would be able to implement a solution.

There are important differences between learning in the process research and pilot development phases. In many pharmaceutical companies, two separate organizations take responsibility for process research and pilot production: often times, chemists hand off their work to chemical engineers. This division of labor is predicated on the idea that each phase of development poses unique challenges. Early on, the goal is to find the appropriate chemistry for the process, and understanding and characterizing the chemistry is paramount. During pilot development, the focus is on understanding scale relationships, optimizing flow rates and the design of equipment, and developing process mechanics.

This division of labor influences the way technical problems are framed and solved. In process research, chemists tend to frame problems in terms of basic chemistry. For example, low yields would trigger a search for a different synthetic route. In contrast, chemical engineers tend to focus their search on physical or mechanical solutions. They would tackle the yield problem by experimenting with flow rates or altering equipment specifications. These differences in problem-solving approaches result partly from educational background, but also from differences in the physical environment of experimentation. In a good research laboratory, equipment is never supposed to be a constraint—equipment is transparent. In contrast, equipment and other aspects of the operating environment are precisely what define a pilot development facility.[9]

Chemists and chemical engineers clearly have complementary capabilities, and it is no wonder that pharmaceuticals utilize both in process development. Given their different orientations, however, two management issues are salient. First, solving technical problems that arise during process development may require input from both chemists and chemical engineers. At the very least, it is imperative to ensure that their decisions are compatible. Second, with regard to the problems left to be resolved over the course of the development project, chemical engineers will play a much more active role once the project enters the pilot plant and moves into commercial startup. This implies that it is critical to identify and solve important chemistry problems before pilot production. A fundamental flaw in the chemistry that results in low yields, for example, may be framed and tackled as a chemical engineering problem. However, changes in flow rates, reactor designs, and other engineering parameters may help, but they will not fix the root cause of the problem—the chemistry. Moreover, attacking the type of issues generally dealt with in pilot development—such as optimization and combining steps (telescoping)—can be impeded if there are deeper problems with the fundamental chemistry. For example, if steps are combined before all the impurities are identified, their exact source will be difficult to trace. Thus, who works on the project, and when, may have a significant impact on performance.

It is relatively common for the synthetic route to change after pilot production has begun. This creates a development strategy choice: How much effort should be put into pilot development before the route has been finalized? How companies approach this issue depends on their overall strategy for route selection. Recall from the previous chapter Atlantic's explicit strategy of cycling through three routes (feasible, practical, and commercial) during development. On the Pressidol project, there was a clear understanding that several of the early steps as well as the final step were commercially viable from the start. With this knowledge, chemists and chemical engineers involved in pilot development could delay optimizing intermediate parts of the process that were likely to change and could focus instead on the finalized steps. Not all companies are so fortunate, however. In some cases, resources are poured into the search for a fix to one problem (say, low yield), whereas the real issue may be a flaw in the basic chemistry of the process (an intermediate that is difficult to isolate). In such a situation, the only solution—a late route change—would delay the project's overall time line, and much of the learning accrued during the pilot development cycle would be lost.

Technology Transfer and Startup

The final phase of process development entails transferring and adapting the technology to the commercial site where it will be used to produce active product, in bulk, for sale. This involves documenting the process in detail and then transferring these documents, along with research chemists, analytical chemists, and chemical engineers, to the manufacturing site. The challenge here is teaching the plant operators and supervisors how the process should be run. Many companies use "commissioning teams" comprising development and plant personnel. Although the problems of technology transfer often feature prominently in the literature on innovation, perhaps the more challenging activity at this stage is adapting the process to the specific conditions of the plant. Plants are complex environments, and the nuances in equipment, procedures, and people that make up its capabilities cannot be fully characterized ahead of time. Operating policies, operator skills, scheduling, and other production routines interact with process technologies to influence performance. Thus, although this stage of development is commonly viewed as transfer, it continues to involve development in terms of adapting the process to the plant and the plant to the process (Leonard-Barton 1988).

Two classes of technical problems require attention during this phase: unanticipated and anticipated. Unanticipated problems arise because of failures at earlier stages of process research and development or because of an unintentional change in the process at a later stage. For example, in one project in the sample, a company discovered an impurity while making its final test batches. Investigation revealed that a minor alteration—using water instead of gas during a single step—had been made after transferring the process to the plant, in order to make the process more compatible with existing equipment. This alteration changed the chemistry of the process and created the impurity.

Ironically, process chemists at the company's process research laboratories were well aware that the presence of water during this step would lead to the discovered impurity. Rectifying the problem was not difficult, but because the problem occurred just before launch, the company was forced to delay market introduction by one month and lost revenues of approximately $40 million.

A second type of problem that can require work at this phase is one that was anticipated but never solved prior to transfer—often because of time pressures. The hope is that the problem can be solved before the required regulatory filings. Unfortunately, this strategy can backfire. Technology transfer and manufacturing startup are inherently chaotic. As the venue changes from the relative serenity of the pilot plant, an entirely new set of variables is introduced—people, equipment, and procedures. Adapting the process to these new conditions is a challenge in itself. The task becomes even more difficult when fundamental process problems are still unresolved. Turning back to the experience of American Pharmaceuticals, the company knew from the start that the last step was the Achilles' heel of the process but transitioned to the factory despite its concerns. Unfortunately, the change served only to confuse matters more.

The commercial startup phase can be challenging because it is where process R&D meets (and often clashes with) plant realities. While process research emphasizes conceptual exploration, deepening fundamental knowledge, generating plausible alternatives to a technical problem, and laying the foundation for further development, commercial startup revolves around the immediate problem of getting the process up and running within rigid time constraints. Technology transfer and startup are considered complete once the plant can produce a predetermined number of batches of materials that meet quality specifications.

The Process R&D Cycle in Biotechnology

Process R&D in biotechnology can be divided into three similar overlapping phases (see figure 5.3). Although the general structure of activities corresponds to those associated with chemically synthesized drugs, the specific issues and the approaches to problem solving are unique. Biotechnology represents a fundamentally different way of synthesizing molecules. Indeed, the molecules themselves are fundamentally different in nature. In chemical synthesis, molecules are "assembled" by appending atoms or chains of atoms to a molecule (or, conversely, by removing chains of atoms from a molecule). The more complex the molecular structure of the compound, the more chemical reac-

FIGURE 5.3 The Process R&D Cycle for a Genetically Engineered Drug

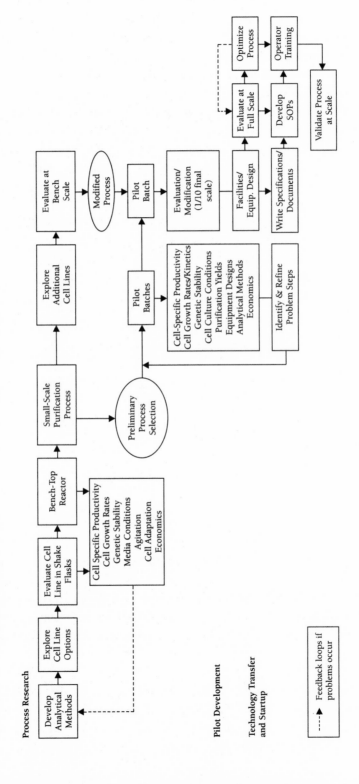

tions are typically needed to synthesize it. In practice, this means that the size of molecule that can be chemically synthesized is limited; past a certain point, the number of required steps would prohibit commercial production. For years, this constrained pharmaceutical researchers' choice of target compounds. Thus, although it was long known that proteins played a vital role in virtually every biochemical process in the body, the use of proteins as therapeutic drugs was limited because they were complex, large molecules, which could not be chemically synthesized. Only a few proteins, such as insulin, factor VIII (a blood clotting protein for hemophiliacs), and human growth hormone (HGH), which were cultured from natural sources, were available as therapeutic treatments.[10] But for the vast majority of the 500,000 proteins found in the human body, these natural methods were far too expensive to produce commercial quantities of a drug.

A critical breakthrough came in 1973 when Herbert Cohen and Stanley Boyer, of the University of California at San Francisco, invented a means of inserting genes into bacteria cells. Genes are responsible for instructing cells how to produce proteins, and each gene in the body is responsible for a different protein. Thus Cohen and Boyer's invention made it possible to insert the human genes responsible for a particular protein (such as insulin) into bacteria cells, which would then become capable of producing that protein.

Process Research

As in chemical pharmaceuticals, biotechnology process research begins once the molecule has been produced in the discovery laboratory. Researchers would have isolated the appropriate genes, inserted them into a host cell (such as E. coli bacteria or mammalian cells), and shown that the desired protein was expressed. Process researchers in biotechnology—including scientists with backgrounds in molecular biology, biochemistry, and protein chemistry—begin their search for a manufacturing process with four pieces of data: (1) the particular protein that needs to be produced (say, insulin); (2) the gene sequence that "codes" for that protein; (3) the host cell that discovery scientists used to express the protein; and (4) the method for isolating and purifying the protein. As in chemicals, this laboratory method is a far cry from commercial manufacturing, and yields are almost inevitably low.

The development of a biotechnology process begins with the design of analytical methods (assays) to detect the presence of the desired protein. These methods are critical because any change in the process may affect the quantity or quality of the protein produced. To conduct meaningful experiments, researchers must be able to measure very precisely the quantity and purity of protein expression. Analytical methods are, as one molecular biologist in the study described them, "the eyes and ears of process developers." The development of analytical methods occurs throughout the project, with later development emphasizing methods applicable to production quality control (where cycle time and ease of use become important criteria).

The economic profile of a biotechnology process is the result of the interaction of three variables: (1) the amount of protein an individual cell is capable of producing ("cell-specific productivity"); (2) the rate at which cells grow in culture (more cells produce more protein); and (3) the purification yield. Numerous factors influence cell productivity, cell growth rate, and yield, but the major process parameters include the type of host cell (such as *E. coli* bacteria versus mammalian cells), the gene sequence, the media in which the cells are cultured (grown), the type of vessel in which the cells are cultured (tanks versus roller bottles), the process flow (continuous versus batch), cell growth conditions (pressure, temperature, feeding regime), and the design of the purification process.

The initial focus for process research is to identify potential "cell lines" and to select one that is optimal.[11] Because a change in the cell line may have ramifications for virtually every other step in the development process, the cell line resides at the top of the process design hierarchy (Clark 1985). In this sense, the cell line is analogous to the synthetic route in chemical pharmaceuticals. Selection of a cell line focuses on four questions: Which produces the precise form of the desired protein? Which is most genetically stable; that is, do the genes mutate after a certain number of generations and cause changes in the protein produced? Which is most productive in terms of output per cell? Which requires the least costly and complex nutrients to grow? Unlike the search for a synthetic route, there is little scientific theory guiding the search for cell lines. As pointed out earlier, genetic engineering has flourished only in the last twenty years. Researchers in the field emphasize that "every protein is different," even if made from similar host cells. To answer the above questions, researchers must iterate through many prospective cell lines ("clones") and collect experimental data on the performance of each.

After a promising cell line or set of cell lines is identified, process researchers begin to experiment with basic process parameters in shake flasks, 1-liter bottles, or even 10-liter "bench-top" reactors. One challenge at this point is to identify and manage interactions across process parameters and outcome effects. For example, a new cell line might have higher cell-specific productivity but express the protein in a form that is much harder to purify, thus offsetting any gain. Similarly, slight changes in the genetics of the cell line might require significant changes in the cell growth conditions. Some types of cells will not grow in a tank unless they are genetically adapted to that environment. Here again, the process is highly iterative, with trial and error predominating. For example, one type of media in which to grow cells is blood serum from fetal calves. Because serum-rich media are very expensive and the use of blood serum creates purification problems, process developers try to use serum-free media whenever possible. But there is no theory to dictate when serum-free media will work. As one researcher interviewed during the study described it, "For one product, we could easily switch to serum-free media. Another product—which used the exact same host cell—will die completely when switched to serum-free. You just can't tell ahead of time what is going to work."

Another difference between chemical and biotechnology synthesis is the researcher's ability to develop a complete understanding of each process step. As discussed earlier, chemical process researchers can analyze a process reaction by reaction. Each intermediate from each step can be isolated, analyzed, and characterized, allowing chemical process researchers to track down the source of any problem (such as an impurity because of a reaction step). Such precision is virtually impossible in the biotechnology context, where each process is composed of literally thousands of reactions. With the exception of a few chemical modifications made to the final product, however, almost all of these occur inside the host cell. In fact, the motive for genetic engineering is that it harnesses the enormous power of cells to construct highly complex proteins. Although molecular biologists understand the mechanisms by which cells carry out this task, the precise sequence of intracellular reactions for any given product is not well known. Thus, although researchers might observe that slight changes in the genetics of the cell or the cell media have a large impact on cell productivity, they generally cannot trace the impact to a specific reaction undertaken by the cell.

Pilot Development

As in chemical synthesis, pilot development involves scaling up the process to an intermediate level. However, the function of this phase is very different in the context of biotechnology. Whereas pilot production runs in chemical technology validate extensive conceptual and empirical knowledge generated in the laboratory, pilot development in biotechnology is much more exploratory. As in chemical processes, scale can influence the performance of biotechnology processes. However, unlike chemical process technology, biotechnology scale-up effects are difficult to predict because there is little theoretical or conceptual knowledge about what environmental variables might affect the process. For example, how well a cell will grow in a tank depends on factors that are not understood or are difficult to model. The protein that the cells have been genetically engineered to produce may actually be toxic to the cell itself. Researchers know that a critical mass of cells must be grown before the concentration of protein will reach a set point, but there are no models spelling out the necessary level of growth or the desired relationship between protein concentration and rates of cell death. Lacking theory, heuristics, and practical experience, only trial and error at larger scale can be used to generate the requisite empirical data.

Although laboratory experiments generate data on the conditions needed to make the cells grow and express the proper protein, failure of pilot batches is a common thread in the interviews conducted during this study and in published accounts. In a published interview discussing Genentech's early efforts to scale up human growth hormone, company cofounder Robert Swanson noted, "Scientifically, we began at square one by taking microorganisms out of the laboratory scale and putting them into much larger stainless steel tanks. You know, learning how those organisms worked in that new environment wasn't easy. The first time we did it, they all dropped dead—they didn't like it."[12] One researcher interviewed during the study emphasized how process performance might vary between laboratory and pilot scale, recalling his experience on a project: "According to research, clone number 53 would express at 30 to 40 picograms per cell per day (pcd). But once we scaled it up, performance went down to about 15 pcd." Compounding the scale-up problem is the lack of understanding of how the processes operate even at small scale. In the example above, researchers could not explain what made clone 53 express 30 to 40 pcd in the lab, let alone identify the factors that caused the yield to drop in the pilot plan.

Much of the problem solving during pilot development revolves around identifying and rectifying the underlying causes of problems revealed in initial pilot runs. Changes in media composition, reactor design, cell growth rate, fermentation conditions, and purification method are a few of the levers used to improve process performance at this phase. Occasionally, the cell line will be changed to gain a major leap in performance. But because such changes can be disruptive to both the process development effort and clinical trials, companies generally prefer to avoid them unless major performance improvements are needed for commercial viability. Once the process is stabilized, emphasis turns toward optimization and improvement. Here again, a set of pilot-scale experiments are conducted to determine the influence on performance of a number of process parameters. At this stage, problem solving also focuses on identifying the critical variables affecting the process (What is making the yields go down? Why are the cells dying?) and designing procedures for controlling them. As in any process, getting a process under control requires that a significant amount of data be generated over a number of controlled experimental runs. One company reported that it tended to increase yields by about 25 percent just by getting the process under control.

Technology Transfer and Startup

As in chemical pharmaceuticals, manufacturing startup in biotechnology involves transferring the technology to the commercial manufacturing plant and adapting the technology and the plant to one another. As was the case in chemical pharmaceuticals, changing the venue introduces a new set of process variables—including equipment design, scale, and procedures. However, in biotechnology, the effect of these variables is less well understood. Nor are all the variables themselves fully known ahead of time. Much of the knowledge associated with biotechnology processes appears to be tacit.[13] One process developer interviewed during the study emphasized that it was the nuances of the manufacturing environment that made the transfer and startup difficult: "The subtle things are most difficult—things you would not even think about writing down cause the most problems, such as slight differences in protocols."

As was the case for initial pilot production runs, it is not unusual for the first commercial-scale runs to fail or to encounter serious performance problems, which may stem from many sources. One is that the process technology itself has not been fully communicated and transferred into the manufacturing setting. Given the tacit nature of the process technology, it is understandable how this might happen. Although the variations may be seemingly minor (for example, in a handling procedure), they may have a significant impact on performance. The problem here is not with the process that was developed, but with the process eventually implemented in the plant. A second problem is rooted in the process itself. For technical reasons, the process may be incompatible with the equipment, scale, or procedures of the operating environment. As noted earlier, the effects of scale can be difficult to predict, and further adaptations to the process may be required at full scale.

Even more common in this study, however, were incompatibilities between the process technology and the production equipment. While pioneering biotechnology companies were attempting to develop novel genetically engineered process technologies, vendors were struggling to develop production equipment to handle these processes. In some instances, biotechnology companies found themselves needing to develop the process *and* the specialized equipment needed to operate the process. Given the paucity of production experience that existed in the early days of the industry, it is not surprising that the biotechnology companies and the vendors had a difficult time designing appropriate equipment, or that there were often mismatches between the requirements of the process and the capabilities of the equipment.

The final step in manufacturing startup is process validation. At this point, the company must run a predetermined number of batches to prove that the process can consistently produce the protein at specified quality levels. At this stage, the process must be extremely well understood and fully under control, and all standard operating procedures (SOPs) must be fully documented.

Given the risks of introducing new process variables with a change in venue, biotechnology companies commonly undertake pilot production in the commercial manufacturing setting. Thus, although they have been described here as discrete phases, they are often combined in practice. For example, the pilot plant may simply be an enclosed area (a "suite") within the larger manufacturing facility. Similarly, to help avoid the equipment incompatibilities discussed above, the pilot production facility may be upgraded and adapted over the course of development to meet the scale and regulatory requirements of commercial manufacturing. In addition, as will be discussed in the next chapter, the entire development cycle—from process research through manufacturing startup—generally involves the same development organization. That is, process research is not organizationally split from pilot development and manufacturing startup, and the scientists who develop the process in the pilot plant are responsible for starting up the process in the commercial plant. In some firms, these scientists stayed on to run the commercial process and became part of the manufacturing management infrastructure.

Knowledge in Chemical Synthesis versus Biotechnology

The above descriptions of the process R&D cycles for both chemically synthesized and biotechnology-based drugs indicate that, although they face the same general issues, process developers in chemical synthesis and biotechnology operate from very different knowledge bases, largely related to variations in the maturity of the two technologies. Whereas chemical synthesis dates back more than two centuries, the major discovery triggering commercial R&D on therapeutic recombinant proteins was made in 1973, and only roughly twenty-five biotechnology-based therapeutics have been approved for sale in the United States to date. Furthermore, although there is extensive basic scientific research on molecular biology, cell biology, biochemistry, protein chemistry, and other relevant scientific disciplines, most of this work has been geared toward the problems of finding and cloning molecules with specific therapeutic effects. There has been very little research on the problems of engineering larger-scale biotechnology processes, and the industry has accumulated scant practice with process design and scale-up. Researchers interviewed during this study generally described the development of biotechnology processes as "involving more art than science."

The critical differences between the structure of knowledge in chemical synthesis and in biotechnology projects fall into three categories: (1) theoretical understanding of the basic processes; (2) ability to fully characterize intermediates and final products; and (3) knowledge of the second-order scale-up effects. Each is discussed below.

Theoretical Foundations

Compared to chemical synthesis, biotechnology process technology is characterized by a relatively immature theoretical knowledge base. Whereas the principles and theories of chemical transformation are well developed and articulated, the precise principles governing the production of recombinant proteins is only dimly understood. As a result, problem solving in biotechnology relies much more heavily on physical experimentation than on conceptual modeling.

Ability to Characterize Intermediates and Final Products

Whereas the structure of the relatively small molecules produced through chemical synthesis can be fully characterized, the structure of most proteins cannot. As a result, it can be difficult to trace how a small change in the process might alter the structure of the protein. Moreover, unlike chemical researchers, biotechnology researchers cannot isolate, analyze, and characterize each reaction in the process, because each process is composed of literally thousands of reactions, virtually all of which occur inside a host cell. Although molecular biologists understand the mechanisms by which cells synthesize proteins, the precise sequence of intracellular reactions for any given product is not well known. Thus, although researchers might observe problems in a process, they cannot be traced back to a specific reaction undertaken in the cell. The difficulty of probing the molecular details of the process make it difficult to build deeper knowledge of primary causes and effects. This in turn makes it difficult to build "micro-models" of the process that permit predictions about how changes in parameters or operating conditions might influence process behavior and performance.

Knowledge of Second-Order Scale-up Effects

As in chemicals, scale can have second-order effects on biotechnology processes, but these effects are not well understood in biotechnology. In the world of chemical synthesis, the discipline of chemical engineering and the accumulation of practical experience have yielded a wealth of principles, heuristics, scale-up recipes, and models for simulating scale effects. Process developers in biotechnology operate with few such theoretical or heuristic weapons. Moreover, beyond scale effects, they must confront the novelty and dynamic nature of the production environment itself. Equipment design, operating procedures, even regulatory rules of the game have all been evolving.

The framework presented in chapter 2 would predict that very different development strategies would be attractive in these two environments. Referring back to terminology introduced in chapter 2, the structure of knowledge surrounding chemical synthesis more readily allows laboratory observations to be mapped into future outcomes in a commercial manufacturing environment. The key issue in this type of environment is ensuring accurate generation of laboratory models. We would expect learning before doing to be a much more attractive development strategy in the context of chemical pharmaceuticals.

In the context of biotechnology, creating a representative simulation of the process in a laboratory environment is extremely difficult for the three reasons discussed above. Thus, although some laboratory observations are critical, the real uncertainty lies in predicting commercial performance. Only by generating real data from the actual manufacturing environment can the process be fully understood. In this knowledge environment, we would expect to find learning by doing preferred as a development strategy.

Conclusion

This chapter has suggested that there may be important differences in the optimal development strategies for typical biotechnology and chemical synthesis projects. This issue is examined empirically in the next chapter. However, some of the knowledge and competencies discussed in this chapter also may contain a firm-specific component. Differences among chemical-based organizations are explored in chapter 7, while differences among biotechnology organizations are the focus of chapter 8.

The Determinants of Performance: Development Lead Time and Cost

THE PREVIOUS CHAPTER provided a detailed analysis of the sequence and structure of activities from the discovery of a new chemical or biochemical entity to full-scale commercial manufacturing. Its purpose was to illuminate the technical context in which process development occurs and to highlight critical differences in how problems are identified, framed, and solved in the chemical and biotechnology segments. In offering a composite sketch of development, the previous chapter suppressed discussion of the impact of many salient managerial issues and choices on performance, including: How much relative effort should a company put into process research versus pilot development? When is the best time to transfer a technology to the manufacturing plant? What type of organizational structure is best suited to process development? Should process research be organizationally distinct from process development? This chapter attempts to shed light on these questions, using empirical data from twenty-three process development projects.

During a process development project, literally thousands of choices must be made. Many of these are technical (Should we try running the process at a higher temperature?), but many are also managerial in nature, and the two are not completely independent. Decisions about project management help shape how technical problems are framed and solved. Development is at one level a technical problem-solving process. But, in the context of virtually any development project, few problems are solved by individuals working in complete isolation. Decisions must be coordinated, information shared, and learning integrated across individuals, functional departments, and geographic locations. Thus development is an organizational problem-solving process.

The previous chapter drew attention to fundamental differences in the structure of knowledge surrounding chemical synthesis and biotechnology projects. The framework presented in chapter 2 suggests that these variations would have important implications as companies in either industry orient toward a strategy of either learning by doing or learning before doing. A primary focus of this chapter is to explore, through comparative analysis, how the chosen strategy affects development performance.

Development Lead Time and Cost

The statistical analysis in this chapter focuses on two metrics of performance: process development lead time and process development cost. Process development lead time is defined as the number of calendar months from the initiation of process research to the successful validation of the process at commercial scale, including only the months in which the project is active. This latter distinction is important, because in pharmaceuticals, process development activities may be put on hold for one product candidate while resources are shifted to another, more urgent candidate. This decision is a result of managerial choice, however, rather than a reflection of organizational capabilities. It generally was possible to identify from project records idle periods lasting one month or more.

It is worth noting that organizations capable of rapid process development enjoy an option that slower organizations lack. At highly uncertain junctures in the development cycle, they may choose to put process development on hold until more information is available—without delaying the scheduled launch date. This not only conserves resources and reduces risk but also improves the overall quality of the process development effort by ensuring that all the necessary product information—including dosage, dosage form, potential size of market, and so forth—is used when designing the process. A stylized comparison of two organizations is presented in figure 6.1, to highlight how process development can be used strategically to hedge risk. Although both organizations completed the necessary development tasks 50 months after the project was initiated, organization A used a hold time of 20 months to await

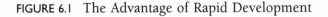

FIGURE 6.1   The Advantage of Rapid Development

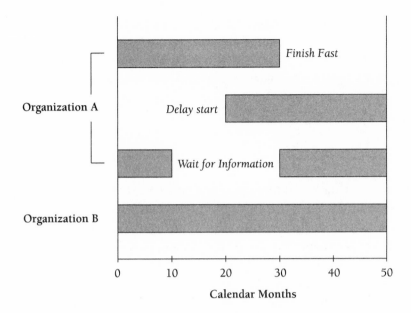

new information on the probability of eventual commercialization, the size of the market, and other variables.

There are other ways in which the ability for fast process development can be strategically valuable. Organization A had the option to start 20 months later than B yet still finish at the same time; conversely, A could have chosen to complete process development 20 months sooner than B (see figure 6.1). Clearly, organization A's development strategy depended on the contingencies of the particular project. For a product candidate with a long clinical development cycle and a high degree of uncertainty surrounding eventual approval, putting a project on hold midway may appear attractive. For a product candidate with a short clinical development schedule, rapid development and an early launch may be the better option.

The second dimension of performance examined in this chapter—process development cost—is defined as the total number of hours spent by scientists and engineers developing the process, again from the initiation of process research to the successful validation of the process at commercial scale. Referring back to Chapter 1, the ability to execute a development project with fewer resources should contribute to a firm's overall performance in a number of ways, most obviously through a reduction in fixed R&D costs (and thus an increase in the return to R&D). However, as was the case for lead time, an organization with efficient process R&D capabilities expands its development options. Virtually all firms in the pharmaceutical industry, including small biotechnology companies, have multiple product candidates in their development pipelines. Given the low odds that most products will reach the market, a critical challenge for managers is to allocate process R&D resources wisely across these projects. An efficient organization can afford to carry out process R&D on more product candidates with the same overall resources, yet with fewer resources on any given project.

Data on Lead Time and Cost

Figure 6.2 contains raw data on lead time and cost (in hours) across projects in the sample. The variations in performance are striking. With respect to lead time, the difference between the fastest and the slowest projects is a factor of 5. The range in development hours is even more notable, with the most costly project consuming more than 66 times the resources of the least costly project.

Clearly, not all these outcomes are a result of management quality. Some can be explained by differences in project content—for example, whether the project involved chemically synthesized or biotechnology processes. The second and third bars in each part of figure 6.2 provide an indication of the performance results by technological class. For lead time, there are significant differences between the two categories: the average biotechnology project took approximately half as much time to complete as the average chemical project (80 months versus 41 months). This is surprising in light of the higher technical novelty of biotechnology projects. For development cost, the average biotechnology project required 15 percent more person-hours to complete.

There are also large differences within categories. In terms of lead time, the slowest chemical project (105 months) took longer to complete than the fastest (39 months) by a factor of more than 2.5. With respect to cost, the least and most costly projects differed by a factor of 17 in the chemical subsample, and by a factor of 66 in the biotechnology subsample. Beyond these broad category differences, the effect of complexity at the project level can be explored using regression analysis.

The Impact of Project Complexity on Cost

Heterogeneity among projects in the sample may contribute to differences in development hours consumed. Scientists participating in the study highlighted a number of project characteristics that might affect overall development cost;

FIGURE 6.2 Lead Time and Cost Performance Data

(a) Lead Time

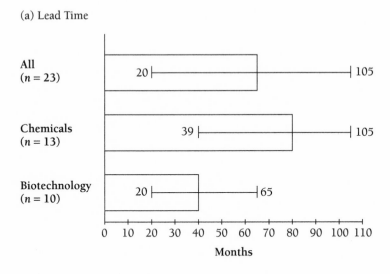

(b) Cost

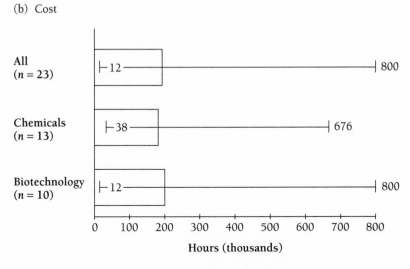

their effects on development hours were statistically analyzed using linear regression. For chemical projects, for example, the number of chemical reactions required to synthesize a molecule was identified as an important factor—a process with more reactions should require more development effort. For both chemical and biotechnology projects, total product output in the first full year of commercial production, or volume, was significant. More development work may be undertaken to achieve better efficiencies for high-volume processes.

Table 6.1 Descriptive Statistics of Project Content Variables

	All (n = 23)	Chemicals (n = 13)	Biotechnology (n = 10)
Chemical Reactions			
Minimum	N/A	4	N/A
Maximum		19	
Mean		10	
Scale (kg/year)*			
Minimum	.01	.300	.01
Maximum	230,000.00	230,000.00	5.40
Mean	12,495.00	22,105.00	1.70
Acute Indication Frequency	5	3	2

* Output in first full year of commercial production.

Finally, the product's therapeutic category can contribute to overall project complexity. Although the small sample size precluded control for therapeutic category at a detailed level, participants in the study suggested that a key distinction was whether the drug was intended to treat a chronic disease or an acute condition. Chronic diseases (such as high blood pressure) require ongoing treatment over long periods of time, whereas an acute condition (such as a bacterial infection) requires treatment over a short time. Because they are administered for a relatively short period of time, acute therapies typically require less lengthy clinical trials to demonstrate both safety and efficacy. A shorter period for clinical trials means there is less time to complete process development, which might lead companies to invest more resources in process development in order to complete the project in the requisite time frame. For instance, to ensure that a commercially viable process is ready in time for launch, the company might invest resources in multiple process technologies in parallel, rather than explore alternatives in sequence.

Table 6.1 provides descriptive statistics of these variables. In terms of chemical reactions, the least complex project involved a 4-step reaction sequence; the most complex, 19. All other things being equal, we might expect the more complex project to require approximately 5 times the resources of the least complex. Volume also exhibited wide variation. Some projects required output of a few grams (of very high-potency material), whereas others involved production in the hundred-thousand-metric-ton range.

Using these control variables in a regression analysis, it is possible to identify differences that may result from managerial factors rather than from technical content (see the Appendix for a description of the method and model used to estimate these differences). Figure 6.3 shows a plot of development cost (in hours) after controlling for project content. Controlling for project content clearly reduces the range of development hours, although the variations are still noteworthy. For example, across the total sample, development hours for the least and most costly projects differed by a factor of approximately 2 (with the range somewhat greater in the biotechnology segment, 2.70, and slightly less in the chemical segment, 2.69). Ranges of this magnitude are consistent with those found by researchers exploring development performance in other contexts.[1]

Although less dramatic than the unadjusted hours, the significance of these numbers can be grasped by recognizing that the most efficient firm could undertake approximately twice the number of projects with the same resources as the least efficient firm. This benefit would be particularly important for biotechnology companies that face relatively severe constraints on their development resources.

FIGURE 6.3 Actual versus Expected Project Hours

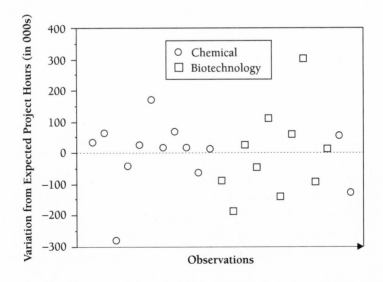

Note: Y-axis is the difference between the actual process R&D hours required and the number of hours expected (after controlling for project complexity, production scale, and therapeutic class).

The Impact of Project Complexity on Lead Time

As for development lead time, a linear regression model using the project content variables described above was estimated; then differences in the residuals were analyzed (see the Appendix for these regression results). Again, although some of the variation between best and worst performers can be accounted for by project complexity, large differences remained after adjusting for project content. For the overall sample, the fastest and slowest projects differed by a factor of 1.75; for the chemical sample, by 1.68, and for the biotechnology sample, by approximately 2. To keep this in perspective, consider that these projects typically span multiple years; thus the fastest organization enjoys a substantial advantage in getting its process technology ready for commercial launch. In a business in which monthly marginal revenues for a new product can be in the multimillion-dollar range, the financial impact of improvements in lead time is noteworthy.

One interesting finding from this analysis was that project complexity did not correspond to lead time within the chemical and biotechnology projects. In other words, the number of chemical reactions, the volume of output, and the therapeutic category—all of which affected development cost—had no statistically significant effect on lead time. This suggests that companies in the study absorbed increased project complexity through additional resource expenditures, but held lead time constant. To illustrate this idea, consider chemical reactions. As the number of needed reactions increases, firms increase development expenditures in a relatively predictable fashion. However, to keep the extra work from delaying the project's completion, firms work on multiple stages of the process in parallel. Thus, on average, a twelve-reaction process would take approximately the same amount of time to develop as a much simpler six-reaction process. However, the twelve-reaction process still consumes more resources than the six-step process.

Traditionally, the literature on R&D management and product development has posited a trade-off between lead time and resource expenditures; that is, lead time can be accelerated only at a cost. Recent empirical studies have called this trade-off into question, suggesting instead that time and cost may be positively correlated.[2] Because this debate is critical to R&D and development strategy and there is little existing data, the relationship between lead time and development cost was investigated here using essentially the same methodology. This entailed using regression analysis to estimate measures of lead time and development cost adjusted for project content differences. The residuals

FIGURE 6.4 The Time-Cost Trade-off Revisited

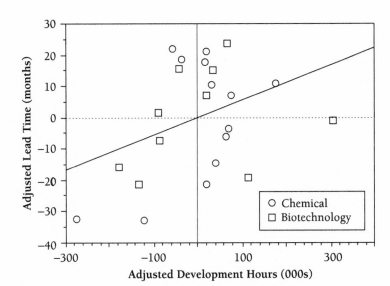

Note: Adjusted lead time and adjusted development hours take into account differences in project content, production scale, and therapeutic class.

of these two equations (the variance in lead time and cost that cannot be explained by content alone) are plotted in figure 6.4. For purposes of illustration, the biotechnology and chemical projects are highlighted.

As indicated in figure 6.4, the relationship between adjusted lead time and development cost is positive (although not statistically significant). These results add credence to the argument that, once you adjust for project complexity, there is no trade-off between cost and speed. Indeed, if anything, it appears that projects with longer-than-expected lead times also tend to consume more than the expected level of resources. Such a pattern would result if there are common underlying project strategy factors contributing to both lead time and costs.

One concern with a small sample of heterogeneous development projects is the possibility that uncontrolled-for differences in content and complexity remain—simply put, we may not be comparing apples with apples. (This issue, of course, is not unique to this study; given the complex nature of development projects, it would be virtually impossible to identify all possible variables.) Uncontrolled or unobserved heterogeneity is a concern for two reasons. First, it can muddy the interpretation of statistical analysis about the effect of one variable on another. Second, apparent differences in project performance may not be the result of better or worse organizational capabilities. If this were the case, there would be no performance variation left to explain with managerial actions.

Within the current sample, three pairs of projects involved development of essentially the same molecule. Assuming no significant observation errors, performance differences within an identical pairing should be attributable to competence rather than content or complexity. Although three pairs are too few for statistical analysis, these data provide a kind of "reality check" on the underlying thesis that organizational capabilities contribute to performance.

Comparing the development cost and the lead time within each pair revealed some striking differences in performance. The ratio of development hours consumed within each of the pairs was 5:1, 1.09:1, and 2.23:1 (thus, in the first pairing, for example, one product consumed five times as many resources as the other). Note that the average ratio of 2.77 across these pairs is very close to the difference estimated statistically across the entire sample (2.70). Similar findings appear for the lead time comparisons, with ratios of 3.25:1, 1.23:1, and 1.39:1. The average ratio of 1.96 is again close to the difference estimated statistically across the entire sample.

The substantial variations in performance observed across the sample after adjusting for project content appear to be of similar magnitude to those found among technically similar projects. Together, these findings help validate the assertion that significant differences in performance may be related to project execution, strategy, and other managerial factors.

The Effect of Organizational Structure and Learning Strategy on Lead Time and Cost

We now turn to an analysis of the organizational factors that may affect process development performance, focusing on organizational structure and learning strategy. Exploration of organizational structure was motivated by previous literature on development (Clark and Fujimoto 1991, and Iansiti 1995) as well as by input during field research from managers who were deeply interested in the question of how they should organize process R&D. Exploration of learning strategy was motivated by our interest in learning and problem solving during process development.

Organizational Structure and Project Performance

In the course of the field research, two organizational models for process R&D were identified (see figure 6.5). In some firms, tasks are divided functionally among a process research group (which handles the initial development phase) and a process development/engineering group (responsible for pilot development and manufacturing startup). This model is referred to as *specialized*. In others, a single process development function or department is responsible for carrying out all tasks—from process development through manufacturing startup. This model is referred to as *integrated*.

In the specialized model, the group responsible for process research typically reports through the R&D side of the organization, whereas the group responsible for development and manufacturing startup reports through operations or manufacturing. The project moves through a distinct "hand-over" phase, wherein responsibility is transferred from process research to process development. This hand-over entails not only a transfer between two distinct groups of technical personnel, but also a formal change in oversight from R&D to manufacturing or operations.

In an integrated model, one group maintains full responsibility for the project, from process research through manufacturing startup. In the companies studied in this project that used this integrated approach, key scientists remained involved throughout all phases of the project. Indeed, in some cases, the process scientists who initially explored basic technical alternatives in the laboratory were on the factory floor several years later, explaining the nuances of the process to operators and even supervising the production of initial test batches. A number of managers pointed out that avoiding a midproject hand-over was the chief benefit of the integrated model.

Evidence from current product development literature indicates that an integrated approach to development helps avoid potential problems of coordination and miscommunication, which can plague more specialized organizations (Clark and Fujimoto 1991, and Iansiti 1995). However, no studies link project performance and organizational structure for process development. The data from this study permit investigation of this issue. Table 6.2 highlights the striking differences between the chemical and biotechnology projects along this dimension. All the biotechnology projects used an integrated structure, whereas less than a third of the chemical projects did so.

The integrated structure used for biotechnology projects differed from that used for chemical projects. As discussed in chapter 5, biotechnology processes

FIGURE 6.5 Organizational Models for Process R&D

(a) Specialized Model

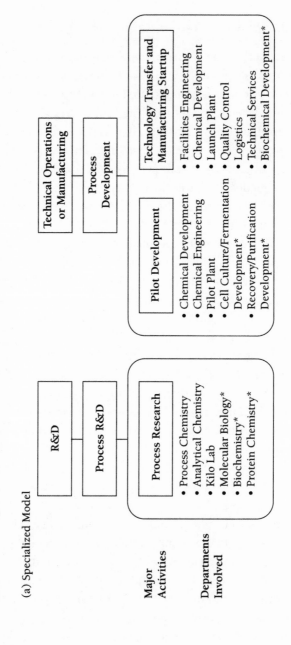

(b) Integrated Model

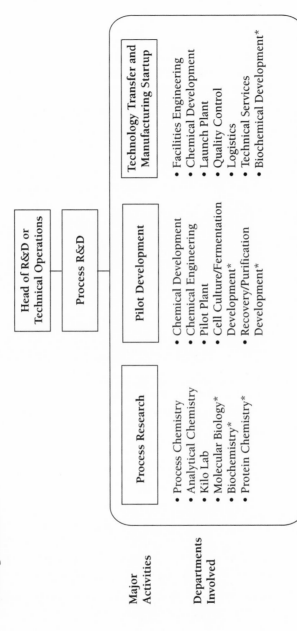

Head of R&D or
Technical Operations

Process R&D

Major Activities	Process Research	Pilot Development	Technology Transfer and Manufacturing Startup
Departments Involved	• Process Chemistry • Analytical Chemistry • Kilo Lab • Molecular Biology* • Biochemistry* • Protein Chemistry*	• Chemical Development • Chemical Engineering • Pilot Plant • Cell Culture/Fermentation Development* • Recovery/Purification Development*	• Facilities Engineering • Chemical Development • Launch Plant • Quality Control • Logistics • Technical Services • Biochemical Development*

* Refers to department name for biotechnology processes only; department names vary by company, and those shown are meant to be representative.

Table 6.2 Frequency of Integrated versus Specialized Organizational
Structures

	All ($n = 23$)	Chemicals ($n = 13$)	Biotechnology ($n = 10$)
Integrated Structure	14	4	10
Specialized Process Research Group	9	9	0

are made up of two production stages: fermentation or cell culture processes (in which genetically engineered cells are grown and produce the desired protein) and recovery processes (in which pure quantities of the protein are isolated and purified from the cell culture broth). Because these processes derive from unique science bases (molecular biology versus protein chemistry), biotechnology processes are divided as well, with one group responsible for fermentation or cell culture processes and another responsible for recovery processes. In the biotechnology organizations studied here, both groups were responsible for their process in entirety, from process research to manufacturing startup. Thus each group essentially employed an integrated approach for its own stage of the process. Because our focus here is on the approach used to coordinate vertical phases of process development (process research through manufacturing startup), the biotechnology organizations are categorized as following an integrated model.

There was significant disparity in the frequency of organizational modes among biotechnology and chemically based projects. One possible explanation for this difference may be firm size. Even the largest and most mature biotechnology enterprises are relatively small in comparison to an established pharmaceutical firm. They also have far fewer drugs in their development pipelines, and thus dividing process development between a research group and a development group may not be economically feasible. With relatively few drugs under development and significant uncertainty associated with each project, there is a high probability that one group would experience significant idle time waiting for a project. An integrated approach allows for more flexibility in balancing development resources, because personnel can be reallocated more easily across projects at different phases of development.

A second explanation draws from the learning framework presented in chapter 2. The use of integrated structures for biotechnology process R&D may reflect the relatively immature and unstructured knowledge base characterizing biotechnology processes. What is hypothesized at lab scale can really only be verified at full production scale. Moreover, the interactions between the underlying biochemistry of the process and the physical production environment are at best poorly understood, and it is difficult to partition problem-solving responsibilities between the two.[3] In such an environment, effective problem solving is more likely to require integration and iteration across all phases of the development cycle. An integrated structure may facilitate direct contact and feedback among the process research scientists and the production requirement. Although integration is also important in chemical projects, the knowledge environment there allows problems to be more readily partitioned across well-developed subspecialties (such as process chemistry and chemical engineering).

The Impact of Organizational Structure on Process Development Lead Times and Costs

The relationship between organizational structure and process development performance in terms of lead time and cost was examined through regression analysis. The statistical models, methods, and detailed results are presented in the Appendix.

On average, integrated organizations completed process development projects eight to ten months sooner (approximately 16 percent) and with 104,000 fewer person-hours (approximately 54 percent) than did firms in which process research and process development were separated. Although this appears to be consistent with prior research, the effect was highly inconsistent, and the relationship is not statistically significant at conventional levels. For the chemical projects, closer examination revealed that only in the final development phase—transfer to the plant—did the integrated structure provide a significant lead time advantage of seven months versus twenty-four months.[4]

Under an integrated structure, the same chemists who develop the basic structure are involved in technology transfer, scale-up, and startup in the factory. It is easy to see why this approach might facilitate technology transfer. The process chemists' intimate knowledge of the process helps them to teach the plant engineers and operators and to spot potential deviations in how the process is being operated. As discussed in the previous chapter, technology transfer and manufacturing startup often involve adapting the process to the plant. For example, if a plant has been experiencing a bottleneck in drying capacity, it may try to accelerate that stage by using a slightly higher temperature or less liquid in a previous stage. In some instances, these seemingly minor alterations can affect the process's basic chemistry. Having the chemists involved, however, helps ensure that procedural modifications do not result in fundamental process changes.

In addition, experience with manufacturing startup helps process research chemists gain a deeper understanding of the plant's constraints and complexity. This should presumably make them better able to anticipate technical needs and to design processes that require less adaptation to scale up and operate commercially. It is important to note, however, that integrated structures are not consistently faster or more efficient than specialized structures over the entire development cycle, which suggests that some of this advantage might come at the expense of high development costs and longer lead times prior to the transfer.

Field observations suggest another reason why integrated structures may lack a consistent advantage for the duration of the project. Lurking beneath the formal specialized organizational structure are informal relationships linking separate process research and process development groups. These infrastructural ties appear to have a powerful impact on problem-solving performance. For example, one of the highest-performing projects in the study was carried out by an organization where process research and process development were not only organizationally separated, but geographically split across three sites (two in the United States and one in Europe). Projects essentially went through two transfers: from the process research group to the process development group (both in the United States, but separated by a few miles); and from process development to the European plant.

What made this organization operate so effectively was an infrastructure that facilitated a high degree of communication and coordination across sites. Moreover, although each site focused on one stage of the development cycle, there was a fair degree of overlap in the technical backgrounds of the personnel involved. Thus the process chemists were not isolated in the process research group, but instead were employed at all three sites. When technical problems arose, researchers from any location could be called upon. Interestingly, the process chemists at the manufacturing plant were considered so able that their colleagues in research routinely asked them to help solve difficult chemistry problems.

Overlapping technical competences helped smooth communication and coordination across sites because they provided a common language with which to frame problems. On one project, for example, when difficulties arose during technology transfer, the plant had its own integrated chemistry and chemical engineering capabilities to solve the problem and avoided having to bounce the project back to one of the development organizations. Organizations without this consistent level of technical competence were faced with problems that escalated into conflicts, with the process research organization blaming process development for ineptitude in implementing the chemistry, while process development blamed process research for flawed chemistry. In this environment, it was difficult and time consuming to agree on the root cause of a problem, let alone come to quick resolution.

Another factor that contributed to the successful performance of this non-integrated organization was the experience of its senior management. The directors of the process research and process development groups both had experience with other companies in their counterpart's position. As a result, each had a broad perspective on the development process and recognized firsthand the challenges and pressures of each position. This shared outlook at the senior level was a catalyst for cooperation and integration at the working levels.

Learning Strategy and Project Performance

The framework presented in chapter 2 suggests that learning strategies may have an important effect on development performance. Two types of learning strategies were identified: learning before doing, in which experimentation is conducted under laboratory conditions or through other forms of simulation, and learning by doing, in which experimentation is conducted under conditions highly representative of the final production environment. In reality, the strategies an organization may use during a development project range from purely conceptual exploration at one extreme through test runs in the actual production plant at the other. However, organizations can choose to emphasize different approaches. For example, an organization that does very little process research and moves development projects quickly into the manufacturing environment emphasizes learning by doing. In contrast, one that spends significant resources doing laboratory research and developing detailed simulations of the process in order to avoid problems later on adheres to a learning before doing strategy.

The appropriate balance between these two strategies has received very little attention. Many today argue that process technologies should be transferred to the plant as early as possible to avoid mismatches between process designs and manufacturing capabilities. Is this always a good idea? The framework in chapter 2 hypothesizes that the appropriate balance would depend on the underlying process knowledge. As noted in the previous chapter, chemical synthesis technology and biotechnology represent two very different knowledge environments. We should therefore expect to see high performance in each segment associated with a different learning strategy.

There are various ways the concept of a learning strategy can be made operational and measured in the context of development projects. Two basic approaches were taken in this study. One looked at the relative length of each phase of the process development cycle. From this perspective, the extent of learning by doing is reflected in the relative amount of calendar time spent undertaking development activities in the manufacturing environment. Using this approach, two related indexes were constructed. One index captures the timing of technology transfer to the manufacturing plant relative to the total length of the process R&D project, on a scale between 0 and 1 (values closer to 0 indicate that the project was transferred to the plant earlier in the development cycle and reflect an orientation toward learning by doing). Figure 6.6 graphically compares two projects, both of which had a total lead time of 50 months. In project A, technology transfer to the plant began in month 40, or at the 80 percent completion point. In project B, technology transfer started at month 20 (or after 40 percent completion). This heavier emphasis on development after transferring to the plant is more reflective of a learning by doing strategy.

A second index of overlap is the ratio of the length of the technology transfer phase to the scale-up lead time. Because scale-up takes place during both pilot development and technology transfer, the total scale-up lead time is from the beginning of pilot development to the end of the project. Using figure 6.6 as an example, project A's scale-up began with the start of pilot development at month 20 and ended with the successful completion of the project at month 50. With this total scale-up lead time of 30 months, including a 10-month technology transfer phase, the index of overlap for this project would be 0.33 (10 months of technology transfer divided by 30 months of scale-up). For project B, the index of overlap would be 0.75 (30 months of technology transfer divided by 40 months of scale-up). In other words, for project B, about 75 percent of the scale-up occurred simultaneously with the transfer and startup of the process in the factory, an approach more oriented toward learning by doing than that used in project A.

Both the above metrics are based on calendar time (in months) spent during various phases of the project. A second approach to capturing learning strategies in development uses the relative number of person-hours consumed. Although this metric is akin to the one described above, it uses relative person-hours rather than relative calendar months. Unfortunately, reliable and consistent data were not available on the precise breakdown of hours by ac-

FIGURE 6.6 Comparison of Development Strategies

(a) Project A—Learning Before Doing

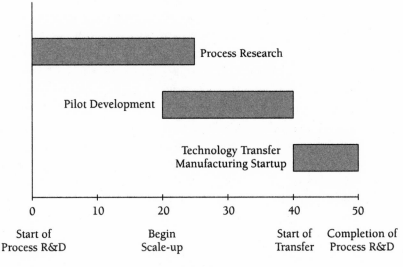

(b) Project B—Learning By Doing

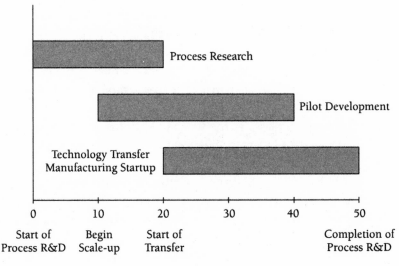

tivity at distinct points in time.[5] Thus, where there was overlap between phases, it was impossible to distinguish how much effort was being invested in one activity or another. This made it impossible to construct a meaningful measure of overlap for person-hours akin to the index of overlap described above.

Figure 6.7 provides an overview of the three metrics of learning strategy. The data reveal marked contrasts between the typical chemical synthesis and biotechnology projects, particularly with respect to the timing of technology transfer and the amount of development investment prior to that transfer. As shown in part (a) of the figure, the typical chemical project was transferred to the factory at a much later phase (in calendar months) in the development cycle than was the case for biotechnology projects (79 percent versus 57 percent). Moreover, these chemical synthesis projects made a significantly greater investment in process R&D resources prior to the transfer (68 percent versus 40 percent in part [b]). Finally, biotechnology projects appear to have involved a much greater degree of overlap between scale-up and technology transfer, as shown in part (c).

These patterns are consistent with the idea that process development in biotechnology requires a much greater reliance on learning by doing than in chemical synthesis. For the typical biotechnology project, it appears that much of the action (in terms of development and scale-up) occurs during the transfer and manufacturing startup phase. In contrast, the typical chemical project seems to involve the transfer of a relatively more complete process design to the factory. Although transfer and manufacturing startup are not trivial (with respect to either amount of time or resources expended), they represent a much smaller share of the development cycle in chemicals than in biotechnology.

The data shown in this figure portray the typical project based on statistical averages. Lying beneath these averages, however, are significant differences in approaches within each class. There are chemical projects, for example, that transfer the process to the factory relatively early in the development cycle; conversely, there are biotechnology projects where the process technology was transferred quite late. These differences in strategy within each class are noteworthy for two reasons. First, they indicate that any possible environmental differences (such as the nature of specific regulations pertaining to chemical and biotechnology projects) are not strictly responsible for differences in strategy. Second, closer examination of technologically similar pairs reveals large differences in strategies. Thus, unobserved heterogeneity in complexity is not driving these differences. Managerial choices appear to be at work. These variations permit investigation of the impact of a particular learning strategy on development performance within each category. Below, we first examine the

FIGURE 6.7 Learning Strategy

(a) By relative amount of calendar time spent in each phase

Chemicals

23%	56%	21%
Process Research	Pilot Development	Tech. Transfer/ Mfg. Start-up

Biotechnology

24%	33%	43%
Process Research	Pilot Development	Tech. Transfer/ Mfg. Start-up

(b) By relative amount of resources expended in each phase

Chemicals

13%	55%	32%
Process Research	Pilot Development	Tech. Transfer/ Mfg. Start-up

Biotechnology

15%	25%	60%
Process Research	Pilot Development	Tech. Transfer/ Mfg. Start-up

(c) By index of overlap between scale-up and technology transfer/manufacturing startup

Chemicals

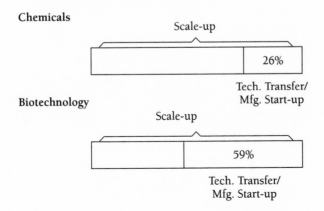

Biotechnology

FIGURE 6.8 Adjusted Hours versus Technology Transfer

(a) Chemical Sample

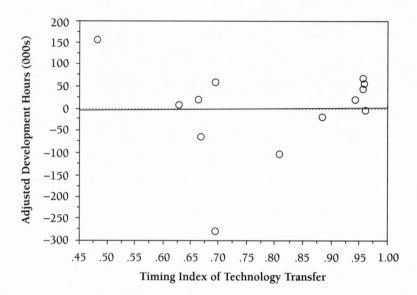

(b) Biotechnology Sample

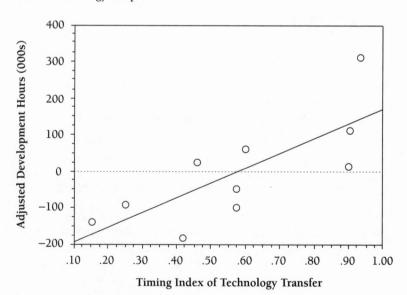

impact of learning strategies on development costs. We then turn to their impact on lead times.

The Impact of Learning Strategy on Development Costs

The relationship between learning strategy and development costs was estimated for chemical and biotechnology projects using linear regression. According to the framework developed earlier, there should be an interaction effect between the class of technology and the learning strategy on development performance. (A description of the statistical method, the specification of the full statistical model, and the results are presented in greater detail in the Appendix.) Figure 6.8 graphically depicts the relationship between the timing of technology transfer and development hours (adjusted for project content and complexity) for both the chemical and the biotechnology subsamples. In these graphs, projects appearing on the left-hand side of the x-axis were transferred to the plant earlier in the development cycle than projects on the right, and the associated companies can be thought of as following a learning by doing strategy. Figure 6.9 shows the relationship between the extent of overlap and adjusted development hour performance for both subsamples. In these figures, projects with greater overlap (more learning by doing) appear toward the right-hand side of the x-axis.

Both sets of figures demonstrate the powerful role of learning by doing in biotechnology projects. There is a statistically significant relationship between later technology transfer and higher development costs in biotechnology. There is also a statistically significant relationship between the amount of overlap and development costs; in biotechnology, more overlap between scale-up and technology transfer/manufacturing startup is associated with lower development costs (holding other factors constant). These results confirm the hypothesis that, when the knowledge base is sufficiently immature (as it is in biotechnology), learning by doing is a more efficient problem-solving strategy.

The patterns for the chemical-based projects are quite different. Here, the need for learning by doing is less clear, and there appear to be no systematic advantages to transferring the process to the plant at an early stage. Nor is there any advantage to be gained by engaging in scale-up while transferring and starting up the process in the plant. In chemical synthesis, learning by doing is neither necessary nor sufficient for high development efficiency. Moreover, although learning before doing is a viable problem-solving strategy in this arena, there appears to be room for much greater diversity of approaches. Closer analysis of specific outlier cases reveals some interesting firm-specific

FIGURE 6.9   Adjusted Hours versus Overlap

(a) Chemical Sample

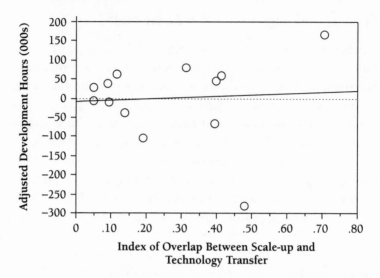

(b) Biotechnology Sample

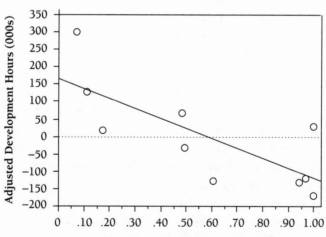

effects and provides additional insight into the role of knowledge and competence in development performance. Two contrasting cases are highlighted below.

Case 1: The Problems of Early Transfer. This project, which had the greatest number of development hours, also involved the earliest transfer of the process to the plant. Although one outlier does not constitute a trend, it at least raises a question: Can transfer to the plant occur too early? Closer examination of this particular case reveals that many of the technical issues associated with the product revolved around the underlying chemistry. Yields were extremely low because of the design of the basic chemistry. Because the product was to be produced commercially in relatively small volumes, chemical engineering issues such as scale-up and equipment modification were less important. Although the plant had a very strong development organization, which employed both chemists and chemical engineers, its experience had been largely in solving scale-up and process engineering problems.

The process was transferred to the production site relatively early for two reasons. First, the development organization on the production site had spare engineering capacity at the time and wanted to get a head start. Second, during the early phases, the process technology produced only a low yield. In order to manufacture enough materials for clinical trials, the process had to be run in commercial-scale vessels. After the transfer, process research remained involved on the project in conjunction with the plant development group (although the two were geographically separated by a drive of several hours). Participants hailed the project as a case of successful collaboration between research and manufacturing. The data indicate, however, that this success came at a high cost. Early transfer to the plant may have cost the firm its ability to fully exploit the process research laboratory's comparative advantage in solving chemistry problems.

Case 2: The Power of Early Transfer. The second noteworthy case involved a project for which development costs were low and transfer to the plant occurred early. This runs counter to expectations of the model and represents a far different picture from that described above. Why, in this case, did early transfer not contribute to lower development efficiency? This organization, described earlier in this chapter, had a relatively unique set of organizational and technical capabilities: it distributed its process chemistry capabilities across all its development sites, including its European-based plant for launching new products. Although other companies in the study also used "launch plants" specializing in new products, this company's plant-based development group was relatively unique in having a strong capability in both process chemistry and pilot development. (In the other pharmaceutical companies studied, technical capabilities at plant sites were in chemical and facilities engineering and were oriented toward refinement and optimization.)

As a result of this organization's capabilities within the plant, the start of technology transfer was uneventful. The plant was involved in the design and development of the basic process architecture and actually had explored alternative synthetic routes—a task that was the sole province of the research laboratories in every other pharmaceutical company in the study. Because of the organization's strong process research and pilot development capabilities, the character of development and the nature of the problem-solving process did not change dramatically at the time of technology transfer. Learning before doing, through laboratory research and pilot simulations, continued to be an integral part of the project even after the factory became involved.

These two cases highlight the need for organizations to match their specific approaches to their repertoire of skills and capabilities. For the first company, exploiting opportunities to learn before doing would seem to require a much longer process research phase because only the process research organization had the requisite technical capabilities. In the second organization, early technology transfer to the plant was not inconsistent with a strategy of learning before doing because of the plant's strong research and pilot development capabilities. The power of process research in creating a lead time advantage is explored in greater depth below.

The Impact of Learning Strategy on Lead Time

The impact of learning strategy on lead time was explored using the same statistical approach applied to development cost. Figure 6.10 highlights the relationship between the percentage of process R&D resources spent prior to technology transfer and lead time performance for both types of projects. Although the effects are not as precise, the results parallel those found for development cost performance (the statistical significance of coefficients on this variable for the biotechnology projects was, depending on the particular specification, approximately $p < .15$). In biotechnology, longer lead times are associated with projects in which a greater proportion of development investment occurred prior to the technology transfer.

The fact that the lead time "penalty" for late technology transfer was less consistently severe than it was for development costs illustrates some interesting aspects of how biotechnology firms manage process development projects. Lead time almost always took precedence over resources. Thus, in cases of

FIGURE 6.10 Lead Time and Extent of Development before Technology Transfer

(a) Chemical Sample

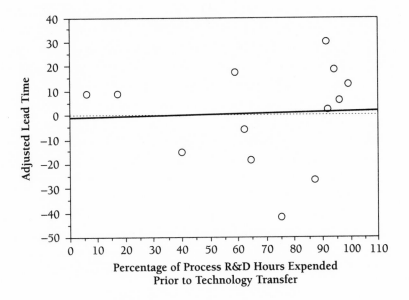

(b) Biotechnology Sample

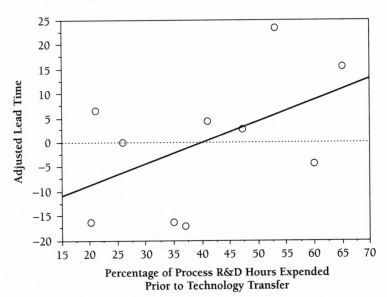

firms' involving plants relatively late, they partially offset potential delays by adding resources. This was particularly apparent when major problems with the process technology were discovered late in the development cycle. To avoid delaying a regulatory filing or product launch, the vast majority of a company's process R&D personnel might be reassigned to fix the process. This would result in a greater expenditure of development resources, but it would also help decrease overall lead time. Late plant involvement also tended to have a smaller lead time penalty because of the nature of the problem-solving processes in laboratories and in small-scale pilot plants. Experiments conducted at laboratory pilot-plant scale have a shorter cycle time than those conducted in full-scale manufacturing plants. For example, a test of a cell culture process at 1-liter scale might take between a few days and a week to complete; the same process run at 2,000 liters might require a month or more. Thus, although smaller experiments are less effective in terms of providing representative feedback, they are fast.

It should be stressed, however, that the lead time effects of late plant involvement are only *partially* offset. In the pharmaceutical industry, adding one or two months to a project schedule can be extremely costly. In addition, empirical data suggest that the impact on development costs in biotechnology is not trivial. Transferring a process to the plant after it is 90 percent complete, as opposed to doing so when it is 60 percent complete (which was the average), would be expected to add 100,000 person-hours, or approximately 50 person-years, to the project. Given that the average biotechnology project in the study required approximately 200,000 person-hours, this represents an additional 50 percent expenditure on process development. For the highly resource-constrained biotechnology firm, this can represent a significant additional resource burden.

Once again, the pattern for chemical-based projects was quite different. Focusing development resources on technology transfer and manufacturing startup does not accelerate the project in the same manner as it does in biotechnology. On the other hand, as was the case for development cost, a relatively wide array of approaches seemed to work equally well, with most of the variance related to individual firms' capabilities.

Because there were no statistically significant trends for the chemical projects in the above analyses, it would be easy to conclude that project strategy does not matter in that context. Although there are clear advantages of involving the plant as early as possible in biotechnology, the opposite did not appear conclusively true for chemical projects. There appeared to be no harm in doing too little development before technology transfer, except in some isolated cases. Does this mean there is no benefit to doing it right the first time, even in a mature technological context such as chemically synthesized pharmaceuticals?

To answer this question, a more detailed probing of the effects of specific development activities prior to technology transfer was conducted. An important milestone in process development is the first batch of production at pilot scale. Because this offers developers their first feedback on process performance outside the laboratory environment, it is a potentially important tool for identifying problems in the commercial manufacturing environment. A critical development strategy choice is the amount of process research to undertake prior to the first pilot batch. One strategy would be to invest heavily, with the goal of achieving a very high-fidelity process. This approach attempts to root out problems before the test and emphasizes learning before doing. An alternative strategy would be to test a relatively undeveloped process, with the goal of getting quick feedback and reiterating the process design—an approach more akin to learning by doing.

The most appropriate approach will depend on how well the pilot simulates the eventual production environment. If the pilot test generates data that can be usefully extrapolated to future performance in a commercial plant, then testing a well-developed process offers advantages; any performance problems that surface can become the focus for subsequent development and refinement. If the process is not well developed in such a context, then feedback from the pilot batch will be "noisy." For instance, if the process is poorly understood and out of control, it will be difficult to interpret the data from the pilot test. Because so little of the process is understood, the root causes of poor performance will be difficult to isolate, and this will in turn impede subsequent progress.

In environments in which pilot production is highly unrepresentative of commercial manufacturing conditions, or in which pilot test data cannot be usefully mapped into commercial performance, it would seem to make little sense to invest heavily in a high-quality pilot process. The process might perform extremely well in the pilot plant, but this would tell developers nothing about how well the process will perform or what problems might surface in the future plant. Here, a "quick-and-dirty" pilot run might provide basic feedback on the viability of the process, but most learning will take place in the commercial production environment.

The data shown in figure 6.11 confirm the expectation that the representativeness of the first pilot run (as measured by the relative amount of process research performed to that point) has a very significant impact on

FIGURE 6.11 Process Research and Lead Time

(a) Chemical Sample

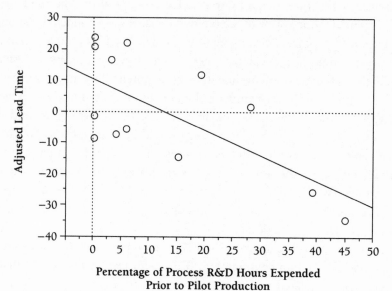

(b) Biotechnology Sample

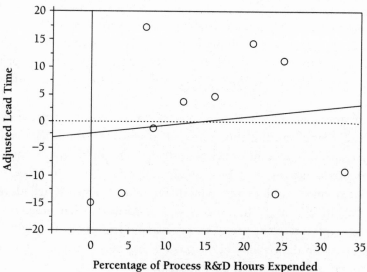

development lead time (after adjusting for other factors) in the chemical environment. Investing in a higher-quality first pilot batch tends to shorten overall development lead time. However, no such relationship exists in biotechnology, and attempts to learn before doing through process research appear futile. Although the relationship for biotechnology is not statistically significant, there are clearly a number of cases where additional spending on process research is associated with longer development lead times. A deeper exploration of these differences is provided in chapter 8.

These results are consistent with those reported for technology transfer. In chemicals, where reasonably accurate predictions of future factory performance are possible, exploitation of opportunities to learn before doing is critical to development speed. In contrast, the statistical results suggest that, in the biotechnology environment, attention is more productively focused on downstream phases of development, where opportunities for learning by doing can be exploited. In this context, fidelity of small-scale or laboratory experiments is less valuable because much of what might be learned will not predict future problems. The findings also suggest different roles for pilot production in the two environments. In chemical synthesis technology, pilot production acts as a quality control checkpoint. Given the opportunity to explore the chemistry at laboratory scale and to model future performance accurately, only poorly developed processes should fail or encounter severe difficulties at pilot scale. In biotechnology, however, pilot production serves a much more proactive problem-solving role. Given the difficulties of accurately simulating a process in a laboratory environment, failures in pilot production are neither unusual nor unexpected. Pilot production generates critical information about the behavior of the process, which cannot be obtained at small scale.

Conclusion

The important lesson to take away from this chapter is that superior development performance requires different practices in different environments. Although the notion that manufacturing should be a seamless extension of the R&D laboratory has gained credence in recent years, statistical results show that this prescription is likely to be beneficial in certain types of technological environments, but not in all. In chemical pharmaceuticals, the role of the plant in development may be less critical because developers can anticipate and respond to manufacturing issues without actually working in the plant. The well-defined structure of knowledge provides a mechanism of integration. In biotechnology, it is simply impossible for developers to anticipate and respond to manufacturing concerns without actually doing their work in the production environment.

The reader is cautioned not to misinterpret the results as implying that there are situations in which developers can ignore manufacturing concerns or develop unmanufacturable processes with abandon. In all contexts, whether the technology is mature or immature, developers must understand manufacturing concerns. Indeed, the framework outlined here was predicated on the assumption that developers should develop processes that perform well in the plant. The findings merely show that, in certain environments, process developers may be better able to anticipate and respond to manufacturing issues, without actually performing their work in the plant. In such environments, most of the learning that needs to take place can be done before the process is transferred to the plant.

The results have implications for thinking about the roles of the plant, the pilot plant, and the research laboratories in the development process, as well as for thinking about how quality in the context of development is defined. In recent years, the idea that development processes—like production and every other type of business process—should be designed for high quality has taken root among practitioners and academics. A high-quality development process is generally defined as one that resolves problems quickly and avoids costly and time-consuming rework. The idea of doing it right the first time has a certain appeal, whether "it" refers to the production of a car, the delivery of a fast-food hamburger, or the development of a novel process technology. In the context of development, however, how does one do it right the first time? In general, literature on the subject has focused on design methodologies such as design for manufacturability and quality function deployment, extensive and rapid prototyping, and the use of cross-functional project teams (Clausing 1993). At their heart, all these approaches attempt to generate new information or to reshape the flow of information so that potential problems are identified (and presumably resolved) earlier in the development cycle. In seeking to avoid future problems, they are really attempts to learn before doing.

The results presented above, however, call into question whether this approach is universally applicable. In biotechnology, the first production runs in the commercial plant often experience serious problems or even fail completely, regardless of how much development work has taken place prior to the transfer. Given the paucity of knowledge about how these processes operate at full scale and under actual manufacturing conditions, it may be impossible, perhaps even futile, to develop a problem-free process outside the actual manufacturing environment. In this type of environment, it is important to make mistakes and, more importantly, to learn from those mistakes. Here, a high-quality development process does not mean catching mistakes before they reach the factory; instead, it means using the factory to uncover potential problems as early as possible. Quality in the development process is rooted in the manufacturing plant rather than in the laboratory (this issue is explored in greater detail in the next chapter).

The next two chapters go into greater detail on learning in the two environments. Chapter 7 examines the underlying organizational processes supporting development process quality in the chemical pharmaceutical context. Chapter 8 examines the underlying processes affecting how biotechnology organizations learn across projects.

Quality in the Development Process—Leveraging Knowledge in Chemical Synthesis

THE PREVIOUS CHAPTER provided evidence that strong knowledge environments make it possible for chemical synthesis organizations to unearth potential manufacturing problems long before the process is transferred to the actual production environment. The data also showed that greater emphasis on early problem solving through intense process research—that is, doing it right the first time—helps reduce overall development lead time. Lead time is, of course, an important indicator of quality in the development process; failure to identify design problems early on leads to rework, which can in turn extend project time lines and consume resources. As discussed in earlier chapters, the ability for efficient and rapid process development is increasingly important in shaping pharmaceutical companies' competitive advantages. However, lead time and efficiency are not the only critical dimensions of development performance. The output of the development process—in this case, the manufacturing process itself—must also be of high quality. It will do a firm little competitive good to be fast and efficient at developing complex, costly process technologies that are difficult to implement. Thus the challenge facing most companies is to create a development process that is fast, efficient, and capable of generating high-quality process designs.

This chapter explores the relationship between the development process and process design quality. Quality in the development process refers to how effectively and rapidly design problems are identified and resolved prior to production. Of course, not all potential problems can be identified at the very start of a project; development is an iterative process involving learning across a series of problem-solving cycles.[1] Effective firms, however, learn to identify, anticipate, and resolve problems at the phase at which it is fastest and least costly to do so. For instance, in chemical synthesis, a strong knowledge base makes it possible to anticipate the potential performance of a synthetic route at the laboratory bench, and a high-quality development process would identify serious route problems at this phase rather than in the factory. In contrast, a problem embedded in the nuances of how a factory operator carries out a specific task may be virtually impossible to anticipate before the fact. Firms also must learn when to stop. Attempts to anticipate every contingency may lead to excessively long development time lines and high costs (and, in the end, probably would not uncover every problem) (von Hippel and Tyre 1995).

A development process should be capable of creating a high-quality process design (or product design, in the case of product development). Quality, of course, is a multidimensional concept, taking on different meanings in different contexts (Garvin 1988). In this context, a high-quality process design can be measured by such indicators as yields, capital expenditures, costs, batch-to-batch consistency, and regulatory compliance. Various studies of performance suggest that a significant portion (as much as 80 percent) of manufacturing process quality is rooted in the product and process design phase.[2] This would suggest a link between the quality of the development process and that of the process design process, but such a link has received little data-driven investigation.[3] That is the primary mission of this chapter.

Because the strong knowledge base underlying chemical synthesis projects permits more proactive problem solving, such projects provide a natural venue for examining issues of quality in development. Thus the analysis here is restricted to the thirteen chemical projects in the sample. Moreover, from a practical perspective, chemical pharmaceuticals offer advantages in terms of data availability and agreed-upon indicators of development quality. The chief disadvantage of focusing solely on chemical pharmaceuticals is that the findings from this chapter are likely to apply only in similarly strong knowledge environments. As discussed briefly at the end of the previous chapter, a far different model of development quality may be required for environments such as biotechnology, where proactive problem solving is inherently difficult.

This chapter is divided into two major sections. The first presents data on the relationship between development cost and lead time versus process design quality. The question to be addressed here is whether there is a trade-off between these dimensions. Data are also presented in the second section on how an organization's approach to process development may influence the quality of its manufacturing processes. A key theme here is the important role of rapid and effective technology selection. The second section of the chapter thus examines the issue of technology selection in detail and probes how organizations manage this process. Before delving into these analyses, however, a brief discussion of the competitive significance of process design quality follows.

The Strategic Value of Process Design Quality

Many managers interviewed during the course of this study believed there was an inevitable trade-off between development speed and efficiency on the one hand, and the quality of outcome on the other. In other words, you might be able to have speed and efficiency *or* a good process technology, but not both. One company's experience is particularly illustrative of this philosophy in action. Recognizing the strategic value of compressing the overall development cycle, the company moved to shorten its process development lead time. Under its new approach, the firm carried out as little process R&D as possible prior to launch—basically only enough to meet regulatory requirements. Explained one senior manager, "It just doesn't pay to delay a product launch to get a better process. We're better off launching with an acceptable process and then investing in process development refinements to drive down costs." The firm's fundamental philosophy could be summarized as "design it fast now, design it right later."

The logic behind this approach appeared sound in many respects. Unless a process is technically or commercially unfeasible or unacceptable from a regulatory perspective, delaying a launch for the sake of additional process R&D is a costly proposition. This company merely chose higher initial manufacturing costs in return for earlier revenue streams on new product introductions. Such reasoning is compelling if a firm lacks the organizational capabilities to develop high-quality designs quickly—quite simply, given its capabilities, it may have no choice.

However, firms that lack the capability to carry out development both quickly and with high-quality results may incur significant costs over the longer run. Consider the advantage held by a firm with the capability for both speed and quality. As shown in figure 7.1, such a firm would have a superior cost structure for newly launched products (rooted in lower capital expenditures and variable costs of production). For a more cost-sensitive therapeutic segment, such as antibiotics or a segment characterized by intense generic or patented substitute competition, such an advantage may be critical to the product's financial success. Interestingly, the company adopting the "design it fast now, design it right later" strategy admitted that profits on newly launched drugs were well below historical rates as a result of higher manufacturing costs and lower-than-expected prices.

A second element of the new pharmaceutical environment also makes it risky to rely on improving process design quality after launch. As discussed in chapter 3, rapid technological change and intense competition are shrinking the life cycles of new drugs. By the time a new process is developed, implemented, and licensed by regulatory authorities, the product may have few years remaining in its commercial life. This means that firms essentially have less time postlaunch to drive down manufacturing costs to profitable levels. Moreover, new molecules are increasingly complex, and the minimum threshold for manufacturing process quality can be quite high. Unless a sufficiently robust manufacturing process is developed, the firm may be unable to produce enough supplies for clinical trials (which leads to delays and can compromise the quality of product development) or to launch the product at even minimal profitability targets. Thus the firm with the capability to develop high-quality

FIGURE 7.1 The Impact of Speed and Quality on Costs

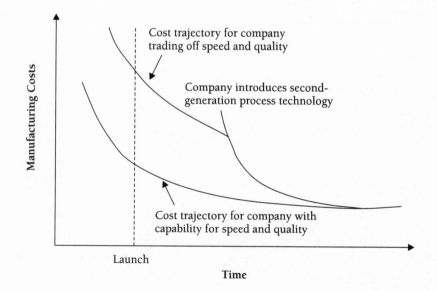

FIGURE 7.2 The Impact of Speed and Quality on Next-Generation Processes

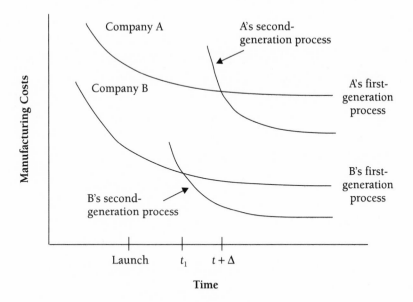

manufacturing processes has additional degrees of freedom when it comes to developing these complex products.

Finally, because process R&D projects done before and after product launch share many characteristics and tasks, a firm with the capability for high-speed and high-quality process R&D on products in development should also have an advantage in improving processes for products already on the market. As illustrated in figure 7.2, a firm with this capability can cycle through more postlaunch process improvement iterations than the firm that must take its time to get the process right. Company B is able to use its fast cycle/high-quality capabilities to sustain its advantage by introducing its next-generation process before Company A can. Perhaps not coincidentally, the pharmaceutical firm in this study with the best performance in terms of both lead time and process quality (as discussed below) was also most aggressive in introducing new generations of process technologies for its existing products.

Defining Process Design Quality

Although the quality of a process design, like that of a product design, is multidimensional, one common way to define process quality is in terms of how well the process meets a customer's or user's requirements.[4] Because the user of a process design is the manufacturing plant, the design's quality can be judged by its match with the plant's requirements, which include ease of operation and maintenance, robustness, reliability, safety, conformance to regulatory requirements, yields, capital investments, and costs. Clearly, an index comprising all these potential data points is impractical. An alternative approach is to focus on a subset of meaningful components. Interviews with plant managers and engineers in this study identified two dimensions of quality that fit this criterion and met the added practical criteria of data availability and comparability across projects: *cost-efficiency* and *complexity reduction*. One additional indicator of process design quality is the frequency and timing of *changes in the synthetic route*.

Cost-Efficiency

Cost-efficiency is defined relative to technically feasible alternatives. Although not all companies were able (or willing) to release cost data, one company fortunately agreed to provide information for its last eighteen development projects.[5] Although limited, these data were useful for examining the sources of cost improvement and their relationship to the firm's development approach.

Complexity Reduction

The second metric of design quality, and the one used more extensively throughout this chapter, is complexity reduction. All else being equal, plants prefer a process technology that has a less complex design. There are a number of reasons for this, including the impact of process complexity on capital and operating costs, reliability, robustness, and regulatory approval. Although cost-efficiency is relatively straightforward to measure, complexity requires additional discussion.

In synthetic chemical processes, the chief way to reduce process complexity is to combine multiple reactions into single steps ("telescoping"). Telescoping essentially reduces the number of intermediate chemicals isolated during the production process and provides a number of economic and operational advantages. First, with fewer steps, less capacity is lost on setups and shutdowns. In addition, because there are inevitable yield losses with each step, reducing the number of steps typically increases overall yields. Finally, because the output of each step—the intermediate chemicals—must go through a standardized set of quality assurance, labeling, and storage procedures, reducing the number of production steps reduces handling costs. Although the specifics of the techniques are peculiar to chemical processes, telescoping has analogies in other contexts. For example, in metal stamping, engineers commonly search for ways to reduce the number of operations required to fabricate the desired shape. In assembly operations, design for manufacturability (DFM) often focuses on reducing the number of assembly tasks or parts. Thus much of what is learned regarding complexity reduction in the context of pharmaceuticals has broader applicability in other contexts.

The degree to which process complexity has been reduced in the present context is reflected in the number of chemical reactions per manufacturing step in the final process. Combining multiple reactions into single production steps results in a higher average number of reactions per step. Using this measure, a process that has not been simplified through telescoping will have a value of 1; that is, one reaction per step. Although the total number of reactions in the process places a theoretical upper limit on the number of reactions per step, no project neared this constraint; in the sample of thirteen chemical projects, the highest number of reactions per step was 3.5—a 7-reaction process manufactured in 2 steps. Furthermore, there was no statistical evidence that the total number of reactions ultimately influenced the number of reactions per step. Thus technical differences across projects do not seem to be driving forces in the degree to which the processes were simplified.

Earlier, we examined whether there might be a trade-off between lead time and development cost. Here we need to investigate whether a time-quality or cost-quality trade-off exists. It may be that some projects are faster or consume fewer hours simply because an organization chose not to focus on developing a more manufacturable process. Figures 7.3 and 7.4 plot content-adjusted development cost (expressed in hours) and lead time against manufacturability.

There is no statistically significant relationship for either development cost or lead time. Indeed, to the extent that any trend can be detected among the noise, there appears to be a positive correlation between development cost and manufacturability (although this is largely a result of one outlier). Although the sample size is too small to yield additional insights through statistical analysis, going behind the regression revealed some interesting patterns (figure 7.4). Although the sample of projects per firm is far too small to draw any statistical conclusions, there appears to be a consistent relationship between lead time and quality *at the firm level*—projects with shorter lead times were associated with a lower complexity. (See the four highlighted projects for organization A in figure 7.4.) This pattern is particularly surprising in light of the perception expressed by many managers that speed and quality were at odds.

FIGURE 7.3 Development Cost versus Manufacturability

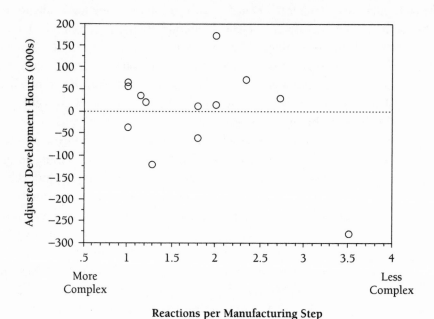

FIGURE 7.4 Development Lead Time versus Manufacturability

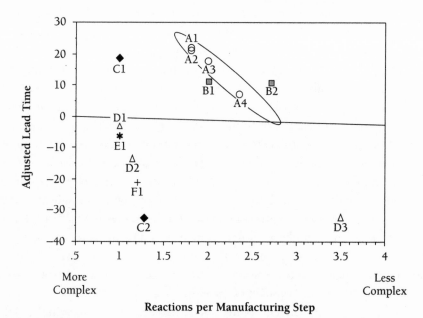

* Each letter identifies a company; each number corresponds to a project.

Further investigation revealed two factors that seem to underlie this relationship. First, the capability for rapid process development allows the organization to spend more time refining the process and making it manufacturable. In projects that ran into technical problems and were behind schedule, the chief concern was getting a process to work consistently in the factory. Ease of operation and manufacturability were considered luxuries to be dealt with only after the process was fully validated and approved by regulatory authorities. A second factor at work was the underlying role of deep process knowledge. As reported earlier, rapid process development in chemical pharmaceuticals hinges on an organization's ability to exploit opportunities in the process research phase. Developing a deep understanding of the chemistry early on enables firms to identify and solve major process problems long before manufacturing startup. This lays a solid technical foundation for optimizing and streamlining the process.

Telescoping a chemical process has strong analogies to systems integration in product development. Integrating multiple reactions in a single process step requires an in-depth knowledge of each reaction, much the same way that individual components of a product cannot be integrated effectively unless each component and its properties are well understood. In projects in which engineers attempted to gloss over problems with the underlying chemistry or had a relatively weak understanding of a particular step, attempts at integrating that step with others simply led to additional noise. High quality in the process research stage is a prerequisite for achieving high quality in the subsequent refinement and optimization stages.

Route Changes

The quality of a development process also reflects how problems are identified and proactively resolved. In the context of chemical projects, a development process that relies heavily on the commercial manufacturing plant to discover and solve major technical problems is akin to a manufacturing process that relies on an inspector to spot defects at the end of the assembly. Major, late process technology design changes are one sign that the development cycle is failing to proactively spot and solve technical problems. In the context of chemicals, the frequency and timing of changes in the synthetic route are one indicator of the quality of the development process. Because route selection draws on basic chemical theories and an understanding of how well routes operate under commercial manufacturing conditions, it is a good reflection of an organization's capability to learn before doing. Problems with synthetic

FIGURE 7.5 Route Changes and Route Selection Time

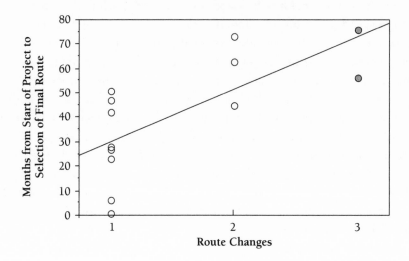

routes can be detected long before a process reaches the factory. Moreover, because synthetic routes represent the basic process technology concept, they have analogies in other development contexts. For example, in product development, concept development and selection represent a critical activity. Learning about route selection and how it affects development performance and quality thus offers broader conceptual lessons. Finally, from a practical standpoint, route changes were very well documented by the companies involved in the study.

As shown in figure 7.5, the majority of chemical projects in the sample experienced one route change (from the original synthetic route used to discover the molecule), and multiple route changes were relatively common. There was also a high degree of variance with respect to how long it took to finalize the selection of a synthetic route. In one project, for example, the final route was selected within a month of project initiation. At the other extreme, a route was not finalized until one project was in its seventy-sixth month. As one might expect, there is a moderately positive correlation between the number of route changes and the time required to select a final route, but there is also a high degree of variance. For instance, two projects underwent three synthetic route changes (see the shaded points in figure 7.5). For one of these projects, however, the route was finalized nearly twenty months earlier than for the other, despite the fact that the molecules under development were very similar. Thus differences in technology cannot account for the discrepancy. As will be discussed later, the ability of the first organization to cycle through routes relatively quickly opened up a number of development options not available to its slower counterpart.

Impact of Route Changes on Complexity Reduction

Because the synthetic route lies at the top of the process design hierarchy, the timing and quality of route selection could have a major impact on overall process design quality, including cost efficiency and complexity reduction. Changes to the synthetic route late in the development cycle can necessitate a significant amount of rework, as equipment designs, process flows, optimization conditions, analytical methods, and operating procedures are revisited and new solutions developed. This not only can be costly, it may also affect the overall quality of the process design if insufficient time remains to complete necessary refinements before the start of production.

Figure 7.6 illustrates the relationship between the timing of route selection (holding overall project length constant) and the quality of process design as measured by the index of complexity reduction. These data suggest that projects with relatively late route selection tend to involve less complexity

FIGURE 7.6 Complexity Reduction and Route Selection Time

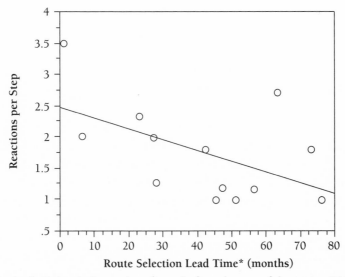

*Route selection lead time is the number of months from the start of the process R&D project to the time when a final commitment is made to a synthetic route for production.

FIGURE 7.7 The Effect of Route Changes on Process Quality

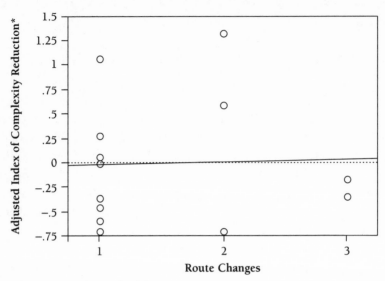

*Holds constant route selection lead time.

reduction. Regression analysis indicates that roughly 42 percent of the variation in complexity reduction is associated with the timing of final route selection.[6] Clinical investigation of the products confirmed that this relationship is driven partly by the schedule compression caused by late route choices. Because telescoping of the process cannot begin until the route is determined, a long route selection process essentially reduces the time available for optimization and refinement activities. To meet time lines, companies then hold off on telescoping and other process refinements that are not absolutely necessary to meet regulatory requirements.

The data suggest that quality in the route selection process—being able to select an attractive route as early as possible—can influence overall process design quality. Where firms made significant route changes late in the development cycle because of chemistry problems not identified early on, they lacked the time needed to refine the process.

Do these data imply that an organization should commit to a single route as early as possible? After all, as shown earlier, more route changes are associated with longer route selection times, which might suggest that changing routes is detrimental to the quality of the commercial manufacturing process. Interestingly, as shown in figure 7.7, a statistical analysis of the independent impact of route changes on complexity reduction (holding constant route selection lead times) indicates this is not the case.

There is virtually no independent statistical relationship between the number of route changes and the degree to which manufacturing complexity was reduced. Combined with the data shown earlier, this indicates that changes in the route per se do not really matter, but the timing of those changes does. An organization can cycle through multiple routes and still achieve design quality as long as it makes its final selection relatively early. This suggests that the capability to cycle through multiple routes quickly may correspond to higher-quality process designs. Before turning to this issue, the next section explores the impact of changing routes on another critical dimension of process design quality: cost.

The Impact of Route Changes on Cost

Route changes may not harm the quality of the manufacturing process (provided they are made early enough), but what benefits do they provide in terms of cost? To gain insight into this issue, data on the cost impact of route changes were examined.[7] Data on eighteen process development projects carried out in one company in the study were used to compare the estimated manufacturing costs of the first route used during development to the manufacturing costs of the final route used in production. Note that in some cases the synthetic route was changed more than once, but data were available only comparing the first and last routes. These data are presented in figure 7.8.

The data show that changes in the synthetic route have a dramatic impact, reducing manufacturing costs by an average of 65 percent (with a median reduction of 74 percent). In contrast, cost reductions through telescoping and other forms of process optimization led to cost reductions of about 40 percent on average. Figure 7.9 provides a more detailed cost depiction of one project that underwent three synthetic route changes. As shown, although some cost reduction occurred with each route, most gains occurred as step changes between synthetic routes. Thus, given a choice between optimizing the initial process and implementing a completely new synthetic route, the limited data here would favor the latter.

The data clearly must be interpreted with care. They represent the experience of only one company and could reflect the firm's unique balance of capabilities between route selection and optimization. For instance, it is quite conceivable that some firms, because of their historical approach to process R&D,

have a comparative advantage in route selection, whereas others have strengths in optimization. However, isolated examples across the thirteen chemical projects in the sample appear to be consistent with this company's experience. For example, changes in the synthetic route were almost universally the preferred option when candidate processes faced severe economic or environmental constraints.

These data shed new light on the relationship between route selection timing and complexity reduction. In some cases, firms may choose to implement a new route relatively late if the cost reduction benefits of doing so exceed the benefits of further optimization. That is, these companies are trading off one driver of design quality (process optimization) with another (a better process architecture). It should be relatively clear, however, that a firm that

FIGURE 7.8 Impact of Route Changes on Manufacturing Costs

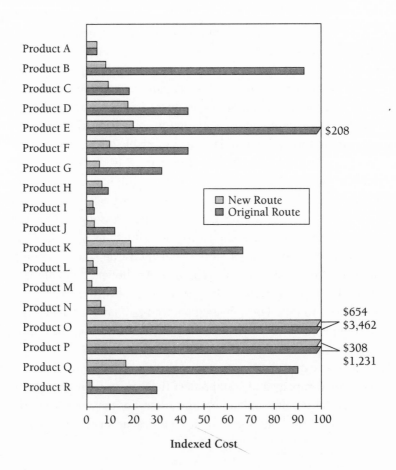

FIGURE 7.9 Three Synthetic Route Changes

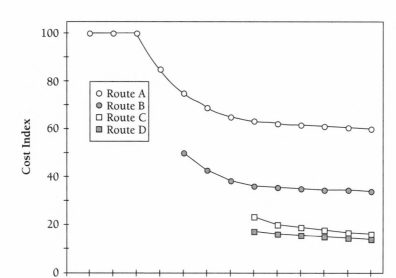

can hone in on the better process architecture early, leaving itself time to optimize and refine, will be in a stronger position. From the data above, process optimization can still account for significant cost reductions (40 percent).

Achieving quality in both route selection (process architecture) and refinement requires a capability for what might be called rapid route cycling. An organization that can rapidly cycle through multiple routes early in the development process can find and implement new synthetic routes (thus greatly reducing manufacturing costs) while leaving sufficient time to optimize and refine the process—without delaying the overall project schedule. As discussed below, these capabilities appear to be rooted in how companies manage and organize the technology selection process.

Creating the Capability for Rapid and Effective Technology Selection

As noted earlier in figure 7.5, there was a relatively high degree of variance in the relationship between number of route changes and route selection time. These data are presented again in figure 7.10, but with specific data points labeled for purposes of illustration and discussion. Using A1 as a benchmark,

FIGURE 7.10 Route Changes and Route Selection Time

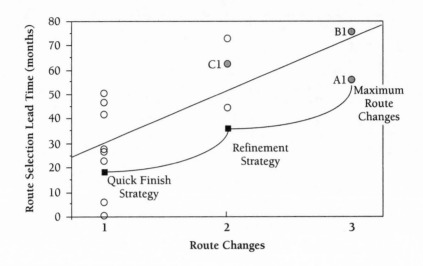

the figure illustrates the various ways a capability for rapid route cycling can be exploited. First, an organization can use its capability to achieve the maximum number of route changes within a fixed time window for commitment to a final route. In figure 7.10, for example, company A was able to achieve three route changes in approximately the same amount of time it took company C to achieve two. Another approach would be to make fewer changes, but to use the additional time for process refinement and optimization. Suppose company A decided to make only two route changes. At its current cycle time of approximately 18 months per route, it could have made two route changes in 36 months (depicted as the "Refinement Strategy"). Now compare this to C1, which required 63 months to go through two routes. Thus company A could have spent an additional 27 months refining and optimizing its process and still have finished in the same time frame as company C. Finally, company A could have pursued a "Quick Finish Strategy," minimizing the number of route changes and finishing the project sooner. For instance, had it made only one route change, A1's route selection time of 18 months would have been faster than seven of the remaining nine projects making one change.

Since A1 and B1 involved structurally similar molecules competing for the same therapeutic market, a direct comparison of these two projects is illuminating. Both projects involved three route changes, but company A completed its route selection in 56 months, compared to 76 months for company B.

Company A utilized its additional 20 months in two ways. It spent 10 months refining and optimizing the process and reducing its complexity, and brought its product to market 10 months sooner. Interestingly, company A used its rapid route cycling capabilities in another way not discussed above. Although the process research group committed to a final route 53 months into the project, it did not stop looking for better routes. Approximately a year later, an even more cost-effective synthesis was discovered. However, rather than delay the project by introducing this synthesis late in the development cycle, the company waited until after it had received FDA approval for the drug using the old route. Within a year, it had its new process fully developed, refined, and validated. Armed with a comprehensive set of data and thorough documentation, the company quickly gained FDA approval for the new process. Thus company A's rapid route cycling development capability provided an advantage not only during the development cycle, but also once the product was on the market.

Detailed investigation of technology selection processes revealed some distinctive characteristics of the projects characterized by rapid route cycling. Although much of the recent literature on development has focused on how parallel processing shrinks lead times, parallel development of alternative routes does not appear to offer a significant advantage. In virtually all the projects in the sample, multiple routes were evaluated at various phases. Indeed, one reason why projects with a single route change often had long route selection times is that the organization was waiting for experimental data from potential alternatives to be fully evaluated. However, what do seem to matter are the way parallel route development is managed and the type of feedback mechanisms used to trigger the search for alternatives.

Product development literature of the current decade offers a variety of opinions on how fluid the concept development phase should be. Traditional models of development advocate early selection of and commitment to basic technical concepts, whereas others have argued that in highly turbulent technical environments it is much more important to maintain flexibility (Iansiti 1995). Rapid route cyclers in this study combined elements of both approaches and adopted what might be termed a *fixed-fluid* model of technology selection. On the one hand, the fact that they continued to search for alternative synthetic routes and commonly changed routes during development suggests a somewhat flexible approach to technology selection. However, not all changes are equal in terms of their impact on development lead times, development costs, and quality. For instance, changing the last step of the synthetic route can require changing all the preceding steps in the process. In an extreme case, the route change can mean starting from scratch—clearly a time-consuming and costly proposition. To avoid this situation, rapid route cyclers tried to fix critical process steps as early as possible, in order to reduce the scope and impact of later route changes. One approach is to fix the final steps of the process, because changes to later steps tend to have ramifications for all preceding steps. Another approach is to exploit the inherent modularity of the chemical process: by freezing the final step or a pivotal intermediate step relatively early, the impact of future route changes can be reduced. The essence of the fixed-fluid approach is that, although major process changes are permitted (indeed, actively sought), each generation builds on the next as much as possible.

A comparison of the three approaches is graphed in Figure 7.11. An example of the *early commitment* approach in action, in which the process is transferred to the plant at an early stage, was discussed in a previous chapter. This project also involved an early commitment to a route. The route was viable, but the development organization had to expend time and resources fixing and adapting to problems inherent in the chemistry. Although there is always uncertainty, a continued search for alternative routes might have yielded a more tractable process. In the *full flexibility* approach, the other extreme, the search for routes continues. But in this case, the search process is viewed in terms of a series of "independent draws," with little technical connection between one route and the next. The fixed-fluid approach attempts to strike a balance. Early on, commitments are made to a class of routes (for example, all routes that use the same last two steps), but the search for alternatives within these bounds is encouraged. This approach avoids the penalties of major late changes while leaving room for improvement. Moreover, rather than waiting for the entire process to be finalized, optimization and refinements can begin on those parts of the process that have been fixed relatively early.

The fixed-fluid approach involves some interesting trade-offs. It reduces the flexibility to change some aspects of the process but at the same time reduces the cost (in terms of lead time, development resources, and impact on quality) of changing others. Paradoxically, organizations following this approach enhance their flexibility to make certain types of changes by reducing their flexibility to make others. Using Upton's (1995) taxonomy of flexibility for manufacturing operations allows us to understand the nature of this trade-off.[8] By locking in one aspect of the process, the organization is reducing the range of future alternatives it might adopt. However, within that range of

FIGURE 7.11 Approaches to Basic Technology Selection

(a) Early Commitment

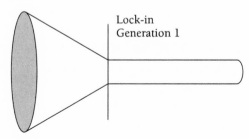

Lock-in
Generation 1

(b) Full Flexibility

Generation 1   Generation 2   Generation 3

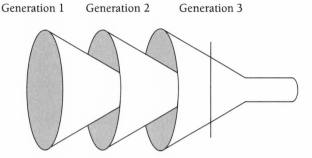

(c) Fixed-Fluid

Generation 1

Generation 2

Generation 3

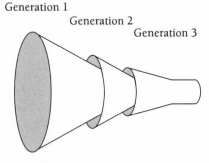

options, it achieves mobility—the ability to change quickly and at low cost between options. Given the time pressures involved in the launch of a new product, lack of mobility can be a serious impediment to any change at all.

Interestingly, much of what has been discussed in terms of the impact of different types of route changes and the desirability of fixing the final step would come as no surprise to the chemists participating in this study. However, many would counter that, given the uncertainty of R&D, it is virtually impossible to get even one or two critical steps of the process right the first time. Here is where differences in organizational capabilities play a pivotal role. In some organizations, the vast majority of feedback about route performance comes through pilot production. Only major problems (such as low yields or steps that are extremely difficult to execute), which cannot be overcome through minor modifications (such as changing a temperature), trigger the search for alternative syntheses.

Companies that successfully pursue the fixed-flexible model follow a proactive approach and exploit opportunities to learn before doing. Rather than wait for feedback from pilot batches, they use extensive laboratory experiments to model the process, make predictions about its performance at a larger scale, identify problems, and explore alternative routes. This approach provides much richer information about the route and its potential weaknesses up front, thus increasing the likelihood of getting critical aspects of the process right the first time. Organizations that know relatively little about the initial route decide whether to go into pilot testing based on technical feasibility (as when the route can produce the desired compound). In companies following the fixed-fluid approach, deeper knowledge about the selected route allows questions to be posed and resolved early on. Is the route likely to be viable in a commercial operation? What specific parts are likely to be sources of problems? Are the pivotal steps problem free? Although fixed-fluid organizations often send processes to the pilot plant with problems, the scope of their impact is generally known in advance. The fixed-fluid organization is likely working on solutions to these problems, whereas the less proactive organization is waiting to discover them.

Another distinguishing attribute of organizations successfully following the fixed-fluid approach is that they not only exploit basic chemical theory and knowledge (which is available to all organizations) but also leverage experience from prior projects. Knowledge acquired through experience tends to be relatively specific to classes of molecules with similar synthetic routes. In a company whose approach typified the fixed-fluid strategy, a process research chemist commented that their two projects included in the sample utilized portions of the chemistry developed for previous projects. Building a deep base of process knowledge is thus a critical element of the fixed-fluid approach.

This has interesting implications for organizational structure. In recent years, much of the development literature has focused on the merits of using cross-functional teams and other functionally integrated approaches to development. The more thoughtful literature has recognized trade-offs between functional specialization and cross integration.[9] The present context, however, appears to be one in which the benefits of specialization—in terms of creating deeper technical expertise—may outweigh the costs of lower cross-functional coordination. Integrated, focused groups clearly provide advantages in terms of communication flow. Often the same process developers worked on a project from start to finish. Because there were no internal hand-overs from one group to the next, the teams were able to develop very detailed knowledge of the overall process.

But integration has its costs in technical depth. Because process scientists in such an organization spend a good part of their time doing downstream development tasks (such as pilot plant experiments, technology transfer to the plant, and validation), they have less time to focus on research. These individuals gain breadth at the expense of depth. Over the course of a career, for example, a process chemist may gain a broader perspective on the development cycle from research to manufacturing but will be involved in fewer projects. Furthermore, although many individuals are doing (or have done) process research on different projects, no one group acts as the reservoir of cumulative process research knowledge. In one project in which an integrated organizational structure was used, a difficult problem with the process chemistry could not be solved internally, requiring extensive consultation and support from another division of the company.

Conclusion

This chapter has explored the linkage between quality in process design and in the development process by which that design is created. Although the analysis was limited to a subset of quality dimensions and projects, the data are suggestive of three basic themes for effective development management. First, there is no apparent trade-off between lead time and development cost, on the one hand, and process design quality, on the other. Firms that were capable of developing higher-quality process designs (as measured by complexity reduction) were equally likely to demonstrate superior speed and lead time performance. Clearly, many other elements of quality should be investigated in future research, but the results here highlight the potential for process development to support an organization's competitive needs for faster development, improved efficiency, and better manufacturing performance.

An explanation for this relationship is rooted in the second theme of this chapter: process design quality is a reflection of development process quality.[10] Process research creates the raw material for development, laying the foundation for subsequent work. Identifying and resolving problems proactively, using well-designed laboratory experiments to simulate future manufacturing performance, leveraging knowledge from prior projects, and minimizing disruptions through commitments to crucial design components help stabilize the basic architecture early, which in turn paves the way for process optimization and refinement. In contrast, when the upstream research stage of a development process is unreliable, inconsistent, or incapable, downstream optimization is a futile and frustrating experience.

Second, there is no sharp trade-off between speed and quality; rather, the two appear to be mutually reinforcing. Fast problem-solving cycles provide rapid and timely feedback about potential problems, a critical factor in proactive problem solving. Strong process research capabilities enable an organization to rapidly simulate process quality in the laboratory phase and to generate quick feedback on potential problems. In an environment where the knowledge base is deep, strong process research capabilities—the basis for learning before doing—drive both speed and quality.

A final theme concerns flexibility in the development process. In a wide range of contexts and industries, many firms debate the appropriate time to freeze a design. Those at the front end of the process—typically researchers or designers—advocate keeping options open as long as possible, arguing, "You can't rush creativity!" Understandably, those responsible for downstream development phases—product and process engineers as well as people in the plant—have a different perspective. A longer upstream phase means less time for process refinement, and they thus prefer an earlier commitment, asserting, "Researchers are never satisfied until *everything* is perfect." Many of the participants in the study struggled with this tension, and the data in this chapter suggest why. Moreover, as development time lines are compressed and groups at each end of the process seek to grab a share of a shrinking time "pie," this debate will only get sharper.

Underneath this conflict are fundamental differences in perspective on the importance of doing (designing) it right the first time versus the need for iteration.[11] On this latter perspective, Reinertsen (1992) notes, "The fastest way to a good engineering solution is to devise simple models first and refine them if they prove inadequate. This may mean doing it wrong the first time, but doing it fast." The discussion here suggests that a mixture of both approaches may be appropriate within the same project. Under the fixed-fluid approach, commitments to those components of the process having the greatest overall impact on other steps are made very early, whereas those with more isolated effects are allowed to float.[12] This approach allows researchers the luxury of iteration for some parts of the process, but forces them to be disciplined in choosing which components are frozen early. Because these choices constrain subsequent search and selection, high quality in process research is even more important under this approach. Whether such an approach is suitable for developing products and different types of processes is an issue that merits further research.

Learning across Projects
in Biotechnology

A CENTRAL THEME of previous chapters has been the relationship between the structure of knowledge and development strategy. In those discussions and analyses, the firm's knowledge environment was treated as exogenous and fixed (within a broad class of technology). That is, all firms operating within the biotechnology environment were viewed as facing the same technological opportunities and constraints; the same was seen as true for chemical projects. This provided a useful way to explore the impact of technological environments on development strategy and performance. However, statistical evidence and field research observations suggest that knowledge bases vary across firms working in the same technological environment.

These variations have important implications in two respects. First, to the extent that some elements of knowledge bases are rooted in firm-specific experiences, firms may differ in their ability to engage in learning before doing versus learning by doing. Second, firm-specific differences in knowledge are widely believed to be a source of competitive advantage.[1] Building deep knowledge that permits learning before doing should be a focal concern of firms in dynamic technical environments. Although most researchers and managers would agree that organizational learning is important and should be promoted, there is far less understanding about how it might be fostered. Furthermore, although propositions abound, empirical research on the topic is scant.[2]

Many questions of importance to both researchers and practitioners remain unanswered. How (and, perhaps more important, why) do some firms create unique knowledge bases? Are some organizations better learners than others? If so, why? How can managers promote learning of the skills and knowledge most critical to their firm's competitive advantage? This chapter attempts to address these issues with observations from the biotechnology subsample of the study. Because biotechnology firms are still relatively young, they provide an excellent context in which to study organizational learning. The projects studied represent each firm's initial efforts at developing commercial-scale process technologies. Tracking differences in performance and practice over these projects allows us to observe organizational learning in action.

The first part of the chapter presents a simple conceptual framework for learning across development projects, which highlights the dual "outputs" of development projects: the technology that is implemented in a new process (or product design) and the knowledge that becomes available for future projects. In most situations, managerial attention focuses on the first of these outputs; getting a new process or product developed as quickly and efficiently as possible takes precedence over building knowledge for future projects. The literature on innovation has reflected a similar bias, focusing largely on the performance of individual projects or firms at a single point in time, rather than on changes in performance over time.[3] Indeed, much of the conceptual and empirical discussion in previous chapters has been oriented toward static performance—how does the approach to managing a particular project influence the performance of that project?

Development projects, however, also create technical and organizational learning that becomes part of a firm's knowledge base and in turn influences the strategies chosen for and performance achieved on future projects. Although many managers would agree that the intellectual by-products of a project lay the critical foundation for upcoming projects, few understand how this learning can be managed or integrated with more immediate goals. The framework in this chapter allows us to examine the dynamic interaction between the organization's knowledge base, its capability for different development strategies (such as learning by doing versus learning before doing), and changes in project performance over time (say, lead time). Drawing from the conceptual and empirical materials presented earlier, the framework suggests that an organization's optimal development strategy may change from project to project as its knowledge base evolves.

This idea is explored through in-depth clinical analysis of the study's biotechnology projects. Comparison across the four firms (where observation over multiple projects was possible) reveals striking variations in the extent of improvement. Investigation of the projects conducted by these firms illuminates how the approach used to manage a project at one point in time influences the knowledge created for future projects. The chapter concludes with a brief discussion of the implications for managing learning across projects.

A Framework for Learning across Projects

There is a long and rich history of literature on organizational learning.[4] The framework presented here builds on the core themes of that literature to explore the specific mechanisms by which organizations learn within the context of process development projects. Although the framework is general enough to be applied to product development as well, process development is examined here for consistency with discussions in other parts of the book.

As noted earlier, every process development project has two potential outputs: the new process technology used in the manufacturing environment and the new knowledge that becomes available for future projects.[5] The three vertical groups at the top of figure 8.1 represent the development processes associated with the creation of a new manufacturing process technology (the factors affecting the performance of these processes were the focus of much of the discussion in earlier chapters). Each group at the top of the figure depicts a project undertaken to develop one generation of process technology. Three potential forces can influence the development process at any given point in time: the firm's existing base of technical knowledge, its existing base of organizational knowledge, and constraints created by existing process technology.

An organization's technical knowledge base—which includes such elements as scientific theories, principles, algorithms, conceptual models, specific analytical or experimental techniques, heuristics, and empirical regularities—has a profound influence on the choice and performance of different development strategies. In some instances, technical knowledge may be well codified in patents, documents, or computer models, but in many cases it is known to be highly tacit.[6] A key ingredient of a firm's technical knowledge base is knowledge about the performance impact of different types of technical solutions. For instance, a firm's scientists may know (from theory or past observations) that mammalian cells grow rapidly between certain temperatures, or that certain types of nutrients work well under some process conditions but poorly

FIGURE 8.1 Framework for Learning across Projects

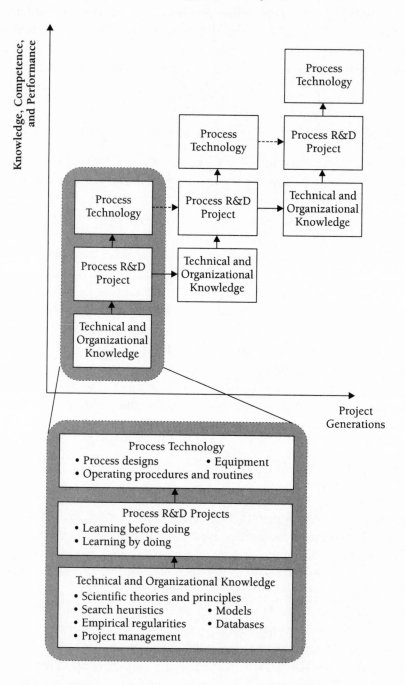

under others. Existing technical knowledge provides a starting point for any given development project and, as discussed earlier, influences the kind of development strategies that should be used during projects.

Organizational knowledge—including how to organize and manage projects, coordinate different problem-solving activities, determine goals and incentives, allocate resources, assign personnel, and resolve disputes—is also likely to influence the choice and performance of different development strategies. Through repeated experience, some firms may develop specialized competences in specific project management approaches or development strategies. For instance, a firm that has historically carried out much of its process development work during commercial production may have built specialized competences in learning by doing, and may continue to follow this approach even if the technological environment lends itself to more efficient development through other approaches.

A third potential influence is constraints imposed by the need to integrate new process technologies with existing process technologies or production capabilities. For instance, new process techniques may be at odds with an existing plant's physical capacity or operational competences. Similarly, a highly automated process would not be a good match for a plant lacking software support and maintenance capabilities. Even when companies implement new processes at a "greenfield site," their existing repertoire of plant management skills and operating philosophies can influence choices of process technologies.

The above discussion calls attention to the constraints that existing technical knowledge, organizational knowledge, and process technologies and capabilities may place on process development strategies and performance. This raises a question: From where do these constraints arise? Thus far, these constraints have been treated as largely exogenous. A biotechnology firm's process R&D strategy, for instance, would be constrained by the structure of knowledge inherent to biotechnologies. However, empirical evidence suggests that, even within classes of technology, there are wide variations in performance and the ability to pursue different approaches.

A resounding theme in the existing literature is that differences in experience account for differences in capabilities across firms.[7] From this perspective, what an organization knows how to do today is a function of what it learned in the course of development yesterday. Thus, referring back to figure 8.1, the horizontal linkages depict the learning that takes place across projects. Each project not only creates a new process technology, it also changes the starting conditions and constraints for the next project. In the course of developing a process technology, the organization engages in problem solving to learn about potential solutions: it conducts experiments, runs simulations, and tests the process at pilot and full scale. A component of what is learned becomes embodied in the process flows, equipment designs and settings, process specifications, operating procedures, and other elements of the process design. Moreover, this knowledge—as well as other knowledge generated during the project—becomes available for future projects. For instance, in developing a mammalian cell process, an organization may conduct a series of experiments to determine how temperature affects protein production. This knowledge is useful for the current project because it enables developers to specify an optimal temperature; more broadly, such knowledge is also useful for future mammalian cell process projects.

A critical component of a firm's technical knowledge base is how faithfully it can model or simulate processes in the laboratory. This knowledge of scale effects can be deepened through experience and feedback about how specific process designs perform in an actual manufacturing environment. For instance, a certain process may work well in the laboratory and in the pilot plant, but wreak havoc in the commercial plant. Analysis of the problem can generate knowledge that might help developers avoid a similar situation in the future (or at least know what to expect under certain conditions).

Organizations can expand their organizational knowledge across projects in much the same fashion. Each project generates data on the performance of different approaches; feedback on gaps between expected and desired lead times, efficiency, and quality performance then triggers a search for new approaches to managing development projects.[8] Management may learn, for example, that certain people need to work closely together, or that more resources need to be allocated during certain phases, if the project is to meet lead time goals. Similarly, they may learn that there is a greater need for learning by doing, which may trigger a change in procedures so that processes are transferred to plants at an earlier phase of the development cycle. Indeed, one need only look around today, at companies in a wide range of industries engaged in wholesale reengineering of their development processes, to see this type of organizational learning in action.

Early theoretical models of learning suggest that technical and organizational knowledge may be tightly intertwined. According to Nelson and Winter's (1982) evolutionary theory of the firm, much of a company's technical knowledge is embedded in its organizational routines. Organizations "remember" new technical knowledge through changes in development processes. For instance, if a firm's development scientists discover an impurity in a given process, they will work to develop a purification step to remove the impurity, as well as an analytical technique to detect the impurity (for quality control purposes). This technical knowledge may be remembered by individuals who worked on the project. But, to ensure that it is "remembered" by others in the organization, the firm may create a standardized list of analytical tests to check for this impurity on future projects. Thus discovery of the impurity added to the firm's technical knowledge base and, by leading to a change in development processes, altered the firm's organizational knowledge base.

The framework and findings from earlier chapters also suggest an evolving, dynamic relationship between technical and organizational knowledge at the firm level. As firms engage in process R&D projects and gain feedback about gaps between laboratory and full-scale performance (and the underlying causes of those gaps), they may become more capable of faithfully simulating processes in the laboratory and discovering problems. Exploiting its deeper knowledge base may require putting greater emphasis on learning before doing. Thus coevolution of technical and organizational knowledge may be critical to sustaining development performance over time.

A number of questions still merit more detailed empirical investigation. For example, what type of knowledge can organizations successfully generate and capture for future projects? Development projects generate both first- and second-order effects. First-order effects comprise the performance of an individual project in terms of lead time, resources consumed, and process design quality; such effects were the focus of chapters 6 and 7. The second-order effect is the impact on the organization's knowledge base. All projects create opportunities for learning, but are unique types of knowledge captured by different organizations? Are some organizations more effective at using their experience to deepen their knowledge bases? Are these differences rooted in how firms approach development projects?

A second set of issues concerns the tension between the evolution of technical and organizational knowledge. On the one hand, as described above, if firms are deepening their knowledge base from one project to the next, there may be very good reasons for their development processes to change as well. On the other hand, organizations are known to be averse to change, even in the face of large gaps between actual and desired performance.[9] As an organization's competence at pursuing a particular development strategy improves with use, it becomes more costly and difficult to adopt alternative approaches. Thus a central challenge of managing learning is to strike the appropriate balance between exploiting existing capabilities and exploring new ones (March 1991). Although there is a long history of theoretical work on this issue,[10] insights from empirical or clinical investigations are generally lacking.

The remainder of this chapter explores these issues with a combination of statistical and clinical data from the subsample of biotechnology projects. The basic approach is to explore the relationship between one dimension of project performance—lead time—and the project strategy across projects within companies. Clinical comparisons across companies are then used to shed light on the mechanisms by which organizations learn across projects, the relationship between a firm's approach to managing one project and its approach and performance on its next, and the forces constraining opportunities to exploit learning across projects.

Learning to Learn in Biotechnology

To get an empirical handle on the issue of learning to learn, we return to the statistical analysis conducted in chapter 6. Figure 8.2 illustrates the relationship between lead time performance and the resources allocated to process research. To facilitate analysis of firm-level patterns, individual data points have been labeled sequentially by organization (for example, project A1 preceded project A2). Overall, there was no statistically significant relationship between performance and process research in biotechnology. However, firm-specific analysis reveals some interesting patterns. Organizations A and B seemed to improve their lead time performance with each project. Organization A, for example, completed its second project about 30 months sooner than its first, and organization B showed an improvement of about 15 months. Although not formally included as part of this study (both projects were completed well after the time frame for data collection had ended), follow-up research on A's and B's next process development projects indicates that this pattern of improvement has continued. Organization A completed its third project in record time, with substantial increases in yields over those for project A2. Organization B also completed its third project with less lead time than was required for project B2. Beating its own record for B2 was one of organization B's explicit goals on its third-generation project. E is one of the most experienced organizations in the sample with respect to biotechnology process development. This might also suggest that it learned to learn before doing across projects. (Unfortunately, this organization was able to contribute only one project to the study, and we thus have no data to track its development strategy and performance over time.)

However, improvement was by no means the norm. Organization C demonstrated significant improvement between C1 and C2, but dramatic deterio-

FIGURE 8.2 Patterns of Lead Time Performance at the Organizational Level in Biotechnology

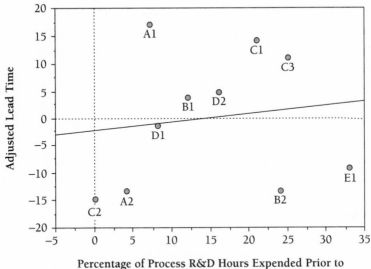

Percentage of Process R&D Hours Expended Prior to
Start of Pilot Production

ration between C2 and C3. Overall, learning appears to be more than simply accumulating experience.

A second noteworthy pattern is that some organizations appear to be better at learning before doing than others. For example, projects E1 and B2 consumed 35 percent and 25 percent, respectively, of project resources in research. The lead time performance of these projects was far superior to that of project C3 (which involved a similar commitment to research) and was on par with that of C2 and A2 (which relied far more on learning by doing). Organizations E and B (by its second project) appear to have developed capabilities to learn before doing.

These observations address one of the questions raised earlier: What might organizations learn to do better across projects? Organizations A and B learned to learn before doing. That is, they used knowledge from previous projects to uncover critical parameters and to create insights about the process technology that accelerated development. First-generation projects appear to have deepened the organization's reservoir of process knowledge that could be leveraged on second-generation projects. But how did organizations A and B do this? Below, we shed light on this question by digging beneath the regressions to explore detailed patterns of behavior and organizational processes. Profiles of the improving organizations, A and B, are first presented, followed by profiles of organizations C and D.

The clinical comparisons revolve around four dimensions. One was the framing of technical problems and the level of analysis at which technical understanding was sought. In some organizations, the challenge of process development was viewed in terms of solving basic scientific problems and understanding the behavior of processes at the molecular level. Others saw the challenge more as solving a specific and narrowly defined engineering problem.

The second dimension was the firm's approach to experimental and analytical methods. Organizations in the study seemed to vary dramatically in the extent to which they emphasized development of high-powered analytical techniques to enhance the quality of feedback from experiments. A third dimension was organizational structure. Although, in the broadest terms, all four organizations had similar structures for process development (that is, all used the integrated approach outlined in chapter 6), there were some fundamental differences in how they operated within these structures. Some used teams to integrate process R&D with other parts of the product development project. Others developed a more functionally centered approach.

Finally, and certainly not least important, were differences in how the organizations integrated manufacturing (more precisely, the plant) into process development. At some organizations, the plant was viewed as an integral part of the development process and a critical venue for experimentation. Others kept the plant relatively isolated from the development process, preferring instead to do most development in the laboratory and pilot plant. Earlier chapters shed light on how this approach influences lead time and cost performance of individual projects. The analysis below illuminates how it shapes the accumulation of specific knowledge.

Organization A

Organization A, a pioneer in the field of biopharmaceuticals, spent its earliest years focused strictly on product research. It followed the common strategy of licensing its first few projects to established pharmaceutical companies for clinical development, manufacturing, and marketing. Although the firm had done some process development on these outlicensed molecules, the bulk of this work was carried out by the licensees responsible for manufacturing. Project A1 represented the firm's first attempt at tackling the entire development process, through manufacturing and marketing.

The challenges facing the firm were both technical and organizational. From a technical standpoint, A1 represented a set of unsolved problems, including media and reactor designs, reaction conditions, purification processes, and analytical methods. Little public scientific knowledge was available; one could not, for example, simply conduct a literature search to determine the best media design for an *E. coli* process. Although many biotechnology firms were developing biochemical processes and solving similar technical problems, they considered this know-how a critical source of competitive advantage and kept it proprietary. Thus, lacking a well-developed knowledge base and access to information at other firms, organization A found itself literally inventing technology to manufacture proteins at larger scale.

The second challenge was organizational. Because organization A had never carried out a complete process development project, it lacked the infrastructure to take a process from research through the factory. On previous projects, process development was undertaken by scientists in the company's product research laboratories. Like many other biotechnology companies, organization A initially underestimated the value of process development, believing that, once an initial process was developed by discovery research, the next step was simply to transfer it to the plant. After A1, the firm's top management recognized the huge gulf between the interests of research scientists focused on finding novel products and the capabilities required to get a process up and running in an actual plant. Two factors were critical in changing management's thinking on this issue. First, during pilot production runs on earlier projects, management saw that growing genetically engineered bacteria at larger scale was not a trivial problem, and scale-up involved more than simply transferring the process to larger tanks. Second, through its collaborations with established pharmaceutical companies on earlier projects, the company was exposed to experienced process development and engineering groups.

Organization A began to build a separate process development group and strategy. It created a new position—senior vice president of process development and manufacturing—and then hired a person with experience in biotechnology process development from one of the company's collaborative partners. One interesting feature of this company's strategy was to integrate process development and manufacturing within the same general organizational structure. The senior vice president explained, "This organization was set up to avoid specific problems. We wanted to have very close links between process development and manufacturing; we did this by integrating them organizationally and physically. The trade-off is that the links between process R&D and product research are not as strong as they used to be."

This structure seemed to have the desired effect on the way process development was carried out and how the manufacturing plant was used in problem solving. As one process researcher noted, "Process development and manufacturing were inseparable. Once we did a few small-scale laboratory experiments to find out what unit operations were required, we immediately went into the plant to try it out. Even at a very early stage we used the plant; we did our development work in the manufacturing plant." Another process researcher added, "From an early phase, we move the process into the pilot plant, which is also our commercial manufacturing plant. There is no distinction between them. It's all one plant, and the same workers do the runs for both. This eliminates the handoff time lag [between development and manufacturing]." These comments are consistent with figure 8.2, which shows that organization A spent only about 5 percent of its project resources before it made its first pilot batches in the plant.

A second noteworthy feature of the company's process development strategy, which evolved during the course of the A1 project, was its focus on developing a detailed understanding of the process technology at the molecular level. Although the ostensible goal was to develop a commercially viable full-scale manufacturing process, technical problems were framed in terms of understanding, at the most micro level possible, the structure, behavior, and characteristics of proteins and the biochemical processes needed to synthesize them. To achieve this level of understanding, the company focused on building a broad base of scientific capabilities in key process technology disciplines such as microbiology, protein chemistry, biochemistry, analytical chemistry, and biophysics. (Interestingly, although process development is sometimes equated with process engineering, the company placed far less emphasis on equipment design, process flows, and other mechanical aspects of the manufacturing system.) Thus the company's problem-solving approach might be characterized as "bottom-up."

It would be easy to imagine that such a group would lack the capabilities needed to develop manufacturable processes. After all, the traditional domain of the scientist is the laboratory, and few scientists have had any exposure to real manufacturing problems or environments. It is the engineers who are supposed to bring a healthy dose of pragmatism to the effort. At organization A, however, the tight integration between process development and the manufacturing plant appeared to overcome any potential dichotomy. As noted above, development took place largely in the commercial manufacturing environment from an early phase, which forced the scientists to deal with the realities of the plant. They learned how the equipment influenced the process and how production workers actually carried out specific steps; the factory became their laboratory.[11] Because they experimented using production equipment, the resulting data were far more representative of final outcomes than typical laboratory results. The statistical evidence presented in chapter 6 indicated that development in the plant has first-order effects on performance: on average, projects taking this approach were faster and more efficient. As discussed later, there were also second-order effects on organizational learning.

A third element of the company's development strategy was heavy investment in analytical techniques. Analytical techniques are chemical or physical methods (such as SDS gels or chromatography) used to characterize the structure of a protein and detect its presence as well as that of potential impurities. Analytical techniques play a central role in the development of all pharmaceuticals because of the need to produce the exact molecule at extremely high purity levels. A critical challenge is to ensure that the process, as it is developed, continues to produce an identical molecule. For instance, a slightly different purification process may filter out the desired form of the protein while leaving in a similar, but biologically inactive, version. Similarly, adding a nutrient to the cell culture process may increase yields but introduce an unwanted impurity. Analytical techniques thus play a critical role in evaluating process R&D experiments.

Such techniques are particularly vital in biotechnology process development because of the sheer complexity of protein molecules and the high potential for biological production processes to generate impurities. Because of their complex structures, proteins are difficult molecules to characterize fully. The "same" basic protein may come in a variety of forms, and even slight differences in structure can affect therapeutic impact. In addition, because the desired protein must be isolated and purified from messy fermentation or cell culture broths, analytical techniques are needed to identify potential impurities. Posed in simple terms, high-precision analytical methods allow process researchers to distinguish between good and bad output, a basic requirement for developing or improving any process.[12] With highly sensitive analytical techniques, researchers get better-quality information from each experiment because of reduced observation error. This better information in turn allows process researchers to map the impact of changes in specific process parameters to changes in the character of the product. Thus strong analytical capabilities are essential to developing a deeper knowledge base about underlying cause-and-effect relationships.

All biotechnology firms recognize the critical role that analytical techniques play in process development. But organization A viewed the development of novel analytical techniques as perhaps the most important capability within its process development group. The company's process R&D group took an aggressive posture toward analytical methods development, striving for sensitivity levels that exceeded what was generally perceived to be necessary at the time (although these higher levels of sensitivity became standard practice for the industry some years later).

Organization A's continued emphasis on strong analytical capabilities was an outgrowth of its philosophy that process development problems needed to be framed and solved at the molecular level. Analytical techniques are the "eyes and ears" of process scientists. The more deeply one wants to probe a process, the more powerful the analytical techniques required. Thus personnel hired for A's process development group came largely from scientific fields (protein chemistry, biochemistry, and biophysics), where high-precision techniques are central to research and part of the toolkit of every PhD.

The superior lead time performance of project A2 compared to that of A1 suggests that some type of organizational learning took place across projects. But what was learned, and how was it learned? From a purely technical viewpoint, one would not have expected much transfer of knowledge across projects. Scientists interviewed at organization A, like those at other biotechnology companies in the study, emphasized that each protein molecule is unique and that the process technology must be customized for each. This implies that any "theories of production" in this setting are local, in the sense that they apply to specific molecules. Indeed, this was learned early by organization A on project A2. The organization thought that it could best leverage development resources by using the basic process technology developed for A1. The initial thinking was that the only difference between A1 and A2 would be the specific genes coding for the protein. But when the genes were inserted into the E. coli bacteria cell used to produce A1, the A2 molecule was not biologically active. It was at this point that the company's scientists realized that A2 required a completely different process technology—one that used a mammalian host cell rather than a bacterial cell. Because the physiology of E. coli bacterial and mammalian cells are fundamentally different, much of the specific technical knowledge acquired from project A1 was not transferable.

Yet, despite the fact that few technical solutions could be directly transferred, A1 generated technical knowledge and organizational skills that provided a foundation for A2. These capabilities resulted from the firm's three-pronged approach to development: a strong focus on developing basic scientific knowledge at the molecular level, heavy emphasis on analytical technology, and close interaction between process development and the plant. The company's emphasis on developing basic knowledge of biotechnology processes at the molecular level had important implications for the type of knowledge available for use on A2. With A1, the company developed basic know-how about the structure, character, and behavior of genetically engineered proteins. Thus, although every protein is different, many of the basic principles needed to develop two processes may be the same. Although a new set of technical capabilities was required for A2, to handle the specifics of mammalian cell production, the firm's existing strength in the basic process sciences made it easier to absorb these new capabilities.

In addition, because the problem-solving strategy was to uncover cause-and-effect relationships at the molecular level, A1 generated a set of procedures for measuring and tracking the stability of proteins, characterizing the protein, and identifying impurities. Thus the company's strong emphasis on analytical techniques complemented its micro-level problem-solving strategy. When development scientists started A2, they had at their disposal a set of powerful analytical techniques that identified impurities at a far more precise level than was possible before A1. On A1, the purification process had to go through multiple iterations simply because, as better analytical techniques became available, process researchers found new impurities that needed to be removed. On A2, with a powerful set of analytical techniques in hand, researchers could be much more confident about what constituted good output, and how process changes might influence process performance.

The other component contributing to the knowledge base available for A2 was the close interaction between process development and manufacturing on A1. Direct and frequent contact with the plant taught scientists about such manufacturing issues as viral contamination, batch-to-batch variability, and degradation of proteins in larger-scale systems. On the A2 project, process scientists were able to anticipate some of the manufacturing problems and FDA expectations for a process technology. As one process scientist described it, "We knew what to look out for . . . and we knew what data and assays would be needed."

Although process development remained very much an art on A2, organization A had deepened its knowledge base in a way that allowed process scientists to anticipate problems. Organization A's process know-how was by no means highly codified or theoretical; however, by building basic scientific capabilities and integrating practical knowledge about the actual manufacturing environment, organization A began to take some of the art out of its biotechnology development. Although learning by doing in the actual manufacturing environment was still absolutely necessary and critical to the success of A2, the firm had begun to build more global theories of biological production processes that could be used proactively. In this way, the firm began the process of learning to learn before doing.

Organization B

Like organization A, organization B initially lacked a formal process development group. The company's process development capability evolved in response to the need to develop a full-scale manufacturing process for its first potential commercial product. To avoid concluding that organizational learning takes place only within narrowly prescribed organizational types, it is important to note some important differences between organizations A and B. Most noteworthy, whereas organization A built up a relatively large process development group, B's explicit strategy was to keep the process development group relatively small. The senior manager hired to build the group commented, "The role of process development is to serve as a bridge between basic [product] research and manufacturing. If the group gets too big, it can get in the way. I wanted to avoid a situation where the process development group became a barrier to rapid development. I wanted process development to be a service, not an entity." Although the formal process development group was small, all the major process development steps discussed in chapter 5—process research, pilot development, and manufacturing startup—had to be performed to get projects B1 and B2 to market. To compensate for its small mass, the process development organization made liberal use of personnel from other organizational functions, including research and manufacturing. Process development projects were performed by integrated teams with members from research, process development, the pilot plant, and commercial manufacturing. Thus process development was in reality a cross-functional project-level organizational entity.

Despite their organizational differences, organizations A and B exhibited some striking similarities. Like organization A, B believed strongly that process development required the firm to be at the leading edge of several basic scientific disciplines. The challenge of process development was viewed in terms of solving basic scientific problems. Also like A, organization B put less emphasis on process engineering. As noted by the head of process development, "Some companies like to build Cadillacs. Our plants are more like Chevys: they're small, but can be easily ratcheted up to meet demand." Organizational learning at A and B implied building knowledge about the structure and behavior of proteins, rather than about the physical or mechanical aspects of the process or the broader manufacturing system.

Organizations A and B were also very much alike in their use of manufacturing as a locus of development. Part of the "keep the process development group small" philosophy was driven by the idea that most process development experiments should be done by the plant. Like organization A, B carried out its pilot production runs in a commercial manufacturing setting. Thus the job of manufacturing went well beyond manufacturing the product in compliance with regulatory standards. The plant was expected to play an integral role in process development. To facilitate this interaction, process development and manufacturing were part of the same organization, and the plant was colocated with R&D. A PhD-level scientist who had started in process development and worked on B1 later became head of the manufacturing plant charged with supplying clinical trials. According to process developers, it was helpful to have someone with his background running the plant because he understood how to manage experimentation—there was no hesitancy to change the process technology while products were in clinical trials. A process developer explained, "The key is to be able to show the FDA that the product is exactly the same after you change the process. As long as you can show the data, you're okay. You've got to be able to do good science in the plant. That's where it helps having a scientist run the plant." As part of "doing good science" in the plant, the company began to emphasize the analytical techniques needed to characterize proteins and identify impurities. As noted earlier, precise analytical techniques are critical to experimental integrity in biotechnology, and they are particularly important if the company plans to make changes once a process is running in the manufacturing plant.

Tight integration between process development and the manufacturing plant helped deepen the organization's process knowledge in two ways. First, learning did not end with the successful transfer of the process to the factory. Even after the process was up and running, process developers continued to monitor performance. If yields fell outside control limits, process development scientists were called in to investigate the problem and to collaborate with operators in identifying the root cause. Thus, although product B1 was in its eighty-fifth batch, it continued to provide data on the underlying drivers of process performance. Second, close contact with the plant during development and startup was an educational experience for both parties. As described by the head of process R&D,

The basic research people here are interested in taking a process all the way from their lab into the factory. Because they get involved in the manufacturing startup, they see the actual problems and alter their approaches. The guy who cloned the [B2] in research was also responsible for developing the commercial purification process. Although he was a researcher, he had learned a lot about manufacturing from his previous process development work on [B1].

Tight and ongoing interaction between process development and the plant played a central role in building and diffusing process knowledge. When the company started B2, research scientists and process developers were armed with experience about what had worked in the manufacturing of B1. For example, the purification process developed in B1, although commercially viable, was complex and costly to operate. Research scientists and process developers spent more time up front on B2 designing a streamlined purification process, before ever testing it in the plant. They had also gained a better understanding of the process parameters that tended to vary under manufacturing conditions, and thus could be more efficient in the design of their laboratory experiments on B2.

At an organizational level, organizations A and B appear to have followed dissimilar strategies for building process development capabilities. Within organization A, a large, formally defined process development group was the organizational mechanism for capturing and storing fundamental technical knowledge related to manufacturing processes. Because organization B lacked the infrastructure to act as a storage mechanism, knowledge tended to diffuse throughout the organization and across functions. Although it might be tempting to think that organization B would have had greater difficulty capturing knowledge, such was not the case. Both organization A's more functional approach and B's more team-oriented approach appear to have contributed to organizational learning across projects. This contrast suggests that no single strategy holds the key to organizational learning. However, each strategy represents a different approach to solving a more fundamental problem: how to create an integrated body of technical knowledge for developing manufacturing processes.

Organization C

Organization C was noteworthy for its inconsistency: although significant improvement took place between C1 and C2, performance deteriorated between C2 and C3. This is all the more surprising given that all three manufacturing processes were very similar—indeed, the same manufacturing plant was used. Some of the discrepancy appears to be a result of the development strategy chosen. On C2, the firm employed learning by doing. C1 and C3 represent aberrations from that strategy: the firm undertook more process research (and seems to have paid a price for doing so). Yet there is more here than just a failure to match the project strategy to the imperatives of the technological environment. If we compare C3 and B2, it is clear that organization C did not improve its capability to learn before doing, even with the benefit of two previous projects under its belt. Knowledge generated in C1 and C2 was not captured. Whereas A and B made some headway in creating more global theories of biotechnology manufacturing that permitted learning before doing, organization C continues to be heavily reliant on learning by doing within each project.

As shown in figure 8.2, organization C pursued an extreme version of the learning by doing strategy on C2. There was only negligible process research before pilot testing because the same basic technology was used for both C1 and C2. This also accelerated the project's overall lead time. Thus organization C was capable of learning across projects, at least during the early phase of the development process. C2's excellent lead time performance can be attributed partly to this cross-project transfer of technology. Moreover, by moving the process into the pilot production facility, the firm was able to identify process problems quickly and adapt to the manufacturing environment. Finally, a commercial manufacturing plant had been designed and constructed for C1. Knowing the equipment and configuration gave developers a fixed target for developing the process.

With C3, the company appears to have put more emphasis on laboratory-based process research, primarily for reasons of expediency. Because the pilot and commercial manufacturing plants were completely utilized for clinical and commercial production of C1 and C2, process developers had no choice but to do more of their development work for C3 in the laboratory; that is, they were forced to learn before doing. Technically, because C3 used the same basic process technology as C1 and C2, this should not have presented a major problem. In addition, it was expected from the outset that the product would be manufactured in the same plant as the previous two. C3 should have been able to capitalize on knowledge from earlier projects. Process research should have been the phase when the company used experience from prior projects to anticipate and solve problems. Organization B, for example, performed the same relative amount of process research on B2 as organization C did on C3, yet the lead time performance of B2 was far superior. To understand why performance deteriorated, we need to examine exactly what was learned (and, perhaps more importantly, not learned) from the C1 and C2 experiences.

The fundamental technical challenge on projects C1 and C2 was framed in terms of fitting the process to the existing plant. As one process developer noted, "The whole driver of this project was to push productivity to the point where we would not have to use a new plant." As noted above, having a fixed plant as a target around which to design a process was an advantage in some respects. However, it also led to a narrow problem-solving focus. Only options that were likely to fit the existing plant configuration and equipment were considered, and process developers were forced to work within a narrower envelope of process possibilities.

For instance, the output of the cell culture process is a function of the scale of the reactors, the density of cell growth (number of cells per liter), and cell-specific productivity (picograms of protein produced per cell). Because the plant was outfitted with 1,000-liter reactors, this first process dimension was already fixed. This forced the company's process developers to search for cell lines and other process parameters that met specific targets along the latter two dimensions. These constraints gave process developers less incentive to do exploratory research up front on a broad range of process options. Thus much of the experimentation that might have yielded greater insight into the molecular biology underlying the production process was precluded by the company's development strategy.

Furthermore, once the process was operating in the plant, senior management was adamant that only minor process changes be made, out of fear that larger-scale changes could cause problems with the regulatory filing. As one process developer noted, "We didn't understand much about the molecule, and we worried how process changes might affect its therapeutic properties." Compounding this problem was a lack of analytical capabilities needed to characterize the molecule. Senior management worried that, if the process were changed significantly, it would be difficult to demonstrate equivalency to regulatory authorities without additional clinical trials. To avoid potential regulatory problems, further experimentation was moved to a separate pilot facility outside the commercial manufacturing plant. Thus, once the process was running in the plant, process developers were largely cut off from further performance feedback.

This approach to development stands in strong contrast to those of A and B, which emphasized understanding the process at the molecular level and using the plant as a locus of experimentation and development. Judged by lead time performance, organization C's approach on project C2 was a success. By adopting the technology developed for C1, C2 was completed quickly and met its commercial requirements. However, C1's and C2's narrow problem-solving focus constrained opportunities for broader learning. In some ways, this strategy confined the organization to developing and exploiting local theories of the process technology; the deeper technical knowledge that comes from broad exploration and experimentation in the actual manufacturing plant was lost. Organization C learned how to make C1 and C2 work in the factory but did not know at a detailed level *why* they worked.[13] Without a broader theory of how these processes worked, process developers were not well positioned to use laboratory experiments as a means of modeling. Only after they were able to move to the factory did process developers begin to uncover problems.

The inability to leverage knowledge from prior projects was further inhibited by a change in project management strategy used by organization C. On C1 and C2, the company used a functional structure very similar to that described for organization A: the process development group managed the development and transfer of the process technology. On C3, the firm adopted a project team structure whereby one overall project manager was responsible for coordinating and managing the flow of work across all the development functions. The benefit of such an approach is improved integration across functions. The trade-off is that functional input, including that of process development, is reduced. Technical decisions affecting process development and process development decisions affecting other aspects of development were in the hands of the project team members. Because many project team members from other functions had not been involved in prior process development projects, information and technical knowledge from those projects were not well integrated into the C3 project.

Thus, as in organization A, the process development group at organization C was initially the repository for technical knowledge. The shift to the team structure destroyed the firm's mechanism for retrieving knowledge. And, unlike organization B, which used a team structure right from the beginning, technical knowledge regarding processes was not widely diffused at organization C, nor was this knowledge developed and codified in a way that might have permitted rapid diffusion to others within the organization. Process development at organization C was an art that worked well when the artists were allowed to practice their craft. Because technical knowledge regarding processes was not developed, and because people from outside process development (such as research scientists) had not been exposed to process development, the shift to team-based project management destroyed any opportunities to learn from prior projects.

Organization D

In the case of organization D, lead time performance deteriorated between the first and second projects. As in the case of organization C, some of this deterioration can be explained by a change in the development strategy. In moving into the pilot plant after only 7 percent of process R&D resources had been expended, project D1 followed a learning by doing strategy. On D2, the firm spent 15 percent of its process R&D resources prior to the first pilot batch, indicating a shift toward learning before doing. However, as in the case of organization C, we need to ask why D did not improve its capacity to learn before doing. Had organization D captured knowledge, it might have been able to use process research more effectively. At the very least, the increase in process research should not have hurt performance. Again, the lack of improvement is surprising, given that D1 and D2 were based on broadly similar classes of process technology. Furthermore, some process development scientists within the firm viewed D1 as more challenging because of the molecule's complex structure and inherent instability.

The patterns of behavior that inhibited learning at organization C were also present in D. Again, these can be grouped into two categories: (1) a failure on the first project to develop a deeper technical understanding of the process technology in a way that might offer broader insights for the next project; and (2) a disconnection between process developers and feedback from the manufacturing environment. Because these patterns have already been discussed, we focus here on the specific ways they played out in organization D.

On D1, the firm found itself in a competitive race with other biotechnology firms trying to commercialize the same molecule. Speed to market was viewed as absolutely critical. Furthermore, given the molecule's complexity, developing a commercially viable manufacturing process was viewed as the key challenge to rapid launch. However, the original strategy was to use an established pharmaceutical company to both market and manufacture the drug. Organization D was to be responsible only for supplying clinical trials. In order to commence clinical trials as quickly as possible, the company decided to develop the process technology in two stages. It would initially develop a process suitable to start Phase I clinical trials. Then, as clinical trials progressed, it would develop a second-generation process capable of producing the product in commercial quantities and at commercially attractive costs.

Almost immediately, it was discovered that the protein had innate characteristics that would cause problems in larger-scale production processes. In particular, the protein tended to stick to the cells from which it was produced, and as a result, it was virtually impossible to isolate and purify. Further manipulations to the cell line solved this sticking problem, but unfortunately, the new cell line would grow only if cultured in small-scale bottles (where the cells could physically attach themselves to the surface of the bottle). The cell line was completely unsuitable for larger-scale production, in which cells are typically grown in suspension (that is, floating in the tank rather than attached to the walls of the vessel). Because the first phase of the process development project was focused entirely on getting a small-scale process ready as quickly as possible, the cell line issue was not dealt with at this time. By using a large number of small bottles, the company would be able to make enough product for Phase I clinical trials. To further expedite the process, the company decided to use a contract manufacturer to make the product for Phase I clinical trials. The view at that time was that, once the documentation was transferred, the contractor could begin producing the protein within weeks.

Unfortunately, the transfer of the process was far more complicated than anticipated. The contractor—located 3,000 miles away—did not understand the subtleties of the process technology and had difficulty making it work. Organization D was forced to send some of its scientists to the contractor to teach them the process, and to leave three people there full time for six months to supervise production and troubleshoot. There were so many problems with production that virtually no further process development was possible back at the company. In the course of this extensive troubleshooting, some process developers involved with the contractors gained in-depth knowledge about the molecule, its robustness (in particular, its tendency to degrade), its toxicity, and other aspects of the process. However, this knowledge was not capitalized on for the second phase of the project, the development of the commercial-scale process. One process developer noted, "When we returned home, we were not able to use any of the information or learning we acquired at [the contractor]. The company had its own manufacturing people who had their own way of doing things."

Development of the commercial process involved extensive technical work to find a way to adapt the cell line to a larger-scale production process. At about this time, organization D's corporate partner decided it wanted organization D to do the commercial manufacturing. After a year of intensive laboratory work, scientists found a way to genetically alter the cell line so that it could be grown in suspension in a large tank; the process was then tried at large scale. Although it ran, animal tests suggested that the product was not therapeutically active. Further investigation of the process indicated that the protein was being degraded during the production process, and minor changes to cell culture media resolved the problem.[14] Additional problems were discovered at the purification end of the process. For example, at larger scale, the filters used for purification tended to clog. Changing the filters solved this problem.

After these startup problems were solved, the process ran smoothly at commercial scale. At one level, the process development project was a success: an intense burst of development effort in the later phases of the project led to relatively quick development and scale-up of a very complex process. However, scientists associated with the project commented that the intense time pressure late in the project forced them into a reactive mode of problem solving. According to a key scientist on the project, "Instead of fully understanding changes before they were made, evaluations were typically done 'after the fact' to make sure the product had not been affected as a result of the process change." Thus, as was the case for organization C, specific problems were successfully solved, but broader opportunities for learning may have been forfeited.

Although projects D1 and D2 overlapped somewhat, project D2 appears not to have benefited from learning in the early phases of D1. Additional emphasis on process research did not expedite development on D2, even though the basic process technologies were similar. There were several reasons for this. First, D2 employed the same two-phase development strategy as D1: first develop a bare-bones process to enable clinical production, then go back and develop a full-scale commercial process. This strategy inherently limited the potential for early-phase process research on D2 to use knowledge from D1. The focus at the early phase was on developing an acceptable process. Because larger-scale manufacturing was a future issue, the scale-up problems of D1 were not considered important information for the early phase of D2. In fact, given intense pressures to make enough product to supply clinical trials, much of the early laboratory work was geared toward supply rather than development.

The second factor that inhibited the transfer of knowledge across projects was a difference in the manufacturing strategies. Although D1 was eventually produced in-house, commercial production of D2 was performed by a corporate partner. The distance between organization D and its corporate partner's plant—more than 3,000 miles—inhibited ongoing interaction between process development and manufacturing throughout the project. This made it difficult for process developers to anticipate future manufacturing conditions and constraints. Moreover, experience from D1, which involved the company's own manufacturing plant and people, was essentially useless. The corporate partner's manufacturing environment, operating procedures, skills, and experience were different. When the corporate partner experienced difficulty starting up the process, it blamed the problem on the process technology ("it was unmanufacturable"), while organization D's scientists blamed it on the plant ("they were incompetent").

Finally, as was the case for organization C, D was undergoing changes in its approach to project management. On D1, the company used a largely functional structure, and D2 used a team approach that increased cross-functional participation and coordination. Although many of the same scientists were involved in D1 and D2, the management of the projects was very different. In particular, senior process development management had far less influence on decisions—even when those decisions had a direct impact on process development activities. For instance, at one point, a decision was made to dramatically increase the size and scope of clinical trials: approximately 50 mg of the molecule were required. This seemed like a relatively small quantity to most members of the project team and to senior management in the company. However, considering that no one, anywhere in the world, at any time, had ever managed to make more than 1 mg of the molecule, 50 mg actually represented a huge quantity. By the time senior process development managers discovered this, the decision (and contractual commitments) had already been made. Process development scientists then spent several months making hundreds of very small-scale batches of the product and did little technical problem-solving. Thus, as we saw in organization C, changing the approach to project management disrupted the informal lines of communication that allowed the firm to exploit existing technical and organizational knowledge.

Conclusion

Every development project can generate multiple outputs: a process technology used to manufacture a particular product or set of products, technical knowledge about underlying cause-and-effect relationships, and organizational knowledge about appropriate development procedures and strategies. Development project performance can therefore be evaluated at multiple levels. In earlier chapters, the emphasis was on first-order performance effects; that is, on how quickly, efficiently, and effectively the process technology was developed. The current chapter has focused on second-order learning effects across projects—in other words, how well did one project generate useful technical and organizational knowledge for the next?

Every project must strike a balance between the immediate goal—getting the process developed as quickly and efficiently as possible—and building knowledge for future projects. In judging biotechnology firms, one must be careful to recognize that these firms, particularly on their earliest projects, operated under intense pressures. In almost every case, if the first project failed, the firm would have no opportunity to try a second. Thus there was a natural—even a healthy—tendency to focus on getting the first project done, even if that meant sacrificing future performance. Yet amid these pressures, some firms managed to complete first projects successfully and build knowledge for future use. The comparison of the four biotechnology firms in this chapter highlights the following elements.

Building Global Theories of Process Technology

As described in chapter 5, the knowledge base surrounding biotechnology processes is immature. Throughout the study, scientists in almost every company used the term *art* when describing biotechnology processes. In all four of the biotechnology companies analyzed in this chapter, process development indeed involved extensive trial and error. Yet there appear to have been significant differences in how and what organizations learned from those trials—and, more importantly, from their errors.

In organizations A and B, initial projects not only succeeded in developing new manufacturing process technologies, but also laid technical and organizational foundations for future efforts. Whereas other organizations succeeded in developing process-specific know-how, or "local" process theories, A and B were able to achieve a deeper understanding of underlying cause-and-effect relationships and to build more "global" process theories that could be leveraged across projects. Of course, biotechnology process development remains on the "art" end of the spectrum for both organizations. However, their experience suggests that it is possible for firms to begin to build process knowledge that transcends individual projects, and to use this knowledge to anticipate and resolve problems on future projects. Thus A and B developed an understanding of both how and why the processes worked as they did.[15]

One implication of this finding for managing learning is the need to use development projects as vehicles to deepen fundamental technical knowledge. Interestingly, neither A nor B conducted stand-alone research projects aimed at advancing their basic process knowledge. Their experience would seem to run counter to prevailing wisdom that "invention" or fundamental research should be separate from development. In a context such as biotechnology, however, where so much learning occurs through doing, stand-alone projects may not be fruitful, and it may be necessary to integrate fundamental research into development projects.

But simply undertaking development projects will not automatically lead to deeper knowledge. Specific approaches and practices used in the management of development at organizations A and B appear to have enabled them to exploit opportunities for learning across projects better than did their counterparts. These included hiring (and retaining) people with strong scientific research capabilities, focusing on measuring and tracing cause-and-effect relationships, and experimenting broadly. This approach can be costly in the short term for some development projects; indeed, lead time and costs on early projects may be greater. For example, organization A's first project (A1) was a relatively low performer because it shouldered responsibilities for nurturing technical knowledge and organizational capabilities for future projects. Managing learning across projects requires an understanding of these trade-offs. If managers become too fixated on individual projects, they risk limiting their ability to create such capabilities across projects.

The Manufacturing Plant as Part of the Scientific Infrastructure

In many companies, even those in high-tech industries, there is a sharp distinction between the worlds of R&D and of the plant. Problem solving, learning, and experimentation reside in the world of R&D. Manufacturing is geared toward meeting supply needs and cost targets and conforming to the process specifications laid down by R&D. This dichotomy was particularly pronounced in organization C. However, we saw that in A and B the manufacturing plant was an integral part of process development. This not only had first-order effects in terms of making it easier to identify and solve problems on the current project, it also gave process scientists a much richer understanding of the production environment. This in turn enabled better anticipation of problems on future projects. In addition, the experiments conducted in the plants fed higher-quality information back into the firm's knowledge base. Developing deeper insights about how biotechnology processes operate and behave cannot be done in isolation from the actual manufacturing environment. Learning by doing on one project helped build the knowledge required for learning before doing on the next.

The process of making the manufacturing plant part of the organization's scientific infrastructure and exploiting feedback loops from manufacturing to R&D has a number of implications for both R&D and manufacturing management. One of these has to do with plant location. Much is made of the benefits of colocation for facilitating the transfer of technology from R&D to manufacturing. Colocation is also critical—perhaps even more so—for facilitating information flows from manufacturing back to R&D. Of course, colocation only sets the stage for information transfers; unless R&D scientists actually spend time in the plant (scaling up processes, conducting test runs, training and supervising operators, and troubleshooting), they will not learn how the manufacturing environment works, nor will they develop the capability to anticipate problems. Making manufacturing part of the development infrastructure requires a more novel mind set than is often found in plants where the sole focus is on physical production. Setting aside capacity and time for development runs, training operators in experimental design so that they will be better able to work with R&D scientists, and implementing appropriate controls and documentation to enable experimentation without threatening the quality of commercial production are some of the prerequisites for making plants producers of knowledge as well as of products.

Creating Repositories of Knowledge

In recent years, much has been made of the appropriate way to structure organizations—in particular, the development process. Functional structures are "out," and teams are "in." In the present study, however, the two firms that demonstrated the most improvement (A and B) employed radically different organizational approaches. Organization A used a functional structure, whereas organization B employed a strong team approach. Both firms developed the capacity to capture knowledge and utilize it on subsequent projects. Different organizational processes evolved to match the organizational structures of the firms, yet both approaches led to the creation of integrated knowledge bases. Some of the problems experienced by organizations C and D appear to have been related to their change in organizational structure. By changing approaches, existing patterns of interaction and behavior, which can have subtle but important effects on the development process, were disrupted. Firms that embark on restructuring or reengineering run the risk of disrupting or even destroying patterns of behavior and informal connections where much existing knowledge may reside.[16] This highlights the benefits of evolutionary organizational change over more radical approaches. This issue is certainly ripe for future larger-scale empirical research.

The Role of Senior Management

Much of the recent literature on organizational capabilities contends that learning is "path dependent"—basically, that history matters. This idea suggests that we can understand a firm's current strengths and weaknesses only by examining what its capabilities were yesterday. This argument is compelling, given how difficult organizational change appears to be. However, when taken to its extreme, the idea of path-dependency suggests that managers can do very little to shape current capabilities. This situation is analogous to one doctor's comments about the three keys to living longer: "Don't smoke. Wear seat belts. Most important, pick parents with good genes!" Discussions of path dependence in organizational learning often create the uneasy sense that the best a manager can do is work for a firm with good lineage.

By examining young biotechnology firms, all of which commenced operation in approximately the same time frame and all of which faced similar environmental constraints, we have had a chance to observe organizational history in the making. What stands out is the powerful role of senior management in the process. Interestingly, if all the scientists interviewed at the four biotechnology firms discussed here were seated at a table and asked about the key to high development performance, they would say approximately the same things, and it would be difficult to tell who was from which firm. Yet these scientists found themselves behaving very differently because they operated in disparate organizational settings and faced unique constraints and opportunities. These organizational environments were shaped largely by senior management's actions and decisions regarding investments for process R&D, capital expenditures on pilot and manufacturing capacity, the physical location of production facilities, outsourcing, development time lines, and the processes used to manage development projects. Moreover, managers can use path dependencies to their organization's advantage by investing in learning on early projects that lay the technical and organizational foundation for future efforts. Organizational history matters, but it is important to keep firmly in mind that managerial actions like these create (or destroy) the conditions needed for organizational learning.

The Concepts in Action—
Case Studies

OVER THE INTRODUCTION and the last seven chapters, this book has provided conceptual frameworks, probed the pharmaceutical development process, and presented detailed qualitative and quantitative evidence on the factors driving high performance across a sample of process development projects. The goal was to make a compelling case for the strategic role of process development and to provide insights of use to both scholars and managers interested in development processes, the management of knowledge, and the creation of organizational competencies. Ultimately, however, the goal of this research is to build knowledge that will improve the quality of the decisions made and the actions taken by managers in specific situations.

This chapter attempts to go one step further. To demonstrate the power of these findings to inform management decisions and influence actions, this chapter presents a series of case studies, each of which portrays a unique management dilemma related to process development. Based on actual situations, these case studies give a flavor of the broader organizational context in which process development issues arise, and the associated management challenges. The concepts developed in the earlier chapters are then brought to bear, framing the managers' problem, illuminating the alternatives, and providing insight into the appropriate course of action. Although the case studies do help illustrate the applicability of the concepts, they go beyond this purpose to provide new insights into the concepts themselves.

Five case studies and associated analyses are presented in this chapter. All five are drawn from full-length published cases written or supervised by the author and have been used in MBA and executive courses dealing with issues of product and process development, technology management, and operations strategy. Not surprisingly, three cases are from the pharmaceutical industry: two from Eli Lilly and one from a small biotechnology company.[1] To help demonstrate the broader applicability of the findings to other contexts, however, two cases come from the automobile and automobile components industries. One describes the situation faced by BMW in launching its 1994 7-Series sedan, and the other describes ITT Automotive's development of a new antilock brake system. Each case presents actual situations and dilemmas (although some information may have been disguised to protect confidentiality). In total, the five cases highlight a set of issues that are central to development in a wide range of industries.

Eli Lilly: Process Development Investment Strategy

One of the most important process development strategy issues facing companies today is the allocation of resources during the development and commercial life cycle of a product. In October 1991, a group of senior-level managers within Eli Lilly confronted this issue head-on.[2] Traditionally, Lilly had focused the bulk of its process development resources for chemically synthesized products on improving processes for products already on the market. These improvements were the responsibility of the process engineering group at the plant where the products were being manufactured. For new products under development, investments were relatively modest and were generally concentrated during the later stages of clinical trials. The perceived advantage of such investments was that the company avoided wasting resources on products that never made it to market. Furthermore, because production volumes generally increased throughout the first several years of a new drug's commercial life, the current approach allowed the company to focus its resources on the period when variable cost reduction would have the greatest financial impact.

Lilly's process R&D activities were shared by two groups: process research and process development. The process research group, responsible for identifying and selecting synthetic routes, as well as for making small quantities of materials for preclinical and early clinical testing, was located in Indianapolis,

Indiana. In Tippecanoe, about two hours from Indianapolis, the process development group was responsible for scaling up and optimizing the process when it was transferred from Indianapolis (this is essentially the pilot development phase described earlier). Once large-scale manufacturability was demonstrated, the process was transferred to one or more of Lilly's commercial bulk manufacturing plants located in various parts of the world. Within these plants, technical service groups were responsible for routine troubleshooting and for making incremental improvements. The process development group was also involved in these efforts.

As the group of Lilly senior management (known as the Manufacturing Strategy Committee, or MSC) began to think about the competitive and institutional changes just beginning to grip pharmaceutical companies in the early 1990s, they saw that improved process technology represented a potentially important strategic opportunity for the company. Although Lilly typically achieved significant manufacturing cost improvements during the first five to seven years of a new product's life, process engineers believed that additional gains could be realized by devoting more resources to process improvements after the launch. However, as the MSC collected and analyzed data, it began to recognize that increasing process development investment *prior* to launch could also have significant benefits.

Because Lilly had never pursued process development investment opportunities aggressively, there were no historical data with which to evaluate and compare possible courses of action. The company decided to retain a consulting firm to undertake a historical analysis of a Lilly product that had been introduced to the market in 1984. Working with internal staff, the consultants conducted interviews and brainstormed to estimate the impact on costs of increasing process development investments at various phases of the product life cycle. From this analysis, three basic proposals emerged.

Plan 1

Increase investments to improve the manufacturing processes for successful products already on the market. These could be products facing price pressure from generics because of anticipated patent expiration, or products for which lower prices might win greater market share. A typical product that might benefit from this option would be a drug with about four years remaining before patent expiration. Under this proposal, the company planned to double the process engineering resources assigned to a product during the first six years following commercial launch, from five to ten full-time equivalents, or FTEs. For any given product, this would increase development costs per year from the current level of $580,000 to $1.6 million. Total additional process development expenditures under this proposal came to $2.9 million. These additional resources would allow the plant to intensify its efforts to improve existing processes through such approaches as combining steps in the production sequence ("telescoping"), changing catalysts and solvents, developing additional process controls, modifying equipment, and optimizing reaction conditions and operating procedures. Through resulting improvements in yields and process throughput times, these additional resources were expected to reduce variable production costs by an additional 3 percent (over what could be expected under existing investments).

Plan 2

Commit to process improvements for a product (or set of products) that is not yet on the market but appears overwhelmingly likely to succeed. Such a product might have six years of additional testing and approval time before market introduction, and approximately nine years of patent protection after introduction. Under this proposal, Lilly would assign an additional five FTEs beginning six years prior to launch. This proposal did not increase the amount of resources invested in process development compared to Plan 1; it simply shifted the timing. Rather than spend an additional $2.9 million in the six years after launch, this plan spent it during the six years prior to launch.

Obviously, spending the resources earlier was risky. Even with an estimated approval probability of 80 percent (a figure the company was thinking of using as a threshold), significant resources would be spent on some projects that never resulted in commercial products. However, there appeared to be great benefits from intensifying process development prior to launch. Because the basic process technology would not yet be locked in by the regulatory filing, process developers had more freedom to explore a broader range of alternatives. This was expected to lead to significant cost reductions in the years prior to launch, the cumulative effect of which might be quite large. For instance, with either the existing approach or Plan 1, manufacturing costs in the year of launch were estimated at $9,000 per kilogram. Under Plan 2, the manufacturing costs at launch would have been only about $4,690 per kilogram; similarly, the manufacturing cost of the drug under the existing approach was $2,000 per kilogram six years after launch, and only $548 per kilogram under Plan 2.

Table 9.1 Resource and Cost Reduction Profiles

Year	Annual Production Volume (kg)*	Current Strategy		Plan 1		Plan 2		Plan 3	
		Unit Cost ($/kg)	Annual Proc. Dev. Expenses (1990 $m)	Unit Cost ($/kg)	Annual Proc. Dev. Expenses (1990 $m)	Unit Cost ($/kg)	Annual Proc. Dev. Expenses (1990 $m)	Unit Cost ($/kg)	Annual Proc. Dev. Expenses (1990 $m)
1977	0		0.00		0.00		0.00		1.60
1978	0		0.00		0.00		0.00		1.60
1979	5,000	15,000	0.00	15,000	0.00	12,000	1.16	7,800	1.16
1980	1,000	14,000	0.00	14,000	0.00	10,320	1.16	7,150	1.16
1981	1,000	13,000	0.58	13,000	0.00	8,731	1.16	6,500	1.16
1982	1,000	12,000	0.58	12,000	0.58	7,334	1.16	5,850	1.16
1983	1,000	11,000	0.58	11,000	0.58	6,014	1.16	4,550	1.16
1984—Launch	10,000	9,000	0.58	9,000	0.58	4,691	1.16	3,250	1.16
1985	10,000	7,000	0.58	6,790	1.16	3,283	0.58	2,600	0.58
1986	10,000	6,000	0.58	5,820	1.16	2,725	0.58	1,950	0.58
1987	10,000	5,000	0.58	4,850	1.16	2,180	0.58	1,300	0.58
1988	10,000	4,000	0.58	3,880	1.16	1,635	0.58	650	0.58
1989	25,000	3,000	0.58	2,910	1.16	1,096	0.58	520	0.58
1990	25,000	2,000	0.58	1,940	1.16	548	0.58	390	0.58

* Includes prelaunch clinical supplies.

Plan 3

Commit additional process development resources to selected products during the earliest phases of development. This plan called for essentially the same level and pattern of investment as Plan 2, but with an additional investment of $1.6 million in each of the prior two years of the development project. Thus, under Plan 3, total process R&D investments would be increased by $3.2 million. The additional spending at this early phase was expected to lead to even greater improvements in yield, throughput, and efficiency than were obtainable under Plan 2. Because the process R&D groups would be involved at the very earliest stages of the project, they could conduct an even more thorough exploration of alternative synthetic routes. Cost savings were expected to be significant. In the year of launch, for example, manufacturing costs per kilogram were estimated to fall to $3,250 (instead of $9,000 under the current approach and Plan 1, and $4,690 under Plan 2).

Analysis

A full comparison of the cost and expenditure profiles of each option is presented in table 9.1, and an illustration of how each option would have affected cost behavior over the life cycle of the drug is provided in figure 9.1. The data on Lilly's traditional strategy indicate that the company saw process R&D and its leverage in terms of incremental cost reduction after launch (via the learning curve) rather than as an integral part of product development. However, as was analyzed in chapter 4, the MSC learned that the effect of earlier process development expenditures is to shift the learning curve down, with significant cost savings. Lilly, like every other company, had many investment opportunities and needed to develop a process development strategy consistent with its broader portfolio of options. Because drug development is both expensive and risky, investments must be timed well.

However, an important theme in this book is that the competitive value of process development goes beyond cost savings (although, as demonstrated here, these can be quite substantial). Thus, although Lilly's senior management had to weigh the potential cost savings of the three plans carefully, it had also to consider the impact of process development on such dimensions as lead time and the project outcome (see table 9.2 for an overview). Viewed from this angle, Plan 1 appeared the least desirable. Because it focused strictly on existing products, Plan 1 had no potential to use process development to enhance product development outcomes. Plan 2 may have had some potential to do so.

FIGURE 9.I Pharmaceutical Costs over Cumulative Volume

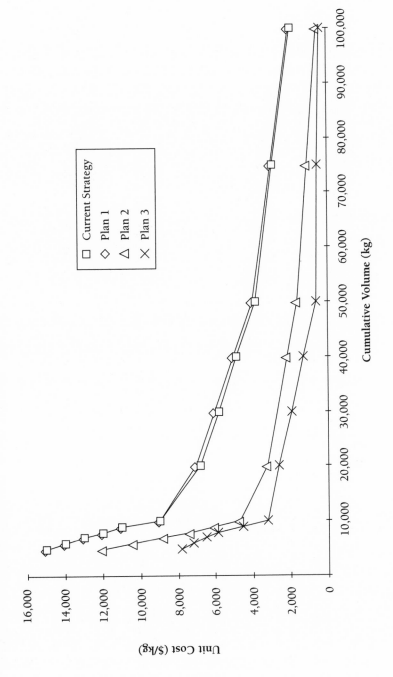

Table 9.2 Summary Profiles of Plans 1, 2, and 3

	Resource Expenditure Profile* (additional resources only)	Risks	Impact on Manufacturing Cost Structure	Influence on Product Launch Times	Influence on Capabilities	Implementation Challenges and Barriers
Plan 1	• $2.9 million • Postlaunch	Very low	Low	• None	• Process refinement • Learning by doing	• Very few • Reinforce existing approach
Plan 2	• $2.9 million • Late-stage development	Moderate	Moderate to high (for successful projects)	• Limited	• Process optimization and scale-up	• No major changes required in pattern of interaction between process R&D and other groups • Builds on existing process optimization capabilities
Plan 3	• $6.1 million • Early- and late-stage development ($3.2 and $2.9 million, respectively)	High	High (for successful projects)	• Can shrink lead times to start clinical trials by alleviating early supply constraints • Helps keep process development off the critical path by solving process problems early	• Process research • Selection and development of process architecture • Learning before doing	• Requires process R&D to develop new perspective on its role • Requires new patterns of coordination and communication between process and product researchers • Requires R&D to develop technical and organizational abilities for rapid cycling and proactive problem solving

* Additional resources only

By making more resources available for process development during the later stages of the product development cycle, it would help ensure that supply bottlenecks or scale-up problems would not cause delays. This is particularly important during Phase III clinical trials, which involve the largest number of patients and thus have the highest material requirements. The chief problem with Plan 2 was that it did little to prevent potential process technology problems from arising in the first place. Moreover, if major process redevelopment had to be carried out during late–Phase III trials, there would be regulatory ramifications.

Thus, although Plan 2 made resources available to react to process problems, there was some potential for the added process development effort during later clinical trials to extend launch lead times. One way to offset this would be to focus later process R&D work on a second-generation process to be implemented postlaunch (under the auspices of a supplemental NDA). This would allow the company to reap the significant cost savings of a new process earlier in the life of the product. But whereas it would remove the risk of delaying the initial product launch, it also would do nothing to accelerate it.

Plan 3 offered potentially the greatest scope for reducing development lead time and also created an improved set of options for clinical development. Essentially, Plan 3 would give Lilly a two-year head start on process R&D relative to the other alternatives. With this advantage, Lilly could accelerate the early phases of the product development cycle. For example, the discussion in previous chapters suggested that synthesis of test materials is on the critical path during preclinical trials. By initiating development early, a company can alleviate the materials bottleneck and reduce the time lag before clinical testing. This can be a particular strategic advantage for molecules requiring difficult syntheses or where being "first to clinic" creates a competitive advantage.

Additionally, Lilly could use its head start to complete process development sooner. This might be particularly important for drugs with relatively short clinical development times, such as drugs for acute conditions. Here, finishing process R&D earlier would translate into a faster product launch. If the project were one in which clinical development lead times were long but low manufacturing costs were critical, then a third option would be to use the additional time at the end of the cycle to continue improving the process.

The above analysis may understate the potential for Plan 3 to enhance Lilly's development options, because it assumes that starting process R&D sooner would have no effect on the length of the process development cycle. In fact, as the data are presented in the case, it appears that Lilly assumed that Plan 3 would increase the time for process R&D (prior to launch) by two years—that is, the extra project activities up front are added to the total process R&D cycle. However, depending on how Lilly chose to invest the resources, total process R&D lead time could be shortened. The statistical results from chapter 6 indicate that a higher percentage of spending focused on the process research phase should lead to less lead time to complete pilot development and manufacturing startup.

The case does not break out the allocation of process R&D spending across different phases of the process development cycle, nor does it state how Lilly intended to spend the money. The results from chapter 6 clearly suggest that, in order to maximize the lead time advantage, the extra resources should be invested in process research (in research prior to the first pilot batch of production). Compared to the other options, Plan 3 had the greatest potential to shrink overall process R&D lead time by making resources available at a stage in the project when thorough process research creates a foundation for rapid and smooth pilot development and manufacturing startup.

A second dimension of the plans that can be evaluated is their respective effects on the evolution of technical and organizational capabilities. As discussed in previous chapters, process development projects provide an opportunity for organizational learning. Because each of the proposed plans created a unique pattern of process development activities, they should have led to unique capabilities over time. For instance, given the regulatory constraints on making major process changes for products already on the market, Plan 1 was likely to lead to additional process engineering projects geared toward process refinement and incremental improvement rather than major new development efforts. This would help reinforce Lilly's engineering capabilities to squeeze additional yield and throughput performance from an existing process technology. In contrast, Plan 2 would shift the emphasis of process development toward pilot development and scale-up, and would help Lilly strengthen its capabilities in these areas. Plan 3, by providing additional resources at the earliest phase of development, would speed up the accumulation of capabilities in process research.

Lilly's management had to ask itself which of these capabilities would create the most value for the company. The answer to this question depended on the company's broader product development strategy going forward. An improved ability to squeeze incremental performance improvements out of existing processes would be valuable in situations in which the company had to defend its existing products from market incursions by lower-cost generic substitutes. If Lilly's product portfolio were aging and its product development pipeline becoming thin, this capability could be very valuable. However, as discussed in chapters 3 and 4, opportunities for product innovation are accelerating in the drug industry. If Lilly were to exploit these opportunities, it should instead pursue a strategy that built capabilities to identify novel processes needed for complex molecules, and to develop and scale up those processes to support aggressive development time lines. Plan 3, by intensifying efforts in the process research phase (where alternative architectures are explored and where the foundation for rapid process development is laid) appeared to fit best with a product development strategy geared toward the aggressive pursuit of product innovation.

If we assume that Lilly opted to move ahead with Plan 3, there are a number of issues to consider. First, the choice of investment strategy for process R&D must be put into the appropriate organizational context. Plan 3 would build new capabilities precisely because it represented a significant departure from the existing process development routine. In other words, given its past focus on improving processes already in production, Lilly was probably particularly good at learning by doing. Plan 3 would entail a dramatic step in the direction of learning before doing. Such a step would require new process R&D capabilities, changing the mix of technical skills in the organization, and putting in place mechanisms for integrating process R&D into the overall project.

Second, moving to a new strategy for process R&D would change the interactions of people involved in product-related activities (such as research, toxicology, formulation, clinical trials, and regulation) and in process R&D. Under Plan 3, there would be much more process R&D activity during the project; moreover, it would take place at an earlier stage. There would likely be cultural barriers to overcome, particularly if process R&D has historically been viewed as less important than product R&D. There would also be a need for both product and process researchers to expand their technical understanding of the other's problems. For instance, discovery chemists would need to learn what information is relevant for process chemists, whereas process chemists, for their part, would need to develop an understanding of the search strategies used by discovery chemists, in order to focus their early efforts on the elements of a compound that are least likely to change.

Third, the process R&D organization would need to build new capabilities to make the best use of the added resources available with Plan 3. Under the old strategy of focusing on postlaunch process development, the process research and process development groups worked quickly to ready a process that met all regulatory requirements and had the potential for significant cost reductions through additional process engineering at the plant. In contrast, under the new plan, cycling through multiple synthetic routes, for instance, would become much more feasible. This would in turn require coordination between process research and process development, as well as integration of capabilities in process chemistry and in chemical engineering. Specifically, Plan 3 would shift the locus of learning from the plant back to process research. It would be crucial for the process research chemists to develop a detailed understanding of the manufacturing environment; otherwise, Lilly would risk spending its additional resources on the development of synthetic routes that were not operationally viable in the plant.

Lessons

Analysis of the Lilly case has amplified three themes from earlier chapters. First, process development prior to launch can have a significant impact on the manufacturing cost structure. Data presented in earlier chapters suggest that, at least in the context of pharmaceuticals, learning curve effects are driven largely by cumulative investments in development rather than by the simple accumulation of production experience.

Second, the competitive value of process development investments must be framed broadly to include their impact on lead time and product development quality. From this perspective, more aggressive product development spending early in the overall cycle should be justified in terms of how much it contributes to launching better-quality products more quickly and efficiently.

Finally, the pattern of investment in process development influences the evolution of technical and organizational capabilities. Changing the allocation of resources is one of senior management's most important levers in building new development capabilities. Choosing among investment alternatives requires understanding the impact of each on the creation of new capabilities, and then determining which alternative best fits with the company's broader strategic mission.

Eli Lilly: Manufacturing Facilities Strategy, 1993

An integral activity during a new product launch is the design, construction, and preparation of the manufacturing facility or facilities. In pharmaceuticals, facilities planning has a particularly challenging complexion. First, the plants themselves can represent a significant share of the total costs of bringing a new drug to market (see chapter 4). Second, facilities planning involves a difficult trade-off: on the one hand, the capital expenditures required and the high uncertainty surrounding product introduction argue for delaying construction as long as possible; on the other, waiting too long to start development risks delaying the drug's launch date if approval is eventually gained. Traditionally, facilities decisions were framed in terms of how to time the capital investment in order to balance these risks. Developing a strategy for facilities that might circumvent this trade-off was the task that confronted Eli Lilly's Manufacturing Strategy Committee in November 1993.[3]

In 1993 Lilly divided process R&D projects for new chemical entities into three stages. In the first, little development was carried out on the process; instead, the focus was on making sufficient quantities of materials to allow preclinical and Phase I clinical development to proceed quickly. In the second stage, which began during early clinical trials, the process research unit (located in Indianapolis) undertook more extensive process research to identify the most attractive synthetic route. Once the route was selected, the process was transferred to the process development group (located in Tippecanoe), where it would undergo further development and optimization in the pilot plant and later be transferred to a commercial manufacturing site.

Faced with an increasingly competitive environment in the early 1990s, Lilly senior management set two goals: to reduce manufacturing costs by 25 percent and to reduce the lead time required to bring a new drug to market by as much as 50 percent (historically, it had taken Lilly between eight and twelve years to develop and launch a new chemical entity). To meet these targets, several managers thought the company would have to substantially change the way it developed processes and approached facilities decisions. Under the company's existing strategy, a new manufacturing facility was built (or an existing one retrofitted) for each new drug coming to market. New facilities were almost always built or modified at one of Lilly's existing "bulk chemical" plant sites around the world; each site had multiple facilities, and each facility was dedicated to a specific product.

The chief advantage of such an arrangement was that layouts, equipment, and operating procedures could be optimized for each product. The major disadvantage was timing. Because facilities were designed around specific products and processes, facilities design and engineering could not begin until process development activities were complete and the process technology was largely finalized. Additionally, because a specialized facility could produce just one product, the company preferred to start construction only when there was reasonable certainty that the chemical compound would reach the market. The director of facilities engineering commented, "With the specialized plant, we're

Table 9.3 Overview of Cost Structures Based on Requirements of Three Typical Products

	Specialized Facility*	Flexible Facility
Capital Expenditures (facilities design and construction)	$37.5 million	$150 million
Annual Operating Expenses (not including depreciation)	$6.8 million	$9.48 million
Volumetric Efficiency (annual output per rig of capacity)	20,000 kg/year	7,500 kg/year

* Data for specialized facility strategy includes cost for all three products combined.

always under time pressure. There's always a crunch, and facilities wind up on the critical path [for product launch]."

As Lilly strove to reduce development lead time, this crunch would only get worse. To avoid delaying product introductions, specialized facilities would have to be designed and constructed earlier in the product development cycle. This was risky, as it would also require an earlier commitment to the process technology. A department head within process R&D noted, "We'll have to do a lot of development very early. We'll also have to finalize the manufacturing process much earlier, even if this means we wind up with less-than-optimal yields."

To avoid these time constraints, an alternative strategy—calling for the deployment of a "flexible facility"—had been proposed. The idea behind this concept was to build one facility that could accommodate virtually any of Lilly's future synthetic chemical compounds and that would serve as a launch plant for all new products. When volume escalated (generally after the first few years of commercial life), a product could then be transferred to its own specialized plant. The chief advantage of the flexible facility strategy was that, by removing facilities design, construction, and startup from the critical path, finalization of the process technology did not have to occur until later in the development cycle.

Unfortunately, a flexible facility would entail much higher capital and operating expenses than was the case for product-specific facilities (table 9.3)—Lilly staff estimated capital expenditures of $150 million and fixed operating expenses (not including depreciation) of $9.48 million per year. Such a facility would have the capacity to produce three "typical" products in the early years of their lives. In contrast, the total capital expenditures for a set of specialized facilities to produce these same three products were estimated to be only $37.5 million, with annual operating expenses of $6.8 million.

A flexible facility was costly to build and operate for two primary reasons. First, in order to accommodate the widest possible range of process technologies, chemistries, and parameters, it would need to use tanks and piping made of complex alloys or lined with glass; such equipment was far more expensive than stainless steel equipment. Moreover, the plant would have to stock relatively exotic pieces of equipment in case they were needed for a particular process. Second, because the equipment and operating procedures of the flexible plant were not optimized to specific products and because operators would have less opportunity to build in-depth knowledge of a single product, yields and productivity were expected to be significantly lower. According to one estimate within the company, a standard unit of capacity (known as a "rig") would yield 20,000 kilograms of product per year in a specialized facility. The same process technology operating in a flexible facility would yield only 7,500 kilograms per year.

Thus, although the flexible facility looked attractive in terms of helping Lilly reduce its development lead time, moving forward with the plant appeared to counter senior management's goal of reducing manufacturing cost. This was the conflict facing the Manufacturing Strategy Committee and its staff.

Analysis

Changing the physical structure of manufacturing facilities alone would not resolve Lilly's dilemma. Were Lilly to adopt a flexible facility launch strategy and change nothing else, it would achieve more rapid product launches but saddle itself with significantly higher manufacturing costs. Were Lilly to remain with its specialized facility strategy, it would be hard-pressed to reduce its development lead time substantially unless it could reduce process R&D lead time, facilities lead time, or both—dramatically. The fundamental challenge for Lilly was to alter its cost-speed trade-off by building new development capabilities. The choices confronting Lilly's management should perhaps be framed as improvement paths rather than discrete choices: the firm could implement flexible manufacturing and then build the capability to dramatically reduce costs, or conversely, it could continue to use product-specific facilities but create the capability for rapid process technology and facilities development. Each of these two paths is examined below.

Path 1

Reduce the cost structure of flexible facilities. The flexible facility strategy raises an interesting paradox. On the one hand, it gives process R&D more time to do its work, which should in theory lead to the development of more efficient and productive process technologies. On the other hand, benefits of this extra work—in terms of lower costs, higher yields, and other performance dimensions—may be partially or fully offset by the inherently higher cost of the facility. Thus Lilly's process R&D group would have to use the extra time to develop much higher-yielding process technologies so that it could compensate for the structurally higher cost of flexible facilities. For instance, to offset lower productivity, Lilly's process R&D group would have to develop processes slightly more than two and a half times as productive as was possible under typical process R&D time lines.

Whether this is possible depends on whether the process R&D organizations are currently developing high-yield processes. This question cannot be resolved in the current context. However, the data reported in chapter 7 (although admittedly limited to the experience of one company) suggest that the leverage for reducing manufacturing costs resides in the selection and development of new synthetic routes (the basic chemistry) rather than in optimizing an existing route. This would suggest that, if Lilly were to adopt the flexible facility strategy, it would want to have a relatively long process research phase to enhance its chances of finding a superior synthetic route. Given the extra time made available by avoiding facilities design and construction, the search for alternative routes could continue throughout the project, with a final commitment to a specific route only made very late in the development cycle (as late as regulatory constraints allow).

It is interesting to note that, with a flexible facility strategy, the manufacturing startup phase should be relatively short. If the plant is designed to accommodate a wide range of process technologies, technology transfer should not involve many difficulties (such as an unexpected incompatibility between the process and the equipment). Although no plant is infinitely flexible, process developers should know the technical and operating constraints ahead of time and be able to design around them. Thus the process should transfer relatively easily to plant, and the process R&D group should have even more time available on the front end of the development cycle to search for high-performing synthetic routes and to engage in pilot-scale optimization (both of which should contribute to a lower cost structure). Here again, the critical issue would be how Lilly opted to use the extra time bought by a flexible facility. The results from this study suggest that the company should use the extra time at the front end of the process R&D cycle to engage in additional cycles of route selection and optimization.

Finally, the cost of constructing and operating flexible facilities may decline across future units (presuming the company builds additional facilities in the future) and over time within the same facility as a result of learning effects. Lilly may, for example, learn that a flexible facility designed to accommodate 80 percent of all potential processes is far less expensive to build than one that must be capable of producing every extreme.[4] Similarly, through experience operating a flexible facility, plant management may learn how to increase productivity through better scheduling or shorter setup times for batches. Given that Lilly had no experience with flexible facilities, the magnitude of future learning effects was difficult to predict with any degree of accuracy. In this sense, the flexible facility would be an experiment in new organizational technology for Lilly and should be evaluated as such.

Path 2

Accelerate lead times for process development and product-specific facilities preparation. The dilemma created by specialized facilities illustrates the power of having the capability for rapid process R&D. If the development cycle is short enough, the company can buy itself sufficient time to permit the use of lower-cost specialized facilities while meeting its time lines. Thus the strategic challenge for process R&D created by a specialized facility strategy is very different from the one raised by the flexible facility. With a flexible facility, the process R&D group's challenge is to find ways to use the extra time available to drive down manufacturing costs dramatically. With a specialized plant strategy, the challenge is to complete process R&D as quickly as possible in order to accelerate the start (and completion) of facilities development.

In order to exploit the low cost potential of specialized facilities while keeping process R&D off the critical path, Lilly would need to find ways to reduce process R&D lead times. That is, rather than simply developing a less mature process in less time (which is how the R&D manager quoted earlier viewed the challenge), Lilly needed to develop a mature process in less time. Interestingly, the fear that having less time will result in a less optimized process was not borne out by the data presented in chapter 7. The reader may recall that across the sample there was no statistically significant relationship between process R&D lead times and the degree to which the process technology was streamlined (via reducing steps) over the course of the project.

A fundamental change in process R&D strategy would be required if Lilly wished to stay with specialized production facilities. Under the current process R&D strategy, little substantive process development was carried out early on. Instead, the focus was on making materials, and extensive process research began only when the product was in clinical trials. Unfortunately, this approach may not be compatible with reductions in product development lead time. As noted above, to meet the envisioned product launch lead time, facilities design and construction would have to begin very early in the overall development cycle. If Lilly continued to follow its existing process R&D strategy, very little process R&D would be completed by the time facilities design needed to start.

This clearly has ramifications for both process R&D lead times and manufacturing costs. The results from chapters 6 and 7 suggest that, in chemical pharmaceuticals, intense process research lays the foundation for rapid and smooth development of the process technology at pilot and commercial scale. Lacking a deep understanding of the process chemistry, Lilly risked encountering problems later in the technology transfer and manufacturing startup stage, the resolution of which could delay the product launch. In addition, by developing a plant around a relatively immature process technology, Lilly might lose some of the cost leverage of specialized facilities. The data presented in chapter 7 on the impact of route changes on cost structure indicate that the major share of cost reduction comes through changes in the synthetic route, rather than through optimizing a given route. If Lilly were forced to finalize process technology early, it would risk locking itself into a high-cost route. Although optimization after transfer to the plant could reduce costs incrementally, major cost reductions through changes in the synthetic route would be precluded. Thus, unless Lilly were to change its approach to process R&D, keeping with the specialized facility strategy would severely constrain opportunities to learn before doing in process R&D.

To accelerate its process R&D cycle without compromising the quality of the process, Lilly would need to be much more aggressive in pursuing process research early in the project. Thus, rather than simply making materials at the outset of the project (its current approach), the process research group would have to become actively involved almost immediately in exploring and evaluating alternative synthetic routes. Indeed, it may be critical for process research to start during the discovery phase in order to get a jump start on the project. The challenge would be to identify and select the commercial synthetic route at a much earlier stage in the project than had historically been the case. Because the company would not have time to cycle through multiple routes during development (as it would with a flexible facility strategy), it would be imperative to ensure high quality in the choice of routes early on. Failure to identify a fatal flaw in the process during the research stage could have expensive and time-consuming implications when the process was transferred to the plant.

A version of the fixed-fluid approach to route selection may be appropriate for Lilly in this situation. As outlined in chapter 7, this approach involves selectively committing to a family of related synthetic routes relatively early on. For instance, some companies determine the final steps of the process first, and then only changes consistent with that family are permitted. By committing early to a family of routes, Lilly could use that information to initiate plant design. The search for a superior route could continue, but it would be focused on routes compatible with the chosen plant design. Process researchers and developers would need to be well aware of these constraints, and facilities engineers would need to be kept abreast of potential changes in the process. In addition, Lilly may be able to use the quality of its process R&D to help reduce lead times for designing and building specialized facilities. Under the current approach, facilities design begins only after the process technology is finalized. It is then presumed to take a fixed period of time to design, build, and start up the facility. However, process R&D is really the starting point for facilities design.

A high-quality process lays the groundwork for the facilities phase in two ways. First, the nature of the process technology determines the facility's design complexity. For instance, a process technology that is less complex (say, with fewer steps or a simpler layout) and requires relatively common process equipment may be faster to design and build than one with complex process flows and using esoteric equipment. In many companies, process chemists envision their task as distinct from that of facilities engineering; in reality, however, the two are closely linked. Process chemists need to build into their process evaluation criteria such issues as facilities complexity and lead times. The second way in which the quality of process technology may affect facilities timing is through its impact on technology transfer and manufacturing startup lead times. By developing processes that anticipate the requirements of the manufacturing environment, process R&D should be able to reduce the lead time for technology transfer and startup.

Lessons

Analysis of the manufacturing facilities decision confronting Eli Lilly illustrates the highly complementary relationship between manufacturing strategies and the creation of new technical and organizational capabilities. Improving development and manufacturing performance and altering trade-offs between different performance dimensions require more than simply changing the physical nature of plant and equipment. It also requires that new capabilities be nurtured. Furthermore, decisions about facilities and process development capabilities must be matched. A useful analogy here is the relationship between computer hardware and software. Just as hardware designers cannot do their work without knowledge of the software design (and vice versa), strategies for facilities (the hardware) cannot be planned in isolation from the organization's development capabilities (the software). Each facilities strategy will require the development of unique process R&D capabilities if the organization is to meet its lead time and cost goals. Facilities decisions clearly affect trade-offs between performance, such as cost and flexibility, but they also can be powerful tools to shape the evolution of the organization's capabilities.

Nucleon, Inc.: In-House Manufacturing Capabilities

A critical dimension of commercialization strategies for new technologies concerns the organizational locus of manufacturing: Should manufacturing be performed in-house or contracted to another party? Traditionally, most companies make such decisions on narrow cost considerations. For a young company that lacks in-house manufacturing capabilities, this decision is really about building a new set of capabilities. The question then becomes one of how an organization should value internal manufacturing capabilities. This was the issue facing Nucleon, a five-year-old biotechnology company, in 1990.[5] Its first drug, CRP-1 (a treatment for burn wounds), was nearing the start of Phase I clinical trials. Since its founding by a university scientist, Nucleon had focused entirely on R&D pertaining to CRP-1 and related molecules. Because it had no commercial products, it had no manufacturing capabilities of its own. Now, however, the company's senior management had to decide how it would produce CRP-1 for clinical trials (see table 9.4 for a summary of the options).

One option was to build a small-scale pilot plant capable of supplying the initial phases of clinical trials. The second option called for using a contract manufacturer (an independent company specializing in the production of biotechnology drugs). A third option was to license the manufacturing rights to a joint venture partner who would also be responsible for taking the product through clinical trials and into the marketplace.

To pursue pilot manufacturing in-house, the company would have to invest $3.1 million to build a bare-bones, small-scale plant capable of making enough

Table 9.4 Summary of Nucleon's Manufacturing Options for Initial Clinical Trials

Option	Impact on Cash Flow (Phases I and II)	Short-Term Financial Risks	Manufacturing Options for Phase III/Commercial Manufacturing
Build pilot plant	• $3.1 million to build plant • $2 million in plant operating expenses • All other development costs	• Failure leaves company with idle plant	• In-house commercial scale manufacturing ($20 million in capital expenditures, plus $1 million in development costs) • License all further development and manufacturing to a partner
Contract manufacturing	• $2 million contractor fee for fixed quantity of clinical supplies • All other clinical development costs	• Failure may leave company with some liability under any "take-or-pay" provision in contract	• In-house commercial-scale manufacturing ($20 million in capital expenditures, plus $1 million in development costs) • License all further development and manufacturing to a partner
License all development, manufacturing, and marketing rights to corporate partner	• Receive $3 million signing fee, plus 5 percent of future gross sales • No further development or manufacturing costs	• None	• No options

CRP-1 to supply the needs of Phase I and Phase II clinical trials; variable production and overhead costs would add $2 million to this sum. If the drug reached Phase III or beyond, a much larger plant that met more stringent regulatory requirements would be needed. Although exact numbers were difficult to determine at this phase, the company estimated capital expenditures of roughly $20 million and additional development and scale-up expenditures of about $1 million to build such a plant. Given the young company's precarious cash situation, a full-scale plant was well beyond its means. However, if the drug showed promise in the clinic, the company expected to be able to raise enough extra capital (either from private investors or through an initial public offering) to fund the required development and to build a commercial plant.

If the contract manufacturing arrangement were chosen, Nucleon would pay a fixed price for a prenegotiated quantity of CRP-1. The company estimated that it could procure the requisite quantity of CRP-1 for approximately $2.0 million. The chief financial advantage of contract manufacturing was that it required little cash up front and had low financial risks. Were CRP-1 unsuccessful in clinical trials and eventually canceled, the company would not be saddled with an idle plant. In addition, contract manufacturing gave Nucleon the option to bring manufacturing back in-house for Phase III trials and commercial marketing.

The third option, licensing CRP-1 to an established pharmaceutical company for all subsequent development and manufacturing, clearly entailed the lowest downside risks. Under this option, Nucleon would receive an up-front payment of $3 million, plus royalty payments of 5 percent of gross sales if and when CRP-1 was approved as a burn treatment. This was the only option that generated cash in the short term, but it also precluded Nucleon from ever developing, manufacturing, or marketing CRP-1 on its own, and thus limited the potential of the project.

Analysis

Each approach involved a different financial profile in terms of risks, returns, and option value. Again, although a full-blown financial analysis is beyond the purpose of this chapter, a brief overview may be helpful. For instance, licensing CRP-1 was virtually risk free but offered only modest returns. Building a pilot plant entailed the greatest risk because it consumed extremely scarce cash that could be allocated to other R&D projects. From a financial perspective, using a contract manufacturer appeared to be an attractive compromise: it required little capital up front while maintaining for the company the option to bring manufacturing in-house for Phase III trials and commercialization.

One way to frame the decision facing Nucleon is to ask why it might want commercial manufacturing capabilities in-house at some point in the future. Today, a common tenet of management thinking is that companies should "stick to their knitting." For many large firms, determining exactly what their "knitting" constitutes is a major challenge in itself. For a young company such as Nucleon, however, its core competency (indeed, its only competency) is relatively easy to identify: R&D. One plausible strategy—in fact a common strategy being pursued in biotechnology today—would be for Nucleon to stay focused on R&D and to use outside partners or contractors to handle commercial manufacturing tasks.

Under this strategy, Nucleon would capture rents on its unique R&D capabilities and knowledge through R&D contracts, licensing and royalty arrangements, or participation as an equity partner in joint ventures. By focusing its management attention and financial resources, this strategy would lead to a deepening of Nucleon's R&D capabilities over time; this would in turn provide a renewed source of rents. However, the logic behind specialization would work only if Nucleon's R&D and manufacturing groups could be organizationally separated without causing a deterioration in the value of R&D competencies, manufacturing competencies, or both.

In biotechnology firms, where product and process R&D are closely linked and where learning by doing in the actual production environment plays a critical role in effective process R&D, the case for organizational separation is suspect. Thus the strategy of specializing only in product R&D while moving process R&D (and manufacturing) to another party may be problematic. In the course of doing product R&D, Nucleon would develop highly specialized knowledge about the molecule and its production process. Even a highly competent outside party would be at a disadvantage in attempting to develop the process technology independently. The only option would be to bring in a partner at the embryonic stage of the project so that both parties could develop the process simultaneously. In theory, Nucleon's scientists could focus on the product technology while its partner focused on the process technology. Such codevelopment, however, raises a number of complications related to ownership and division of intellectual property, allocation of risks and returns, and issues of project governance. The reality is that most companies in Nucleon's position do not want to involve outside partners at such an early stage, because of a desire to protect intellectual property.

Given that it is difficult to separate product and process R&D in biotechnology, one alternative would be for Nucleon to simply turn over production to an outside partner (while holding onto process R&D). Here again, the organizational separation of process R&D and manufacturing may not be easy. The data presented in chapter 6 demonstrated that the production environment is a critical venue for biotechnology process R&D. Developing a process in one environment or firm and then transferring it to a manufacturing site will likely lead to higher process development transfer costs. From an early stage in the project, therefore, Nucleon needed unlimited access to the commercial manufacturing facility. Although it might be able to strike a deal with a partner that would grant it early access to the plant, a number of practical and institutional constraints might hinder such an arrangement.

First, Nucleon would have to convince its partner to build a new plant precisely when certainty about the project's ultimate success was lowest. A second potential problem would be the geographic distance between Nucleon and its partner's plant. If the partner already had a plant, it would be highly unlikely to happen to be adjacent to Nucleon's R&D facility. A third issue concerns Nucleon's access to the manufacturing plant. Unless Nucleon's process scientists had extensive access to the plant, discretion over experiments, and even control over initial pilot runs, experimentation and on-the-floor learning would be extremely difficult. Again, one must wonder how much free rein one firm would be willing to give another's process R&D scientists inside its plant.

Finally, even if all these barriers could be circumvented through well-specified contracts and significant trust and cooperation, there remains the issue of learning and appropriation of knowledge. Recall from chapter 8 that, in biotechnology, the plant and production activity themselves are a major source of technical knowledge about processes. Thus the issue is not just transferring technology from R&D into production, but capturing the learning from production and transferring it back to R&D. Contact with the plant is the means by which some biotechnology companies appear to have deepened their technical knowledge of process R&D. Without an internal manufacturing capability, Nucleon would risk losing access to this source of learning, and over time its process R&D competencies may suffer.

The above discussion suggests that Nucleon should, over the longer term, seek to build in-house commercial manufacturing capabilities. Does this mean it should invest in a pilot plant immediately? Clearly, a critical ingredient of this decision relates to the company's cash flow situation. Beyond this, however, the company would need to examine the pilot plan decision in terms of how it would help build future commercial manufacturing capabilities. From the discussion and analyses of earlier chapters, there appear to be significant costs and complications of bringing commercial manufacturing back in-house after using a contractor for pilot production. In essence, Nucleon would be transferring production to its plant at a relatively late stage in the process R&D cycle. We know from chapter 6 that such a step can be costly. Slight differences between the contractor's and Nucleon's pilot facility and operating methods could have a substantial effect on the process. In all likelihood, Nucleon would find itself needing to redevelop the process to adapt it to its own plant. This would not only be costly (in terms of process R&D investments), it could also put the project time line at risk. Thus, although contract pilot manufacturing appears to have "option value," issues related to the problems of technology transfer would make it a costly option to exercise. With in-house pilot manufacturing, Nucleon would maintain an opportunity to learn from production experience and deepen its knowledge of the process. It would begin to work toward building a commercial manufacturing capability.

Lessons

The traditional method of framing vertical integration decisions like the one facing Nucleon is to pose the question: Should Nucleon make or buy CRP-1? A response would call for a careful financial analysis of the costs, benefits, risks, and option value of each approach. Although these are important dimensions, the above analysis of the Nucleon case illustrates that sourcing decisions can have a tremendous effect on the firm's capabilities. They thus call for a broader framing of the issue. Managers need to ask: What is the value of having certain manufacturing capabilities in-house? Again, financial constraints and considerations are critical, but manufacturing capabilities also need to be evaluated in terms of their broader impact on the firm's core development capabilities. The results of this study suggest that, in a context such as biotechnology, where so much of the process development action needs to take place in the manufacturing environment, internal manufacturing capabilities may be a prerequisite to developing strong process development capabilities. The value of in-house manufacturing in this case lies not so much in the ability to achieve lower-cost production, but in its contribution to building the firm's process R&D capabilities.

ITT Automotive: The MK-20 Project

As companies increasingly pursue global manufacturing strategies, they confront a growing number of issues concerning the appropriate locus and scope of process development activities across geographically dispersed plants and engineering centers. ITT's experience with its MK-20 brake system illustrates some of these issues, as well as the broader applicability of the concepts developed in the context of pharmaceuticals.

In 1994 ITT Automotive was entering the final stage of development of a new generation of antilock brake systems (ABS), the MK-20. As ABS became standard equipment on more cars at the lower end of the price range, suppliers faced increasing pressure to develop systems that could be manufactured in much higher volumes and at much lower costs than for previous generations. In addition, as automotive companies shortened their overall development cycles, component suppliers were forced to shorten development lead times as well. Thus the MK-20 project presented the company with two challenges: (1) design the product and the process technology so that the MK-20 could be sold profitably at approximately half the price of existing ABS, and (2) reduce development lead time by about 40 percent. Product and process development of the MK-20 were carried out at ITT's central engineering department in Frankfurt, Germany, while manufacturing took place in the company's four plants in Mechelen (Belgium), Frankfurt (Germany), Asheville (North Carolina), and Morgantown (North Carolina).

To meet these stringent cost and lead time goals, central engineering adopted a novel strategy for developing and implementing the process technology. In the past, product and process engineers worked in a sequential and largely independent manner. Development focused primarily on product design; once that was completed, process engineers were responsible for figuring out how to manufacture the product. In reality, there was little time to optimize the process before the start of commercial manufacturing, and process improvement and optimization fell on the shoulders of the manufacturing engineers and shop-floor operators. Judging by their steep learning curves for productivity and quality, it was clear that the plants had developed excellent improvement capabilities.

However, the central engineering group in Frankfurt was concerned that this approach would not suffice for the MK-20. It decided that the process must be fully developed in parallel with the product and optimized before it was transferred to the plant. In addition, central engineering believed it absolutely critical for all four plants to use exactly the same highly automated process. (Automation, it was hoped, would offer benefits of low-cost production, rapid ramp-up, and meeting global customer needs.) Process standardization across plants was viewed as a means of facilitating cross-plant learning and accelerating manufacturing startup. The director of central industrial engineering argued, "Using one process allows the machines to become process capable more quickly. You don't have to worry about different problems at each site." In addition, because automobile companies increasingly insisted on certifying the process technology used to manufacture their components, standardizing processes had real advantages in terms of global sourcing and coordination of supply.

The goal of developing a fully optimized, standardized process technology was based on compelling logic. Full optimization is highly consistent with the total quality mantra of doing things right the first time. Moreover, taking steps to promote the exchange of information and learning across a network of plants appears consistent with the idea of creating a learning organization. Finally, standardization was key to having a global manufacturing strategy. Yet the managers of each of the company's plants in North Carolina did not see it this way. They argued that, because each plant faced unique operating conditions (in terms of wages and workforce skills, for example) and had to meet different customer needs, the same process technology would not be appropriate for all plants. A fully automated process might be fine for the German plant, with its high wages and close physical proximity to the engineering group, but they argued that it made much less sense in North Carolina plants, where wages were low and years of effort had created a highly committed workforce. In addition, managers worried that a highly automated process technology would be much more difficult to improve incrementally and would essentially lock the plants into the current state of the art. One manager argued, "If you automate, you stagnate." The requirement that all plants use an identical process technology further contributed to the plant managers' concerns about stagnation.

One cannot ignore the politics of this situation. The new approach represented a shift in the locus of power to develop and improve processes. Under the old approach, process improvement was the domain of the plants; under the new strategy, all opportunities for improvement were theoretically exhausted by central engineering before the process ever reached the plants. The plants became implementors, whereas before they were actively involved in the seemingly more attractive business of development and improvement.

Analysis

While not denying the role of politics, the framework developed in this book exposes deeper differences in engineering's and manufacturing's models of learning and suggests possible actions to resolve the dilemma. It is clear that the traditional strategy emphasized learning by doing in the plants, in the form of *kaizen* (use of grassroots teams to identify and implement improvements on a continuous basis) and other types of online shop-floor improvements. Most resources, at least initially, were focused on finding and correcting bugs that had been overlooked during development. The new strategy emphasized learning before doing, because all potential problems were expected to be found and resolved before the process reached the plant. Thus the crux of the debate was disagreement over which path would lead to the greatest improvement over the longer term. The view from the North Carolina plants was that incremental improvements would lead to lower costs than would be possible by adopting a highly optimized but inflexible process early (see figure 9.2).

The engineering department in Frankfurt assumed a very different position. From their perspective, full optimization before launch meant achieving the lowest cost trajectory from the start. Although the plant could reduce costs through systematic improvement efforts and kaizen, at best it would

FIGURE 9.2 The View from Manufacturing Plants in North Carolina

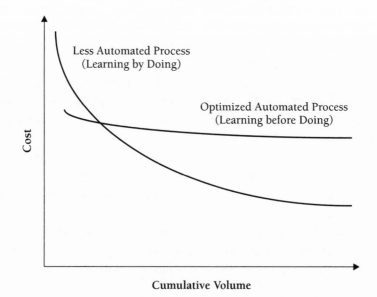

Less Automated Process
(Learning by Doing)

Optimized Automated Process
(Learning before Doing)

Cost

Cumulative Volume

FIGURE 9.3   The View from Central Engineering in Frankfurt

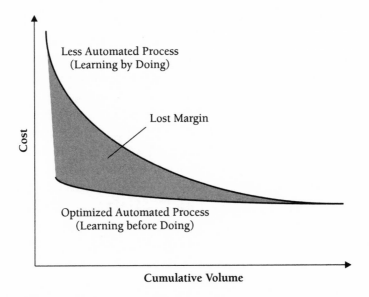

Cumulative Volume

achieve engineering's lowest cost solution. Meanwhile, of course, the company would lose margin equivalent to the cumulative area between the curves (see figure 9.3).

It is interesting to note each model's different assumptions about the potential for anticipating and identifying problems before running the process in the plant. Engineering's learning before doing model assumed that it could find and address most opportunities for improvement by using the right design methodologies, by running tests in a small-scale pilot plant, and by incorporating cumulative knowledge from previous projects. Manufacturing's learning by doing model was predicated on the assumption that there were simply too many subtleties in each manufacturing environment to uncover every problem and exploit every latent opportunity for improvement.

Which one was correct? More importantly, what should the company do? The key to answering these questions is to assess the underlying state of knowledge about the process technology. Although we lack the detailed technical information to make such an assessment, in all likelihood both engineering and manufacturing were partly correct. There were likely to be many opportunities to resolve problems before launch, particularly in light of the fact that, under the old approach, very little attention was paid to process issues during development. However, it also seems unlikely that central engineering in Germany understood all the subtle differences across plants. Thus some aspects of the process could be optimized ahead of time, whereas others may have required learning by doing in the plant.

A strategy for process development involves sorting out which aspects of the process should be developed under each approach. The first question that the managers at this company needed to ask was: How is the environment in which engineering is working different from that of the future manufacturing sites in the United States? In this case, central engineering sought to minimize differences in equipment, production volumes, operating procedures, operator skills, and the quality of raw materials by doing extensive pilot testing in the company's Frankfurt plant. It hoped that any problems that might arise in a real manufacturing environment would be discovered long before the process was transferred to the North Carolina plants. To further enhance the representativeness of the knowledge acquired during development, engineering decided to test the process on the same equipment that would be used in the North Carolina plants (after development was completed, the equipment would literally be crated and shipped to the plants).

These steps essentially eliminated many of the physical and technical variations between the environments. However, infrastructural differences—such as the skills and experience of the workforce, the order mix and volumes, and the quality of raw materials—remained. Thus the next question management needed to ask was: How do these differences affect the performance of the process? It was important to distinguish between differences with known effects and those with unknown effects. For instance, the order mix would likely have an impact on process performance because it would affect setup times and, in a highly automated process, create a need to handle contingent process flows. By and large, however, these effects could be simulated by running the process in Frankfurt with the expected order mix of the U.S. plants for a sufficient period of time. By doing so, engineering could learn that certain order mixes typical in the United States might create bottlenecks at specific process points. The process could then be redesigned by adding extra capacity for those processes. However, the impact of different workforce skills might be harder to model. In a highly complex automated production process, preventive maintenance and quick response to problems are absolutely essential to minimizing downtime and thus to the system's economic viability. These skills are a result of training and experience, and may be hard to quantify accurately. Thus development of maintenance procedures is an aspect of the process technology best left to individual plants.[6]

In this case, the company had to be careful about the first-and second-order effects of its decision. At one level, the debate was about the right process technology and manufacturing strategy for the MK-20. Would automation and standardization lead to faster ramp-up, lower manufacturing costs, and higher quality (first-order performance effects)? However, the strategy choice would also have implications for the evolution of the firm's knowledge base, its organizational capabilities, and its ability to improve across product generations. Adopting the strategy advocated by central engineering would likely lead to an erosion of the plants' process improvement capabilities. The important question, then, was whether ITT would retain its ability to improve processes across generations. Here, central engineering could find itself in a catch-22. By stripping the plants of their ability to change and improve processes, central engineering could lose its key source of feedback needed to identify improvement opportunities for the next generation. However, continuing with the current strategy (having the plants undertake most of the improvement) would create second-order risks as well. Although each plant seemed to be doing a good job of improving its processes, there was no central capability in the company to integrate feedback across plants and to incorporate this collective experience across new process generations. Here, it appeared that the best strategy in terms of improvement across process generations was to use a mixed approach. The only way central engineering could effectively learn before doing was to exploit the knowledge captured by the plants in the course of learning by doing.

BMW: The 7-Series Project

One of the most important, time-consuming, and costly activities taking place during a given product development effort is the fabrication of prototypes.[7] Prototypes—or, more precisely, prototype testing—is how product and process engineers validate their knowledge of solutions. Building and testing prototypes is a natural part of the iterative problem-solving cycle that takes place during development. Although companies often focus on the prototype itself, the process used to fabricate it can have major implications for learning during development. BMW's experience with building prototypes for its 7-series sedan illustrates the ways in which prototyping can be used to learn about potential manufacturing problems well before the start of commercial production.

Roughly two and a half years before the scheduled start of commercial production of its remodeled 7-series sedan, BMW faced a critical decision about how to fabricate the third and final batch of engineering prototypes.[8] BMW's usual approach was to make and assemble its prototype vehicles manually in its in-house prototype shop. Meticulous attention to detail by the company's highly skilled craftspeople resulted in prototype vehicles that closely reflected the form and function laid out in product designers' drawings. Although this process was costly (each prototype cost about $1 million), it resulted in extremely high-quality prototypes. This approach could easily accommodate last-minute design changes. Moreover, because only general-purpose tools (such as mallets, drills, files, and grinders) were used, there were no long procurement times for specialized tooling.

The design team charged with developing the cockpit and interior trim of the car proposed an alternative that it believed would improve the quality of newly launched models. The team proposed that the prototype parts for the cockpit and interior be fabricated using specialized tooling more akin to actual production tools. The team also proposed that the company use its commercial suppliers to make the parts and employ ordinary production workers to handle the assembly. The risks inherent in this approach were numerous. The early investment in specialized tooling—at a cost of approximately $11 million—would have to be written off if design changes were made after this phase of prototyping. More important, because of the long time required to design and procure the tooling, the design team would have to commit to a design much earlier and would not have the latitude to make changes at the last minute (because the tooling could not be changed).

The benefits of the new approach can best be understood in terms of how it affected the nature and timing of learning during the development cycle. Under the traditional approach, prototypes were built so that various attributes of the product design could be tested. How did the car look? Was the interior roomy enough? How did the car accelerate, corner, and brake? Did it hold up well in a crash test? High-quality prototypes enabled the company to simulate product performance and learn about further opportunities for refinement. However, by hand-producing the prototypes with tools, technology, and people that differed significantly from those used in actual commercial production, the traditional approach to prototyping generated virtually no opportunities for simulating process performance. Thus, under the traditional approach, the prototypes were high quality in the sense that they represented the designers' intent, but the process itself was not, because it was not at all representative of the future manufacturing environment.[9] Only once pilot production runs and commercial production started (about nine months prior to launch) did BMW begin to uncover potential manufacturing problems (for instance, some parts might be hard to fit together when machine-molded rather than shaped by hand). BMW relied heavily on the production startup phase to identify and solve such problems. But this learning by doing strategy was costly in two respects: it greatly slowed the rate at which the company was able to achieve full production volume, and it led to a relatively high number of quality problems in production vehicles.

The new approach, which attempted to simulate the production process during development, shifted the emphasis toward learning before doing. With the objective of improving the quality of newly launched vehicles, BMW decided to try the new prototyping approach for the interior of the 7-series. The results were not disappointing. Better simulation of the production process during the development phase led to the identification of many more potential manufacturing problems before commercial startup (see figure 9.4 for a comparative profile of engineering change orders on the 7-series project versus a previous project). With adequate time, the development team was able to correct these, and the new 7-series was launched at the highest quality level in the company's history.

Lessons

BMW learned three important lessons during this experiment. First, the company learned that prototyping could be an effective way to simulate the production process and to identify and resolve certain types of manufacturing problems. Prototyping could be an instrument of learning before doing. The company also discovered that prototyping was not always necessary—in fact it was, in some cases, overkill. For instance, any simple parts (such as speaker covers) never presented a manufacturing problem; for those, there appeared to be little value in trying to simulate the production process during development. On the other hand, there was much to be learned by simulating the process for more complex components and subsystems (such as the instrument panel and the center console). This speaks to the point raised earlier about the need to match problem-solving strategies to the specific nature of problems. Finally, the company also learned that many of the benefits in terms of more manufacturable designs came about because the new approach forced product and process designers to interact and integrate their efforts in completely new ways. Historically, product and process development were highly separate functions within the company. Under the new approach, prototypes became a locus of integration between product and process designers. These new pat-

FIGURE 9.4 Engineering Change Orders at BMW

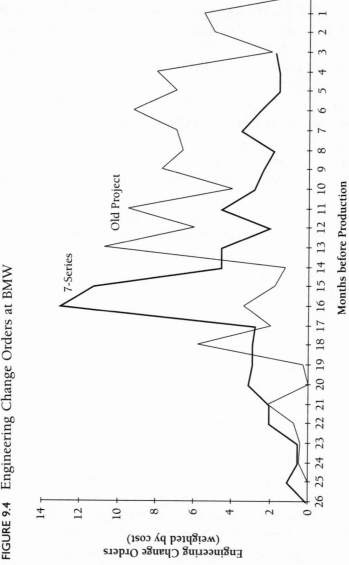

terns of interaction and integration, which made product designers more cognizant of manufacturing issues, represented an important second-order effect of the new approach.

Conclusion

The five cases discussed and analyzed in this chapter have provided perspective on several dimensions of process development strategy: the amount and timing of process R&D investments; technology choices (automation, flexibility); vertical integration; the organization of process R&D (centralized versus decentralized); and the methods of prototype fabrication (see table 9.5 for an overview). We have also had an opportunity to see how these decisions play out in a variety of technological and organizational environments—from chemically synthesized and biotechnology-based pharmaceuticals to automobiles, and from large multinational corporations such as Eli Lilly and ITT to fledgling startups such as Nucleon. Despite these differences, three themes emerge, all dealing with integration. Effective management of process development requires integration at three levels: across multiple dimensions of process development strategy, between the process development strategy and the knowledge environment, and over time.

Integration across Multiple Dimensions

When confronted with a major competitive challenge such as the need to reduce costs dramatically, shrink development lead times, or improve quality, managers tend to focus their attention on a particular element of their development strategy. Indeed, in all the cases portrayed in this chapter, managers initially reached for the lever they perceived to have the greatest impact on the most salient dimension of performance. For Lilly, this was the amount and timing of process R&D spending (and, later, the nature of facilities); for Nucleon, whether to build a pilot plant; for ITT, the extent of factory automation; and for BMW, the prototyping process. Yet what each management team in these organizations came to learn was that their overall development capabilities and performance depended on more than making the right choice along one particular dimension. Indeed, because choices along one dimension typically have implications for options along others, specific process development decisions can rarely be made in isolation. Instead, superior performance depended on integration and coherence along multiple dimensions of process development strategy. Process development is a *system* of activities, organiza-

Table 9.5 Comparison of Case Studies

	Dimension of Process Development Strategy	Nature of Choice	Critical Issues
Eli Lilly Process Development	Amount and timing of process R&D investment	Early versus late spending on process R&D	• Financial risks • Impact on cost structure • Impact on development speed and quality • Impact on capabilities
Eli Lilly Manufacturing Facilities	Facilities and process technology	Specialized versus flexible facilities	• Manufacturing cost–development lead time trade-off • Improvement paths
Nucleon	Vertical integration	Internal versus external sources of manufacturing	• Financial risks • Value of internal manufacturing as source of development competence
ITT MK-20 Project	Organizational and geographic locus and scope of process R&D activities; process technology	• Centralized versus decentralized process R&D • Global versus plant-level improvement • Full versus semiautomation	• Appropriate problem-solving strategies • Low initial costs versus flexibility to improve • Learning across product and process generations
BMW 7-Series	Methods of prototype fabrication	• Hand-built versus production-representative process	• Prototyping as instrument of learning before doing in-process development

tional processes, and assets—both physical and intellectual. Like any system, outstanding performance hinges on achieving a high degree of integration among the components.

One implication of this finding is that managers should take a systems-level view of process development performance. In evaluating their current process development capabilities, auditing approaches along multiple dimensions might be a useful way to uncover glaring inconsistencies and sources of performance problems. For instance, as we saw in the Lilly cases, a strategy of early commitment to a narrowly defined process technology would have been quite inconsistent with the use of flexible facilities. If a company was pursuing a high degree of automation across a geographically dispersed network of plants, each of which lacked significant development capabilities, prototyping the automated process during development would be critical. In addition, a systems-level perspective may be useful in planning and managing the creation of new process development capabilities. Rather than focusing their attention and the organization's resources on one particular area, managers need to frame the problem in terms of designing a system comprising multiple components: levels and timing of process R&D spending, facilities and technology choices, vertical integration, the geographic and organizational locus of process R&D, methods of prototype fabrication, and so forth. To achieve cohesion among these different dimensions, managers need to clearly articulate a set of overarching process development goals and themes.

Integration with the Knowledge Environment

As discussed above, crafting a cohesive process R&D strategy requires understanding how all the dimensions of process development fit together. However, an effective process development strategy must be more than internally consistent among its parts. It must also be consistent with the structure of technical knowledge influencing problem solving. No single process R&D strategy will be right across all types of environments. Lilly's process R&D and facilities strategy problems would have been very different if the case had focused on Lilly's operations in biotechnology, where so much of the learning related to process development must take place within the factory. In that situation, the option of completing process development quickly enough to leave time for facilities design and construction would have made little sense. In biotechnology, the facilities often evolve as the process is developed. Thus process development as well as facilities design and construction need to occur in parallel. Likewise, Nucleon's sourcing decision would have looked quite different had it been developing chemically synthesized molecules. In that case, the need for in-house pilot production capabilities to facilitate rapid and smooth process development would have been much less critical, because chemical processes can be more easily simulated outside the actual production environment.

The ITT and BMW cases provide perspective on managing knowledge in complex systems products. Unlike drugs, which are based on a single molecule, systems products are based on multiple components and multiple technologies, each of which may be characterized by a unique knowledge base. As a result, in systems products, different process development strategies may be required at the component level. For instance, at BMW, the process development strategy for a simple component was very different from that for a complex component or subsystem.

The challenge in this context is to simultaneously manage distinct approaches to learning and problem solving within the same organization (indeed, in many cases, by the same people). For a component based on a complex and highly immature process technology, for which it is difficult to anticipate many potential manufacturing problems, an engineer might be told, "After you do a preliminary design, transfer it to the plant. They will figure out the problems and what needs to be changed." For another component based on a much more mature process technology, the engineer may get just the opposite orders: "Get the design right. Don't transfer it to the plant unless you are sure it is bug free." Clearly, a situation like this would be ripe for confusion unless management framed the process development strategy appropriately.

Finally, as illustrated by the ITT case, getting agreement on whether the same problems can be solved by doing or before doing may not always be easy. The same problem can look quite different to an engineer sitting in one part of the world and a production manager sitting in another. Avoiding such debates is nearly impossible. Management's role is to help structure the debate in a way that makes it informative. One way to do this is to make sure the appropriate (in other words, the most informed) parties are brought together. Managers are also responsible for making sure the discussion of these issues takes place at the appropriate time: during the project planning phase rather than during development—or, worse, at the time of technology transfer.

Integration over Time

All the cases in this chapter echoed the theme that any given process development decision has two effects: the intended first-order effects on performance (cost, flexibility, or quality) and the often-unintended second-order effects on the evolution of future capabilities. In some instances, these second-order learning effects may have a much greater impact on an organization and its performance than first-order effects. What is important to keep in mind is that today's decisions and actions set the stage for tomorrow's options.[10] Individual process development decisions influence the rate and direction of a firm's improvement path.

One implication of this finding is that managers need to frame individual process development strategy decisions broadly. Such decisions not only affect what the organization does today, but over time influence the patterns of behavior in which the organization's capabilities are rooted.[11] At BMW, for instance, adopting a new approach to prototyping helped the company identify problems earlier in the design of the 7-series and led to improved quality. However, the new approach to prototyping also led to a different pattern of interaction between product and process designers. The second-order effect of the prototyping decision—the creation of a more integrated development capability—was likely to have a much greater effect on the quality of future projects than a change in the prototyping process alone.

From this perspective, individual process R&D decisions are not discrete events; rather, they are part of a series of actions over which the firm's development capabilities are built. Evaluation of how individual choices fit into a sequence of decisions, as well as how they influence paths of improvement, are critical to building a coherent set of development capabilities over time. The manager who understands and recognizes the potential impact of current process R&D strategy decisions on future capabilities will be in a better position to lead the organization down more desirable improvement paths.

Conclusion and Implications—Beyond Pharmaceuticals

OVER THE PAST decade, the pharmaceutical industry has seen radical changes in its market and technological environments. These changes have elevated the strategic role of process development and manufacturing capabilities in an arena in which firms have traditionally competed solely on the basis of new product introductions. Established pharmaceutical firms and new entrants alike have pursued various strategies for improving their process development capabilities. The quantitative and qualitative data, statistical analyses, and case studies in the preceding chapters represent an attempt to capture the learning from these natural organizational experiments carried out by managers in the industry. Although the story of pharmaceuticals is fascinating in its own right, the goal of this study is to generate general conceptual insights that will inform future research and managerial practice in a range of contexts.

Distilling these broader implications is the focus of this concluding chapter, which is divided into three parts. The first summarizes three central themes of process development that flow from the analysis. The second identifies areas outside the realm of process development where these themes may apply to future research. The chapter concludes with implications for management.

Three Themes of Process Development

The analysis of process development in pharmaceuticals highlights three themes that have implications for both academic research and managerial practice: (1) the strategic leverage of superior process development capabilities; (2) the relationship between the structure of knowledge and learning strategies; and (3) the dynamics of organizational knowledge and competences.

The Strategic Leverage of Superior Process Development Capabilities

In many high-tech industries, the development of new products captures the lion's share of management attention and scholarly interest. This fascination with products is understandable: innovative and high-performing products are often the source of competitive advantage. Moreover, products are visible and tangible manifestations of an organization's development capabilities. Process development, in contrast, tends to draw attention only in those mature industries or segments where product designs have standardized and low-cost manufacturing has become the primary source of competitive advantage.

Effective process development can also play a very important—albeit different—role in industries characterized by rapid product innovation and intense competition in new product development. Behind many new products in technology-intensive industries such as pharmaceuticals, advanced materials, specialty chemicals, and semiconductors are extremely complex process technologies, the development of which may be as challenging, time consuming, and important to overall commercial success as the design of the products themselves. In such contexts, the value of process development lies in how it contributes to the overall effectiveness and performance of the product development cycle. The capability for fast, efficient, and high-quality process development represents a hidden source of advantage.

In recent years, there has been much discussion and practical application of various tools, techniques, and organizational strategies to better integrate manufacturing into the product development cycle. Design for manufacturability, quality function deployment, simultaneous product-process design, and development teams that include process engineers and manufacturing personnel have become relatively popular ways to achieve a better fit between product and process design. Although these approaches represent an important first step and help eliminate many sources of waste and inefficiency, the power of process development capabilities goes well beyond merely achieving compatibility with product designs. They can contribute to the speed, efficiency, and quality of new product launches.

A firm that can develop sophisticated process technologies more rapidly and with fewer development resources has strategic options that less capable competitors lack. First, a shorter process development cycle moves off the critical path faster and supports aggressive overall development lead times. Additionally, a more efficient organization may leverage its advantage by undertaking more projects, thus hedging risk in an uncertain environment. Rapid process development also offers an organization flexibility in its timing of technical commitments and resource expenditures. In environments where product introductions are fraught with a high degree of technical uncertainty, there are two significant advantages to delaying key technical decisions or resource deployments. First, it can reduce overall development costs for projects that may be terminated. Second, it allows the organization to design the process technology with better information about the product or market while still meeting scheduled product launch time lines.

Process development speed can contribute to product quality by giving designers more latitude in the timing of their commitments. A company with fast process development capabilities, for instance, can freeze its final product design specifications later and still have time to complete all the necessary process development steps. In turbulent technical or commercial environments, the ability to iterate the product design can be critical to achieving market success (Iansiti 1995).

Process development quality can influence product development performance in various ways. Where product and process technologies are tightly intertwined, highly sophisticated process technologies can be an enabling device of product innovation. In organizations where process development can push the frontiers of technology, product designers have more degrees of freedom and are forced to make fewer design compromises in the name of manufacturability.

Although this study used examples of pharmaceutical projects to illustrate the effect of process development on overall development performance, a similar effect is likely to be seen in other high-tech industries. Indeed, given relatively aggressive product time lines, high capital costs, short product lives, and intense competition, effective process development is likely to be an even more potent contributor to product development performance—and overall firm performance—in such industries (Hatch and Mowery 1994).

The Structure of Knowledge and Learning Strategies

Process development involves a wide range of activities, from computer-aided simulations and laboratory experiments to factory-floor implementation of newly developed production techniques. At their core, all these activities are a form of learning: they focus on discovering gaps between actual and desired performance and on uncovering new techniques and approaches to span those gaps. Ultimately, the ability to carry out process development effectively requires an organizational capability to identify and anticipate problems, as well as to harness experience and existing knowledge to find and implement solutions. In short, high performance in process development requires the ability to learn.

Much of the existing literature and management thinking has emphasized learning by doing. In this study, learning by doing involves the development and testing of technology in the final production environment (or a close approximation to it). The advantage of learning by doing is that feedback is highly representative; all the nuances and subtleties of the actual production environment are incorporated in the experiment. However, at the other end of the spectrum, conceptual explorations, computer simulations, and small-scale laboratory experiments can also be used to predict future performance, identify problems, and analyze alternatives. The approaches at this end of the continuum were referred to as learning before doing, because knowledge is acquired before the process is moved to the final production environment.

A particular approach to learning is characterized by more than the physical nature of the apparatus used to conduct experiments. It also includes such elements as the types of people involved at different phases (research scientists or process engineers), the metrics used to assess and validate progress, and the standards used to decide whether to move a project from one development phase to the next. For instance, although on one level a strategy of learning before doing entails preventing a relatively large fraction of problems through extensive process simulation in the laboratory, on another level it means measuring the project's progress along dimensions such as yield improvements and cost reductions before the technology is transferred to the plant. In contrast, an organization adopting an orientation toward learning by doing requires development scientists who understand how to carry out experiments under production conditions; such a firm should also adopt a different set of metrics for evaluating progress. For example, performance improvements after transfer to the factory are a much better indicator than improvements achieved in the lab or pilot plant.

A critical aspect of an organization's development strategy can be framed in terms of the emphasis it gives to different experimental approaches. Again, for almost any development project, a range of experimental approaches may be used—from computer simulations and "thought experiments" to on-line tests of the process in the commercial factory. Boeing, for example, uses extensive computer-aided simulations in designing new generations of aircraft, but it also acquires feedback on designs for certain parts (that do not jeopardize safety) through in-flight tests.[1] Any given development context will require a mixture of experimental modes because of differences in the nature of problems. Some problems can be solved through simulations and other approaches at the "before doing" end of the spectrum, whereas others are much more difficult to anticipate or solve ahead of time. It is an issue of choosing the appropriate mix.

The results of this study indicate that no single approach is best under all conditions. Instead, the appropriate approach in any given situation depends on the nature of problems that need to be solved during development, which in turn depends on the structure of underlying knowledge. There are many ways to characterize the structure of knowledge. Past research has focused on the degree to which knowledge is codified versus tacit. This study adopted a different perspective, focusing on the degree to which knowledge acquired under one set of experimental conditions could be used to predict performance under another.

Effective learning before doing requires that the organization be able to map laboratory observations into a distribution of outcomes in a different environment. Three dimensions of knowledge influence an organization's ability to do this: knowledge of underlying causal variables and their precise relationship to performance; knowledge of the future manufacturing environment (or, more precisely, the new process variables introduced in that environment); and knowledge of how those new variables affect process performance and behavior.[2] The most common variable known to drive a wedge between observed performance and manufacturing performance is scale. However, during the study, other salient differences between laboratory and commercial manufacturing environments were identified, including variations in equipment, the skill level of personnel, and standard operating procedures. Where there are principles, theories, models, or heuristics that capture these relationships, much of what is learned in one environment can be used to predict what will happen in another. Such knowledge allows an organization to do much of its learning in the laboratory, before the process is operated in the plant. In contrast, where relationships between one environment and the next are poorly understood, such representative simulations and experiments cannot be designed, and the only way to get reliable feedback about future performance is to experiment in the final production environment.

The findings reported here suggest that, in an environment such as chemical synthesis, where the bulk of problems can be modeled at laboratory scale, an orientation toward learning before doing enhances development performance. The opposite was true in biotechnology. However, this does not mean that all problems in a chemical environment can be solved before doing whereas all problems in biotechnology require learning by doing. Within any given development project, different strategies may be applied to problems with different characteristics. For example, in chemical synthesis, getting the basic chemistry right can be accomplished through laboratory experiments; on the other hand, fine-tuning an operating procedure that is highly dependent on subtle idiosyncrasies of the plant environment will most likely require learning by doing. As will be discussed later, getting up-front agreement on the types of strategies that can be used to solve problems can help alleviate some of the conflicts that arise between R&D and manufacturing.

The Dynamics of Knowledge and Competences

Technical environments impose broad constraints on what firms do and how they learn. It is important to understand how these environments shape options for development. However, it is also important to recognize that individual firms operating within the same broad technological field do not share identical knowledge bases. Although all firms in a given field might share the same basic competences in chemical synthesis or biotechnology, there are critical differences at the detailed level of knowledge. For instance, some firms appear to have developed more structured and deeper process knowledge bases than others, because of their better understanding of critical cause-and-effect relationships and the factors influencing production processes under commercial operating conditions. Such knowledge—reflected in the type of experiments and analytical tests conducted early in the project, the models and heuristics used to frame technical problems and interpret experimental results, and the patterns of interaction between personnel in the laboratory and factory—allows an organization to anticipate problems or design laboratory experiments early enough to uncover problems long before the process ever reaches the factory floor.

The field research presented indicates that an organization's knowledge bases evolve as a result of past experience and past projects. Every development project has both first-and second-order effects. The first-order performance effect is how well knowledge about a specific process technology is developed and applied. Process development lead times, productivity, and quality are good indicators of how well projects perform in this regard. Development projects can also generate deeper technical and organizational knowledge that is useful for future projects. These by-products are the second-order effects of development projects.

This suggests a dynamic relationship between learning by doing and learning before doing strategies. Initially, when an organization has little experience with a particular technology, it is forced to rely on learning by doing. Each learning by doing experience, however, can contribute to the organization's knowledge base. Over time, as the organization's knowledge base deepens, it can shift from an inductive to a more deductive, or learning before doing, mode of problem solving.

The idea that firms develop their knowledge bases and competences through experience is not new. However, the data in this study indicate that, although experience has the potential to generate learning, some organizations seem better able to make use of their experience than others. Posed differently, some organizations appear to have learned how to learn. The ability to learn across projects can be traced to specific management decisions, including hiring employees with appropriate technical backgrounds, structuring the development process, and managing resources and capacity. For process development, learning is also rooted in how an organization feeds data from manufacturing back into its technical knowledge base. Most discussions of the R&D-manufacturing interface focus on the problems of transferring knowledge from R&D to the manufacturing plant. However, building R&D's capacity to anticipate process problems in manufacturing requires feedback from manufacturing to R&D.

From this perspective, organizational or geographic barriers between R&D and manufacturing can have a significant negative consequence. Over time, as the firm's process R&D scientists become less aware of the plant environment and how specific process choices affect actual performance, they become less capable of designing processes that work well in that environment. In the context of process development, maintaining a capability to learn before doing requires that the firm utilize the plant as an ongoing source of knowledge creation.

Implications for Theory and Future Research

Process development is a fascinating and important activity in its own right. It is hoped that the research presented here has given scholars and practitioners alike a better sense of the potential role of process development in competition and the factors associated with superior process development performance over time. However, the implications and insights go beyond process development. Process development shares a number of characteristics with other organizational activities and raises similar issues. For instance, the structure of knowledge bases features prominently in process development strategies and performance. But knowledge plays a pervasive role in all organizational activities, from product development through distribution and marketing, and has a powerful impact on a firm's competitive strategy. The insights gleaned about learning, knowledge, and problem solving in the context of process development, then, have implications for scholars doing research in various other areas. The discussions below highlight three areas where further research may substantiate and extend the current study's findings.

The Impact of Technological Change

Although not addressed directly in this study, the findings have implications for how changes in technology affect industry structure and firm performance. The idea that changes in technology can have a potent impact on industry evolution and the fates of individual firms has a venerable history in the literature. It has long been recognized that technological change can erode the competitive position of dominant firms while opening the door to new entrants, a process Schumpeter (1934) referred to as "creative destruction." Over the past decade, research has explored the precise mechanisms driving this process. An important theme from this literature is that not all types of technical change have the same impact on existing firms. Tushman and Anderson (1986) found that whether technological change leads to the demise of dominant firms depends critically on whether the new technology enhances or makes obsolete existing organizational competences—what they call "competence-enhancing" or "competence-destroying" innovation. Whereas competence-destroying innovation is likely to lead to the failure of incumbents in an industry, competence-enhancing innovation does not. Henderson and Clark (1990) propose a two-dimensional framework that distinguishes between technical changes at the component and system levels ("architectural innovation"). In their framework, architectural innovation—which affects the relationships between component technologies while leaving the technologies of the individual components largely unchanged—requires the most organizational change and can thus have the most serious consequences for incumbents.

The framework developed in this study suggests another way in which technological changes might be competence destroying and affect competitive dynamics. Over time, we might expect firms to develop patterns of learning that reflect the knowledge environment in which they have operated. For example, firms that have long operated in an environment characterized by a highly mature and well-structured scientific knowledge base would have developed an infrastructure and processes to support learning by doing. By upsetting existing theoretical models, empirical relationships, and heuristics, certain technological changes could essentially make obsolete the firm's capabilities for such deductive learning, and require it to learn how to learn by doing.

Consider the example of a pharmaceutical firm with a long history of developing and manufacturing chemically synthesized drugs. Given the knowledge environment in chemicals that permits future performance to be reasonably well predicted from laboratory results, the company has developed an extensive repertoire of organizational routines to facilitate learning before doing. It structured its development cycle with heavy emphasis on process research; it thoroughly explores alternative synthetic routes through the use of sophisticated computer simulations; it conducts extensive laboratory experiments on processes before ever testing them at pilot scale; and it has implemented a standardized set of pilot-scale tests to ensure that all major technical problems have been solved before the process is transferred to the commercial plant. It has clear criteria for assessing whether a process is ready to be transferred to the factory. In short, the company has developed a capability to design the process right the first time. From the results presented here, we would expect this organization to be a high performer in the world of chemical synthesis.

Now consider the challenges biotechnology presents for the same firm. Biotechnology is competence destroying in two regards: technical and organizational. At the technical level, it requires skills in different scientific disciplines (molecular biology, biophysics, and protein chemistry versus organic chemistry and chemical engineering). The technical challenge is to develop knowledge and competences in these new domains (which requires more than simply hiring PhDs in the relevant fields). The organizational challenge is even more daunting. Given the immature knowledge base in biotechnology, many of the firm's deeply ingrained learning before doing processes, heuristic frameworks, project milestones, and philosophies would no longer be relevant. The firm would need to develop an entirely new set of organizational routines that facilitate learning by doing in the final production environment. This helps explain why most pharmaceutical companies going into biotechnology have created separate organizational subunits or divisions focused on biotechnology.

A similar set of issues can also arise for changes in product technology or markets. A dramatic change in component technology (such as the use of advanced composites instead of aluminum in airframe design) or in the customer base can violate many of the models and heuristics a firm uses to conceptualize designs and assess the potential performance of alternative designs during the early stages of a project.

Clearly, further research is needed to understand how structural changes in knowledge bases influence firm performance. Whether established firms' problems adapting to technological uncertainty are a result of changes in the mix of problem-solving strategies is an open empirical question. The issue is particularly relevant to firms in a range of industries because of recent advances in R&D technologies, such as computer-aided design, computer-aided simulation, and rapid prototyping. In industries such as airplanes, integrated circuits, workstations, automobiles, and even textiles, computer-aided design and related tools are reshaping the economics of product development and have the potential to alter competitive advantages. By attempting to achieve better simulation of final performance at the early design stage, they fundamentally shift the focus of problem solving toward learning before doing, and may require some firms to build fundamentally different internal development processes and capabilities.

A related issue raised by this study concerns the evolution of technological know-how over time. Are structural differences in technological know-how purely a function of maturity, or are there some inherent differences that do not vary with time? Is there a characteristic evolution whereby the learning by doing that is initially required to cope with lack of theory and experience eventually gives way to learning before doing strategies as deductive knowledge accumulates?[3] The static comparisons of chemical synthesis and biotechnology in this study provided only glimpses into these questions; time alone will determine whether biotechnology will follow the same evolutionary path as chemical synthesis. Clearly, more detailed historical comparisons are needed to explore the rich set of institutional, organizational, and economic forces that shape the structural evolution of technological knowledge and in turn influence the approaches to learning adopted by firms over time.[4]

Product Development

The development of a new process technology raises many of the same challenges, issues, and problems as product development. Both require technical problem solving, experimentation, and integration. Both require predicting and simulating how a future customer will respond to the design.[5] In the case of process design, that customer is the factory; in the case of product design, the customer is the end consumer or user of the product. Posed in this way, the fundamental challenge of product design is to learn about customer needs and preferences and, through an iterative process, to close the gap between what the product design offers to the customer and what the customer really wants.

Just as there are many ways to simulate production performance, there are numerous techniques and approaches to discover customer needs and simulate how well products in development may meet those needs. Customer surveys, analysis of buying patterns, focus groups, customer observations, and, more recently, computer-aided experiments are common techniques for uncovering customer needs and preferences. Prototyping—whether using crude clay models or "virtual prototypes"—is the most common method for simulating how well a product might meet those needs.[6] Because these mechanisms for discovering customer needs and generating feedback differ in the extent to which they rely on simulated as opposed to real conditions, they can be viewed along the learning by doing versus learning before doing spectrum.

The results from process development suggest that different approaches would be appropriate in different types of product environments. For example, Sony, in lieu of market research, designs products, manufactures small batches of prototypes, and then sells them in shops in the electronics district of downtown Tokyo (Lorenz 1986). Based on the feedback it gets from these sales, it decides whether to increase production or redesign the product. Sony's approach is really the learning by doing equivalent of the product design domain and is based on the assumption that it is futile to try to discover customer needs. By selling the product in real stores to real customers, Sony gets highly representative feedback on customer needs and how well the design meets those needs. On the other end of the spectrum lies a company like Boeing, which relies heavily on computer-aided design and simulations in designing new generations of aircraft. Part of the difference between Boeing's and Sony's approaches can be attributed to costs. For Sony to build a few thousand Walkmans and distribute them in downtown Tokyo is a relatively inexpensive proposition. For Boeing, it is prohibitively expensive, extremely time consuming, and potentially dangerous to build full-scale working proto-types and let airlines test them in actual flight operations.[7]

The framework from this study suggests that a prototyping strategy can also be driven by structural differences in the knowledge bases. Sony believes that consumer marketing is an art and that no company can ever understand enough about consumer tastes and psychology to predict whether buyers will prefer one design element or another (will they like red buttons or blue? should the corners be rounded or square?). Perhaps by necessity, Boeing operates at the other end of the spectrum. Through years of designing aircraft and collecting data from actual in-flight performance, as well as extensive basic research in advanced materials, electronics, and other key systems, Boeing has developed extensive knowledge about critical design parameters and how they affect such performance characteristics as efficiency, stability, strength, and manufacturing costs.

The idea that different approaches to experimentation during product development are required in different technology settings clearly has implica-tions for practice, but far more research is needed to distill these. A strong implication for research is the need for cross-industry studies and comparisons. To date, most research on product development has been industry focused.[8] These studies have been invaluable in providing a deep understanding of organizational and management issues associated with development in particu-lar contexts. In the future, such cross-industry comparisons may help identify critical differences in the structure of knowledge and the implications of these variations for development practices in a wide range of environments.

Organizational Learning

As portrayed here, process development conjures a host of images: scientists running laboratory experiments with highly sophisticated instruments; engi-neers designing equipment; a group of technicians hovering around a piece of equipment trying to determine why it keeps failing; a team of technical spe-cialists discussing the results of the latest pilot production batch. It is easy to lose sight of the fact that production process is but one of a broader class of organizational processes that operate routinely within companies.[9] Most busi-ness activities follow some type of regular flow and pattern. Some processes—such as those used to take and fill customer orders—affect the way operational activities are undertaken. Others—such as capital budgeting processes—affect the way decisions are made. Even such high-level activities as strategic planning and corporate governance can be viewed as processes. Any attempt to develop new organizational processes and routines—something commonly done under the banners of process reengineering and total quality management programs—represents a form of process development. The study of the development of production technologies provides a window into the broader phenomenon of the development of new organizational capabilities and processes.

Although seemingly quite different in nature, manufacturing process development and organizational process development share many traits (see figure 10.1). Both, for example, are undertaken with the goal of establishing a new routine that meets specific business objectives. Both efforts involve similar activities: manufacturing process development begins with research and concept development; organizational process development begins with background analysis of existing processes and planning. Each is subjected to a pilot test or trial run. For instance, a new logistics process for providing overnight delivery of spare parts is likely to be test-marketed in a particular region. Manufacturing processes and organizational processes typically evolve iteratively through multiple generations and refinements. Both involve scale-up (or rollout) in terms of expanding and replicating the process across sites. Just as a newly developed production process may exhibit unexpectedly poor yields at full scale or in a commercial production environment, a newly created business process may not work as well as originally planned and may need to be revised. Implementing organizational change in any domain can be viewed in terms of process development.[10]

As with manufacturing process development, organizational development presents managers with choices between learning before doing and learning by doing. In an organizational development project, learning before doing implies spending relatively more time and resources exploring, designing, and analyzing options, running small-scale experiments, and selecting and optimizing the design before trying it out under true operating conditions. Consider the following example. An insurance company seeking to reduce the time it takes to approve (or reject) requests for new policies embarks on a plan to reengineer its underwriting process. Following a strategy of learning before doing, it might call in a consultant (or use internal staff) to conduct an in-depth study of its current process, and a set of alternative approaches might then be identified and analyzed. Computer simulations could be run to determine which proposed process offers the fastest turnaround time, and input could be solicited from underwriters, managers, agents, and even customers. After identifying the most promising approach, a small field test might be tried (a

FIGURE 10.1 Parallels between Manufacturing Process Development and Organizational Process Development

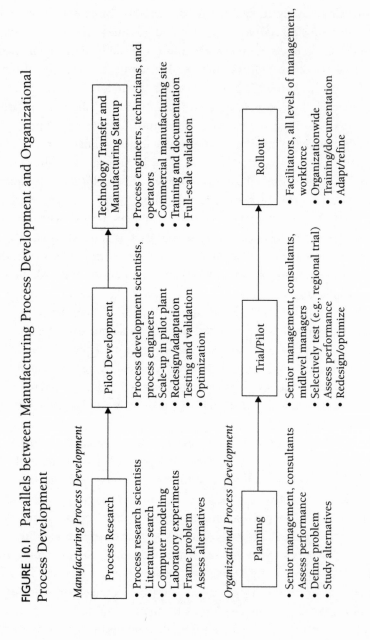

Manufacturing Process Development

Process Research

- Process research scientists
- Literature search
- Computer modeling
- Laboratory experiments
- Frame problem
- Assess alternatives

Pilot Development

- Process development scientists, process engineers
- Scale-up in pilot plant
- Redesign/adaptation
- Testing and validation
- Optimization

Technology Transfer and Manufacturing Startup

- Process engineers, technicians, and operators
- Commercial manufacturing site
- Training and documentation
- Full-scale validation

Organizational Process Development

Planning

- Senior management, consultants
- Assess performance
- Define problem
- Study alternatives

Trial/Pilot

- Senior management, consultants, midlevel managers
- Selectively test (e.g., regional trial)
- Assess performance
- Redesign/optimize

Rollout

- Facilitators, all levels of management, workforce
- Organizationwide
- Training/documentation
- Adapt/refine

prototype underwriting team might process claims for one week) to validate the process. If it met expectations, the new process would be rolled out for use in the rest of the organization.

This approach seems like a perfectly natural and logical way to proceed. Yet the alternative approach—one that relies more on learning by doing in the actual operating context—also has strong merits. For example, a company might believe that it would be impossible to find the optimal design up front because there were too many unknown variables. It might spend little time on up-front analysis and instead try a few obvious alternatives in actual operations. Based on real-time feedback, it then could redesign the process incrementally over repeated iterations. Questions such as "What will the agents think?" and "Will the turnaround time be quick enough?" would be answered from testing the process under actual operating conditions. Again, the distinction between learning before doing and learning by doing is a matter of degree, not of kind.

Choosing the appropriate balance between the two learning strategies is far from an abstract exercise. Consider the debate between proponents of two common improvement programs: reengineering and total quality management. As noted by Garvin (1994), these two movements share many characteristics: both focus on processes, and both contend that most companies' processes have grown inefficient. Yet the two approaches differ in how they propose to develop more efficient processes.

Proponents of reengineering believe in starting with a blank slate. Rather than attempt to improve existing processes incrementally, reengineering strives for sweeping change. Because it involves deep and potentially traumatic organizational upheaval, reengineering tends to be driven from the top down. It also tends to rely heavily on up-front planning, analysis, and buy-in from constituents. The goal is to *re*design it right the first time. In this respect, process reengineering is oriented toward learning before doing. In contrast, total quality management advocates a continuous, incremental approach (Garvin 1994). Only through careful control and measurement of existing processes is it possible to identify opportunities for improvement. TQM tends to be driven from the bottom up, employing tools such as kaizen. In its use of online feedback, kaizen and TQM programs are predicated on the notion of learning by doing.

The results from this study suggest that the choice among TQM, reengineering, and other approaches, when framed as different strategies for learning, hinges on the nature of knowledge in the organizational environment. Like manufacturing processes, organizational processes differ in the extent to which they rest on knowledge bases that are well developed and structured around relatively well-understood and validated cause-and-effect relationships. For instance, consider the example of a company looking to reduce inventory in its distribution channel while preserving existing delivery lead times. Using relatively well-known principles, heuristics, and algorithms, fairly robust models can be constructed to explore system designs and simulate their impact on performance. While such models are by no means perfect, they allow organizations to hone in relatively quickly on promising alternatives. (There is no need to go out and build warehouses in different locations just to see how they affect inventory and lead times!)

Contrast this situation to one in which a U.S. company is contemplating the development of an entire operating and sales capability in China. Without experience operating in China, the company may have difficulty predicting the performance of any system it designs because it lacks full knowledge of critical idiosyncratic variables, such as those related to local culture and custom. Clearly, any firm contemplating such a major investment needs to do its homework, but much more will be learned in the process of starting up operations. In this type of situation, the company might be better off starting out as small as possible and then ratcheting up its infrastructure as it gains experience and information in China. This is essentially learning by doing.

As in the case of manufacturing process development, there is no uniformly right way to design and develop organizational processes. The learning strategy must be matched to the impediments and opportunities created by the firm's knowledge base. Gaining a deeper understanding of the particular organizational learning strategies available to firms, and the type of organizational problems each is best suited to solve, is a rich area for future research.

Implications for Management: Unlocking the Potential of Process Development

After more than 200 in-depth interviews on both sides of the Atlantic, after carefully studying pages of project records and time lines, and after all the statistical analyses and case studies, one theme stands out above all else: High development performance is rooted in what managers do. All the organizations and project teams involved in this study employed intelligent scientists and engineers who worked extremely hard and cared deeply about doing superb work. The established pharmaceutical companies in the study had years of cumulative process development experience and more than ample technical and financial resources at their disposal. The biotechnology firms, although armed with less experience in process development and fewer resources, combined some of the best scientific minds in the field with the high-powered incentives created by the lure of stock options. Yet despite all this, some organizations and project teams were able to undertake comparable process development projects more quickly and more efficiently, and did a better job at capturing and applying experience from one project to the next. In short, they managed to nurture and unlock the potential of process development capabilities. This chapter concludes by addressing the question: What can managers do to create and exploit the potential of process development in their own organization?

Unfortunately, there is no simple answer. Researching, developing, and implementing new process technologies in a dynamic environment is organizationally complex and technically challenging. It employs a wide range of people with vastly different technical backgrounds and work experiences, encompasses venues from the laboratory to the factory floor, and often spans the globe. Part of the challenge lies in making specific decisions (such as the timing of technology transfer). But it also requires organizations with the appropriate capabilities to execute those decisions and to generate improved options for future projects. Building capabilities in this realm is no easy task for managers. Although there is no single formula for success, the field research conducted during this study revealed a number of managerial behaviors that contributed to outstanding development performance. The final pages of this chapter examine three levels of action at which managers can influence their process development organizations: defining the role and mission of process development, architecting the process of development, and managing organizational experimentation and learning. These three activities echo the themes of process development discussed at the outset of this chapter. Defining the role and mission of process development requires understanding the hidden leverage of process development. Architecting the process requires understanding the relationship between the structure of knowledge and learning strategies. And managing organizational experimentation and learning requires an understanding of the dynamics of knowledge and competences.

Defining the Role and Mission

Many managers, either implicitly or explicitly, have adopted a model of process development based on mature industry settings where low cost is the primary driver of competitive advantage. A central theme of this study is that the value of process development, in technologically dynamic settings, should be more broadly framed in terms of providing proactive support for rapid, efficient, and high-quality product development. Unlocking process development's hidden leverage requires that senior management articulate a far different role for process development than is commonly found in many organizations.

Table 10.1 provides a comparison of the essential roles and tasks of process development in a mature industry setting versus one where competition re-

Table 10.1 Two Models of Process Development

	Conventional Model	New Model
Primary Goals	Reduce manufacturing costs of existing products	Proactive support of timely, efficient, and high-quality launches of new products
Technical Focus	• Incremental process improvement • New capacity/ equipment/automation • Troubleshooting • Product modifications for enhanced manufacturability	• Exploration/development of new process architectures needed for new product designs
Product Development Role/Influence	Peripheral	• Central • Process developers as core members of product development teams
Customer	Plant	• Plant • R&D
Key Capabilities	• Process engineering • In-depth knowledge of current manufacturing environment • Minimize product disruptions	• Process science • Ability to anticipate future manufacturing requirements • Responsiveness to project level uncertainty
Learning	Maximize learning curve *within* product/process generations	Capture learning *across* product/process generations
Metrics of Performance	Improvements in yield, cost, quality, and capital over the life of a product	• Improvements in *initial* yield, cost, quality, and capital across products • Lead time, efficiency, quality

volves around new product development. The conventional approach to process development (the left-hand column of the table) focuses on incremental cost reductions through minor adaptations of an existing product's design, process engineering refinements and process optimization, the development and application of automation, investments in new plant and equipment, modifications in standard operating procedures, and substitution of lower-cost or higher-quality raw materials.[11] This approach, although well suited to mature industry contexts where product designs are relatively stable, will not help an organization competing on the basis of product development.

In the high-performing organizations from both segments in this study, senior management clearly articulated the role of process development in terms of its contribution to the firm's product development capabilities. The role of process development manifested itself in two ways. One was the extent of participation on product development teams. Where process development is truly considered a critical element of the development process, process developers are core members of the project teams. This implies more than simply being invited to meetings or attending solely out of fear that process development will be "blind-sided" by a schedule change; rather, process development scientists and managers must help shape critical decisions and provide technical advice on the project.

Process development's role in product development is also reflected in the timing of process R&D activities within the total development cycle. In organizations where process development is expected to contribute to product development, process development scientists are routinely involved at the earliest phases of the project, scouting out major process issues or alternatives for molecules still in the discovery phase, for example, or helping solve complex technical problems associated with product synthesis. Different levels of involvement will obviously be called for in different technical and industry environments. However, an important acid test for evaluating process development's role is the extent to which product designers and developers consult with them and utilize the group to help solve problems at an early stage.

Making process development an integral contributor to product development requires that the entire organization embrace a new perspective on the potential leverage of process development. It also requires that the process development organization develop a set of competences and skills that enables it to be an effective contributor. Management can assist by making adequate resources available. Indeed, one useful data point for companies attempting to evaluate the role of process development in their organizations is to compare the allocation of resources between product and process R&D. A second lever for managers is hiring and recruitment. If process development is to be treated as an equal partner in development, process developers need to be viewed as technical peers to those on the product development side of the organization. Finally, in setting the expectations for process development and defining its mission broadly, management should employ the appropriate set of perform-ance metrics.

Architecting the Process

Defining the role of process development broadly is a critical first step on the path to building process development capabilities. However, unlocking process development's full potential requires designing a development process that is capable of speed, efficiency, and quality. These capabilities are rooted in the organizational processes by which problems are identified, framed, solved, and implemented. Thus an essential task for management in nurturing process development capabilities is to design and influence the organizational pro-cesses used for development. In shaping a development process, the critical choice for managers is the degree of emphasis on different approaches for learning and problem solving. How much emphasis will be placed on learning before doing? What types of problems can be most quickly and efficiently solved in the laboratory versus on the factory floor? What criteria will be used to assess and validate knowledge throughout the project?

The most important lesson stemming from this study is that no uniform development process fits all technical environments or firms. Although there were similarities between biotechnology and chemical pharmaceuticals in how effective managers defined the roles and expectations of process development, there were fundamental differences in how high-performing organizations in these segments operated. As discussed earlier, these differences stem from the fact that process knowledge is structured differently in the biotechnology and chemical synthesis settings. Firm-level differences in knowledge also influence the design of appropriate development processes. The critical challenge for management is to design a development process that fits with the imperatives of the knowledge environment in which the firm operates.

One implication for managers is the need to be highly selective in adopting certain practices, principles, and approaches to development which have been shown to lead to high performance in other contexts and which are then touted as keys to world-class development performance. Although certain approaches and principles of development—such as "design it right first time," the need to transfer process technologies to the plant early, design for manufacturability, and quality function deployment—may make sense in some contexts, they may be completely inappropriate in others.

Architecting an appropriate development process requires a detailed and shared understanding of the technical environment and the firm's specific knowledge base. Questions about the type of problems that can best be addressed at different phases can be difficult to resolve and require detailed analysis of the problems arising on past projects. For instance, what looks like an easily avoidable problem to a process engineer based in the factory may be completely arcane to research scientists working at the laboratory bench. Developing a shared understanding of the firm's knowledge base and its ability to solve problems provides the basis for a development process that is credible to everyone, from the laboratory to the factory.

A crucial piece of creating the right development process architecture is to ensure that the organization has the appropriate mix of resources, people, and physical assets to complement its chosen strategy. Resource allocation across different phases of the development cycle is one powerful way managers can induce (or hinder) the execution of a particular approach. For instance, to pursue a strategy of learning by doing, resources need to be invested in full-scale manufacturing capacity and technical support in order to enable online pilot tests. In contrast, a development strategy oriented toward learning before doing requires that resources be allocated to research and tools (such as CAD) used for sophisticated process simulations. Decisions about organizational integration between process R&D and manufacturing, as well as the physical location of manufacturing plants, also need to take into account the development strategy. Outsourcing or locating manufacturing plants distant from R&D, for example, may create barriers to tight integration between process R&D and manufacturing. Managers need to keep in mind that the architecture of the development process, like that of a building, is composed of many different elements, all of which need to fit together in a coherent system.

Managing Organizational Experimentation and Learning

A third role for management is to manage the dynamic evolution of the organization's knowledge base and competences over time. Each project can be a learning experience and offers an organization the opportunity to deepen its technical knowledge (by gaining a better understanding of critical cause and effect relationships) and discover new procedures and organizational interactions that enhance performance. However, as discussed earlier, learning is not automatic. Management influences both the extent to which projects generate knowledge and how effectively this knowledge is applied across projects.

Thus managers also help determine the extent to which a project becomes a vehicle for building knowledge. For instance, project goals and expectations set by management influence whether developers experiment broadly in search of a more complete understanding of the technology, or whether they focus on the immediate task of completing the particular project. In a related fashion, allocating sufficient resources in personnel and physical manufacturing capacity to enable such experimentation will also play an important role.

Moreover, building an organization's knowledge base will require enhancing the skills of its employees. Individuals, like organizations, often must learn by doing; what individuals do in an organization (and thus what they learn) is largely a function of career paths and project assignments. If such assignments are oriented largely along technical specialties, it should be expected that individuals in the organization will develop deep knowledge in their particular domain but lack an integrated understanding of the technology at a systems level.[12] In more mature technologies, there may be individuals who specialize in systems integration (chemical engineers often play this role in chemical process technologies, for instance). However, in an emerging technology such as biotechnology, ready-made integration specialists do not exist. They must be grown internally through career paths and project assignments.

Ensuring that the organization is exploiting opportunities to learn at the project level is only part of the management challenge. In addition, managers must help ensure that learning is applied across projects. If an organization is doing a good job deepening its knowledge with each project, its development strategies must also evolve to exploit this new knowledge. This requires that management adopt a dynamic perspective on the organization's development framework. Just as no single development strategy is appropriate in all environments, no single strategy is appropriate for the same firm over time.

Managing this evolution requires a delicate balance between the need for a well-defined and widely shared approach to development and the need to alter the process to exploit what has been learned on past projects. Keeping the development process rigid in the wake of changes in the firm's knowledge base will lead to suboptimal performance. On the other hand, restructuring and redefining the development process can be disruptive and, as discussed in chapter 8, can inhibit performance.

One way to maintain the appropriate balance is to adopt an evolutionary approach through which each project incorporates incremental changes in processes or practices to reflect what has been learned from project to project.

This approach permits much better tracking between the organization's development process and its evolving knowledge base. Under this approach, organizational process development is routine activity performed with each new manufacturing process development project.

Few organizations in any industry today have the luxury of sitting still. Success requires the capability to do more proficiently than one's competitors those things that customers value. These capabilities are rooted in processes. The challenge facing senior managers is to create organizations that can improve on existing processes while being able to adapt to rapid market and technological changes. In this type of environment, the ability to rapidly and efficiently develop processes—whether production or other types of organizational processes—may be the ultimate source of competitive advantage and organizational renewal.

Research Methodology

This appendix describes the research methods used in this study. It begins with an overview of the sample (and the methods used to develop the sample) and the data collection process, and then describes the variables used in the statistical analyses. The final section presents the statistical methods, models, and results.

Sample and Data Collection Methods

The sample used in this study's statistical analyses consists of twenty-three process development projects, each of which was associated with the launch of a new therapeutic molecular entity. Ten projects involved proteins made through recombinant biotechnology methods, and thirteen involved traditional chemically synthesized compounds. Five large pharmaceutical companies (including the biotechnology division of one of these companies) and five new entrants participated. Of the five established pharmaceutical firms, three were headquartered in Europe and two in the United States. Given the proprietary nature of the data used in the study, the companies and the individual projects are not identified by name. However, the aggregate profile of the companies participating in the study is relatively typical of top-tier firms. All five established companies ranked among the top twenty globally in terms of sales and annual R&D spending; three were among the top ten. All new

297

entrants were based in the United States. Although all might be considered biotechnology firms, one company's process development project involved largely chemical synthesis, and its project was classified as a chemical-based technology. No Japanese companies participated, because they have played a relatively small role in the global pharmaceuticals industry to date. For instance, no Japanese companies rank among the top fifteen globally, and only one, Takeda, ranks among the top twenty pharmaceutical companies in terms of annual R&D spending in 1993. Future studies certainly may want to include Japanese pharmaceutical firms as they become more central players.

Beyond the companies that contributed projects to the sample, a small number of other companies provided background information on technical and managerial issues surrounding process development. These companies were generally unable to provide systematic data on individual projects, either because they had not completed a project (as was typical for younger biotechnology firms) or because they were unable to dedicate time to data collection. These firms provided information that was extremely helpful—particularly in the early stages of the study—in forming hypotheses and framing the issues.

The choice of potential projects was relatively limited at most firms. Highly productive pharmaceutical companies rarely launch more than one or two new chemical entities in any given year (in 1993, for instance, the most new chemical entities introduced by a single firm was three). Many companies have gone several years without launching a single chemical entity. The choice in biotechnology was even more limited, because only about twenty-five new biotechnology drugs had been introduced since 1982, and few firms have launched more than one or two new drugs. Three criteria were used to select projects. First, process development had to be finished (although the resulting product need not have been launched). Second, the company had to have adequate project records (for instance, on resources and costs). Finally, the key participants had to be available for interviews.

The projects in the study took place between 1980 and 1993. Data for each project were collected between mid-1991 and mid-1993 through three methods: in-depth interviews, questionnaires, and internal company documents. In the early phases of the research, a set of unstructured interviews was conducted to identify the relevant managerial and technical issues, generate working hypotheses, and determine the most relevant metrics for examining those hypotheses. The next phase was to collect systematic data across projects. A questionnaire was administered personally during on-site interviews. In virtually every case, my research assistant or a collaborator was also present at these interviews, and we carefully cross-checked notes to ensure consistency. Any discrepancies were resolved through follow-up communications. At least two rounds of interviews were conducted for each company, with later rounds used to verify or refine data collected earlier. Follow-up telephone and fax communication was also used to fill in missing details. For each project, between five and twenty people—with responsibilities ranging from those of bench-level scientists and technicians to senior executives—were interviewed. In total, approximately two hundred people were interviewed. Internal company documents—including detailed project event reports, technical process information, standard operating procedures, project team charts, accounting reports, and memoranda—were also used to verify information collected through the questionnaire and structured interviews.

Variables

Variables considered in this study include basic measures of performance, allowances for differences in difficulty, and various strategic decisions affecting project outcome.

Indicators of Project Performance

Two key measures of project performance were the number of hours spent developing the process and lead time.

Development Hours. Development hours for each project included the time spent developing the process, from the start of process research through the successful validation of the process in the manufacturing plant. It included the time spent by scientists, engineers, and technicians involved in process research, pilot development, and manufacturing startup, as well as the development of analytical techniques for the process, technology transfer to the plant, and the analytical work required to meet regulatory filings. It did not include any allocation for overhead or administrative hours; time spent by production personnel conducting routine production activities in either the pilot plant or the commercial plant; or hours consumed in plant design or construction. Because this study focuses on the process development required to manufacture active chemical or biochemical compounds, hours spent on formulation process development were excluded (this activity is generally carried out by a separate development group and thus was relatively easy to distinguish). Data on development hours were constructed from detailed interviews with individual participants and from analysis of project reports.

Lead Time. Lead time is the number of calendar months elapsed from the start of process research through successful validation. Process research was deemed to have started when the organization first began to carry out research on a process technology suitable to make the product at larger scale. In most instances, company records pinpointed this date, because it usually coincided with a host of other decisions to begin a broader development effort on a particular drug candidate. Successful validation was also easy to pinpoint because it is a critical regulatory event. Given the long time horizons and uncertainty of most drug development projects, it was not uncommon for process development for a particular molecule to stop periodically during a project. The lead time figures used in the analysis do not include these idle periods.

Controls for Project-Level Differences in Content

Because some projects had a higher degree of difficulty, the study took into account various indicators of difficulty.

Technology Class (CHEM). Projects fell into two broad technological categories: biotechnology-based process technologies and classical chemical synthesis. In the statistical analyses, the dummy variable CHEM was coded as 1 if the project involved the development of a chemically synthesized process.

Number of Chemical Reactions (CHEM*REACT). For the chemical processes, the number of chemical reactions in the synthesis was considered by most participants in the study to be a critical indicator of process complexity and thus of the degree of difficulty of the process development project.

Scale of Process [Log(Scale)]. Scale of process was identified as the estimated output of the process in the first full year of commercial production. Given the enormous range of this variable (from less than 1 kilogram to greater than 200 metric tons in the first year) and the likelihood that degree of difficulty of process development increases at a decreasing rate, scale was measured in logarithmic form.

Therapeutic Class (ACUTE). During the field interviews, it was suggested that the therapeutic category could affect the degree of difficulty of the process. In particular, because drugs to treat acute illnesses were expected to move through clinical trials more quickly, process development faced greater pressure to stay off the critical path of the overall product launch. Without the luxury of time, these projects might be expected to have higher resource expenditures because multiple process options would have to be explored simultaneously.

Development Strategy Variables

The development strategies used for each project in the sample were measured as follows.

Relative Timing of Technology Transfer (TRANSFER). The percentage of total project lead time (in calendar months) elapsed before the start of the transfer of the process to the commercial manufacturing site.

Overlap Between Scale-up and Technology Transfer Phases (OVERLAP). The ratio of the length of the technology transfer phase to the length of the scale-up lead time (which is the sum of the pilot development phase and the technology transfer phases).

Development Effort Prior to Technology Transfer (%PRE-TRANSFER). The percentage of total project hours expended prior to transfer to the plant. This variable is analogous to TRANSFER, but represents the percentage of person-hours rather than the percentage of calendar time occurring before the technology transfer.

Development Effort Prior to First Pilot Batch (RESEARCH%). The percentage of total project hours spent before the first attempt to produce a batch of materials under pilot plant conditions.

Pilot Development Effort (PILOT DEV%). The percentage of total project hours consumed between the first pilot batch and the start of the transfer to the commercial manufacturing site.

Lead Time for First Pilot Batch (PILOT-1 LEAD). The number of months between the start of the project and the first attempt to produce a batch of material under pilot plant conditions.

Organizational Structure (INTEGRATED). A dummy variable set equal to 1 if one organization in the company was responsible for all activities of process R&D (from process research through successful transfer to the plant).

Statistical Models

Three sets of statistical models are presented. The first set presents the models used to estimate the impact of various elements of project complexity and content on both lead times and development hours. The second set focuses on the strategic and organizational determinants of development costs, and the third set does the same for lead time performance.

Content-adjusted Development Hours and Lead Times

To get a content-adjusted measure of both development hours and lead times, the following regressions were estimated:

$$\text{Development Hours}_i = a_0 + b_1 \text{ CHEM}_i + b_2 \text{ CHEM} \times \text{REACT}_i + b_3 \text{Log(Scale}_i) + b_4 \text{ ACUTE}_i + e_i$$

$$\text{Lead Time}_i = a_0 + b_1 \text{ CHEM}_i + b_2 \text{ CHEM} \times \text{REACT}_i + b_3 \text{ Log(Scale}_i) + b_4 \text{ ACUTE}_i + e_i$$

The results are shown in table A.1. The residuals of each model can be thought of as the development hours or lead times that could not be explained by the technical class or content of the projects. These content-adjusted metrics were used in the analysis of the relationship between lead time and development hours in chapter 6.

Development Hours

To analyze the impact of development strategy on development hours and to estimate whether this impact differed between the biotechnology and chemical process technology projects, the following model was estimated using least squares:

$$\text{Development Hours}_i = a_0 + b_1 \text{ CHEM}_i + b_2 \text{ CHEM} \times \text{REACT}_i + b_3 \text{Log(Scale}_i) + b_4 \text{ACUTE}_i + b_5 \text{INTEGRATED}_i + b_6 \text{TRANSFER}_i + b_7 \text{CHEM} \times \text{TRANSFER}_i + e_i$$

where the variables are defined as above. As discussed in chapter 6, two closely related metrics of development strategy were of interest: the relative timing of technology transfer to the factory (TRANSFER) and the degree of overlap between transfer and scale-up (OVERLAP). Because these two measures are highly correlated and represent different ways of capturing the same phenomenon (learning by doing versus learning before doing), they are analyzed separately. Thus a second set of models was estimated, substituting the variable OVERLAP for TRANSFER.

Essentially, CHEM, CHEM × REACT, Log(Scale), and ACUTE are variables designed to control for differences in the technology and content of the projects. The main coefficients of interest are b_6 and b_7. Here, b_6 is an estimate of the effect of the timing of technology transfer on development costs for the biotechnology projects in the sample; b_7, the coefficient on the interactive term,

Table A.1 Adjusting for Project Content Differences

Independent Variables	Development Hours			Lead Time		
	DH-1	DH-2	DH-3	LT-1	LT-2	LT-3
Content	209.3***	225.5***	184.7***	41.4***	40.48***	41.00***
	(56.7)	(54.8)	(43.9)	(6.06)	(6.11)	(6.44)
CHEM	−334.7**	−503.6***	−363.6**	27.3*	39.08**	37.16*
	(142.4)	(168.9)	(137.0)	(15.22)	(18.82)	(20.08)
CHEM × REACT	31.2**	30.2**	23.3**	1.16	1.23	1.32
	(12.2)	(11.7)	(9.3)	(1.31)	(1.31)	(1.37)
Log(Scale)		51.4*	19.7		−3.58	−3.15
		(30.4)	(25.2)		(3.38)	(3.70)
ACUTE			296.6***			−4.07
			(81.2)			(11.90)
R^2	.17	.24	.54	.50	.50	.477
F	3.30*	3.36**	7.49***	11.94***	8.38***	6.024***

* $p < .10$, ** $p < .05$, *** $p < .01$

indicates the *difference* between the effect in biotechnology and the effect in chemicals. A positive sign on b_6 indicates that later transfers in biotechnology are associated with higher development costs (after controlling for other factors that might influence these costs) and would be consistent with the idea that early technology transfer (learning by doing) is an effective strategy in biotechnology. A negative sign on b_7 would indicate that less learning by doing is required for high performance in the chemical environment. The results of these models are presented in table A.2.

Models 1 through 4 include only the variables controlling for differences in project content and complexity. Although these results were provided earlier, in table A.1, they are presented here to facilitate comparisons with the other variables of interest. Models 5, 6, and 7 show the effects of the managerially controllable project level and organizational structure variables, TRANSFER and INTEGRATED. Although the average effect of INTEGRATED is relatively large (Model 6, for example, suggests that integrated organizations require approximately 105,000 fewer hours to carry out a project than organizations dividing process research from process development, compared to an average of 193,864 hours for all projects in the sample), it is also quite inconsistent, and the coefficient is not statistically significant at conventional levels. Models 6 and 7 include the TRANSFER variable. As shown in Models 6 and 7, the effect of TRANSFER across the entire sample of projects is positive (indicating that later transfers to the factory are associated with higher development costs) and statistically significant.

Models 8, 9, and 10, which include the interaction terms, provide insight into how the impact of technology transfer timing on development costs differs across the two technological classes in the sample. In all three models, the coefficient on TRANSFER is positive and statistically significant, indicating that a high degree of learning by doing is essential for development efficiency in biotechnology. As expected, the coefficient on the interactive term (CHEM*TRANSFER) is negative and statistically significant, indicating that learning by doing via early technology transfer is less important for development efficiency in the chemical synthesis projects. Given the relatively small sample size, an analysis was conducted to examine whether any particular points were driving the results. The models were reestimated twenty-three times, each time with one observation excluded. In no case did the exclusion of a point lead to a significant change in the coefficients of primary interest.

Table A.3 presents estimates of the model using the variable OVERLAP in place of TRANSFER. The negative coefficient on OVERLAP indicates that a higher degree of overlap between scale-up and technology transfer is associated

Table A.2 Regressions Results—The Impact of Technology Transfer Timing on Process Development Hours (standard errors in parentheses)

Variables	Model 1	Model 2	Model 3	Model 4	Model 5	Model 6	Model 7	Model 8	Model 9	Model 10
Constant	209.3*** (56.7)	225.5*** (54.8)	184.7*** (43.9)	177.5*** (42.5)	219.5** (101.6)	108.7 (99.6)	33.9 (80.7)	−62.5 (119.0)	−65.32 (91.08)	−72.6 (86.3)
CHEM	−334.7** (142.4)	−503.6*** (168.9)	−363.6** (137.0)	−296.2** (105.3)	−385.1** (151.3)	−508.1*** (141.6)	−429.2*** (128.7)	−120.7 (279.5)	−198.4 (244.1)	30.0 (192.5)
CHEM × REACT	31.2** (12.2)	30.2** (11.7)	23.3** (9.3)	23.1** (9.3)	23.9** (9.7)	25.4*** (8.6)	23.3*** (8.5)	25.8*** (8.1)	24.7*** (7.9)	24.7*** (7.7)
Log(Scale)		51.4* (30.4)	19.7 (25.2)		17.4 (26.5)	16.6 (23.2)	22.9 (23.1)	5.9 (23.2)	7.9 (22.8)	
ACUTE			296.6*** (81.2)	318.5*** (75.5)	288.1*** (86.2)	237.3*** (78.3)	269.1*** (75.2)	238.3*** (74.8)	256.4*** (70.1)	263.6*** (63.3)
INTEGRATED					−34.5 (90.3)	−104.7 (84.1)		−65.1 (84.2)		
TRANSFER†						323.2** (130.6)	268.4** (124.9)	449.3** (148.1)	436.6*** (145.3)	444.5*** (139.7)
CHEM × TRANSFER†								−448.4* (283.0)	−513.3** (266.9)	−545.1** (244.1)
adj.R²	.17	.24	.54	.55	.52	.63	.62	.66	.67	.68
F-value	3.30*	3.36**	7.49***	9.99***	5.73***	7.24***	8.12***	7.1***	8.46***	10.67***

* $p < .10$, ** $p < .05$, *** $p < .01$

Coefficients and standard errors divided by 10^3.

†Statistical significance for TRANSFER and CHEM × TRANSFER are for one-tail t-tests.

Table A.3 Regression Results—The Impact of Overlap on Process Development Hours (standard errors in parentheses)

Variables	Model 1	Model 2	Model 3	Model 4	Model 5
Constant	437.00*** (121.7)	439.4*** (119.5)	444.6*** (115.0)	363.8*** (71.0)	363.3*** (72.7)
CHEM	−501.0*** (138.4)	−560.2*** (143.7)	−544.3*** (131.3)	−501.1*** (121.3)	−527.1*** (136.2)
CHEM × REACT	24.8*** (8.4)	25.7*** (8.3)	25.8*** (8.1)	24.7*** (7.9)	24.7*** (8.1)
Log(Scale)	12.8 (23.0)	7.5 (23.0)			10.4 (22.4)
ACUTE	244.90*** (76.5)	237.6*** (75.3)	243.0** (71.3)	263.3*** (67.3)	254.0*** (71.1)
INTEGRATED	−105.7 (83.0)	−69.7 (86.3)	−74.2 (82.7)		
OVERLAP†	−243.3*** (94.1)	−309.9*** (106.3)	−315.3*** (102.0)	−307.4*** (101.0)	−300.5** (104.5)
CHEM × OVERLAP†		280.3†† (221.5)	293.5%* (211.6)	363.9** (195.4)	339.5* (206.8)
Adj. R^2	.64	.65	.67	.68	.66
F-value	7.49***	6.82***	8.50***	10.15***	8.1***

* $p < .10$, ** $p < .05$, *** $p < .01$

Coefficients and standard errors divided by 10^3.

†Statistical significance for OVERLAP and CHEM × OVERLAP are for one-tail t-tests.

†† $p = .11$ in one-tail t-test.

with lower development costs, a finding consistent with the idea that learning by doing has performance benefits in biotechnology. The coefficient on the interactive term CHEM × OVERLAP is positive, indicating that overlapping has less of a cost reduction benefit for the chemical projects. These findings on the effect of overlap corroborate those for technology transfer.

Lead Time

The same basic modeling approach was used to examine the impact of project strategy on lead time performance, with three sets of minor modifications. First, because the dependent variable in this model is lead time (measured in calendar months), learning strategy was measured in terms of the percentage of total project person-hours consumed at different phases of the project (this avoids the statistical problem of having the dependent variable show up in the denominator of an independent variable). Second, as shown in table A.1, a different set of project content control variables was appropriate in the lead time model. In controlling for technical differences in the projects, the only variable that made any statistically significant difference indicated whether the project was a chemical or a biotechnology project. As shown below, the other variables—including the number of chemical steps in the process, the scale of the output, and the therapeutic class of the drug—did not improve the statistical quality or insight of the models. Because their inclusion also did not have an impact on the other effects examined in the model, they were dropped in order to maximize the degrees of freedom (a critical issue in a sample size this small). Finally, because production of the first batch in the pilot plant is nearly always on the critical path of the process development project, the lead time to produce the first pilot batch was included in the model.

The lead time models focus on the effects of development effort prior to the first pilot batch of production (RESEARCH%) and the effort prior to the start of technology transfer (%PRE-TRANSFER). This latter variable is analogous to the technology transfer timing variable used in the models of development costs. As was the case for the development-hours models, the basic methodological approach is to use interactive terms between the technology class (CHEM) and each of the development strategy variables of interest. The two regression models estimated to explore the effect of each of these variables and their interactive effects with technology class were:

$$\text{LEAD TIME}_i = \beta_0 + \beta_1 \text{CHEM}_i + \beta_2 \text{PILOT-1 LEAD}_i + \beta_3 \text{INTEGRATED}_i +$$
$$\beta_3 \text{\%PRE-TRANSFER}_i + \beta_4 \text{CHEM} \times \text{\%PRE-TRANSFER}_i + e_i$$

$$\text{LEAD TIME}_i = \beta_0 + \beta_1 \text{CHEM}_i + \beta_2 \text{PILOT-1 LEAD}_i + \beta_3 \text{INTEGRATED}_i +$$
$$\beta_4 \text{PILOT DEV\%}_i + \beta_5 \text{RESEARCH\%}_i + \beta_6 \text{CHEM} \times \text{RESEARCH\%}_i + e_i$$

The second version of the model simply disaggregates the effect of pretransfer activities. %RESEARCH is the percentage of total person-hours expended on the project during process research. The purpose of estimating this second version of the model is to glean additional insights into the effect of specific development activities.

Results of this analysis are shown in table A.4. Models 1 through 7 show the results for the models without inclusion of the interactive terms on technology class, thus providing a picture of the effect of the different variables

Table A.4 Regression Analysis—Determinants of Lead Time (standard errors in parentheses)

Variables	Model 1	Model 2	Model 3	Model 4	Model 5	Model 6	Model 7	Model 8	Model 9	Model 10	Model 11
Constant	41.40*** (6.03)	42.57*** (6.25)	46.72** (11.48)	36.96*** (7.39)	44.90*** (14.35)	39.63** (14.64)	35.60*** (9.02)	32.38** (11.94)	30.61*** (8.71)	24.92 (21.93)	25.16 (17.76)
CHEM	38.75*** (8.02)	27.60*** (7.07)	15.91 (9.98)	22.98*** (7.71)	27.77** (12.56)	26.18** (12.40)	34.83*** (9.24)	29.33** (10.61)	40.54*** (9.62)	44.52* (23.79)	48.71** (22.33)
PILOT-1 LEAD		1.21*** (0.34)	1.03*** (0.34)	1.06*** (0.34)		0.53 (0.40)		1.20*** (0.31)	1.28*** (0.33)	0.59* (0.41)	
INTEGRATED			−9.86 (8.91)		−9.76 (11.65)	−8.00 (11.51)		−10.70 (7.95)		−7.41 (11.59)	
RESEARCH%†		−0.886*** (0.27)	−0.776*** (0.28)	−0.776*** (0.28)					−0.202 (0.446)		
CHEM × RESEARCH%								−1.16** (0.499)	−0.996** (0.535)		
PILOT DEV%			0.197* (0.13)	0.180* (0.13)				0.238 (0.12)			
%PRE-TRANSFER†					0.155 (0.17)	0.101 (0.168)	0.143 (0.165)			0.433 (0.40)	0.401 (0.411)
CHEM × PRE-TRANSFER%										−0.406 (0.448)	−0.308 (0.450)
Adj. R^2	.50	.69	.71	.70	.49	.51	.50	.77	.73	.50	.48
F-value	23.34***	17.35***	11.62***	14.04***	8.06***	6.7***	11.91***	13.09***	15.57***	5.47***	7.89***

* $p < .10$, ** $p < .05$, *** $p < .01$

† Indications of significance for RESEARCH%, %PRE-TRANSFER, and interactive terms are for one-tailed t-test.

across the sample at large. The relative investment of resources prior to technology transfer appears to have relatively little impact on development lead time (see Models 5 through 7 in table A.4). The effect was positive (indicating that faster development lead times were associated with more development in the factory), but the statistical significance was not strong. Further disaggregating the pretransfer effects, however, was revealing. More emphasis on process research appears to shorten development lead times, whereas the opposite appears to be true for pilot development. Thus the two independent effects appear to have partially offset one another across the sample. Consistent with the analysis of development costs, the effect of organizational structure is ambiguous. Integrated organizational structures were associated with faster development lead times, but the effect was statistically insignificant.

Models 8 through 11 include the interaction terms to identify differences in effects across the chemical and biotechnology projects. Models 8 and 9 focus on the impact of process research spending prior to the first batch of pilot production, and Models 10 and 11 examine the impact of process R&D spending prior to the start of technology transfer. As shown in Models 8 and 9, the coefficient on RESEARCH% is not statistically significant, which means there is no strong relationship between the spending on process research prior to the first batch of pilot production and lead times *for the biotechnology projects*. The interactive term (CHEM × RESEARCH%) is negative and quite significant, indicating that there is a stronger lead time–reducing effect of process research *for the chemical projects*. This is consistent with the idea that learning before doing (via process research) can have lead time–reducing benefits in chemical projects. In Models 10 and 11, the estimated coefficients on %PRE-TRANSFER and the interaction term (CHEM × %PRE-TRANSFER) had the same signs as those estimated for the RESEARCH% models. However, unlike those models, the significance of the estimate on the interaction term was not high ($p < .20$). Thus, although Models 10 and 11 indicate a correlation between more spending prior to technology transfer and shorter lead times, the relationship is relatively weak.

N O T E S

Chapter 1

1. See, e.g., Imai et al. (1985), Stalk (1988), Clark and Fujimoto (1991), Wheelwright and Clark (1992), Wheelwright and Clark (1995), Iansiti (1995), and Ulrich and Eppinger (1995).
2. *Wall Street Journal,* 28 April 1992, p. A16.
3. *Fortune,* 3 October 1994, pp. 124–128.
4. See, for example, Garvin (1988), Stobaugh (1988), Womack et al. (1990), Upton (1995).
5. The following sources of information were used to develop the Gillette Sensor case: "We Had to Change the Playing Field," *Forbes,* 4 February 1991, pp. 82–86; "How a $4 Razor Ends up Costing $300 Million," *Business Week,* 29 January 1990, p. 62; "Gillette Set to Go on Laser-made Sensor Razor," *Metalworking News,* 15 January 1990, p. 1.
6. See, e.g., Gambardella (1995).
7. Abernathy (1978), Abernathy and Utterback (1978), Utterback (1994).
8. See, for example, Abernathy and Clark (1985), Tushman and Anderson (1986), Henderson and Clark (1990), and Christensen (1992).
9. Abernathy (1978, p. 168).
10. Nevins et al. (1989) and Ulrich and Eppinger (1994).
11. In automobiles, closed steel-body designs were not feasible until several manufacturing innovations were developed in the 1920s, including new processes for manufacturing lightweight, high-quality sheet steel and the introduction of automatic welding (Abernathy 1978).
12. See, among others, Imai et al. (1985), Stalk (1988), Clark and Fujimoto (1991), and Iansiti (1995).
13. See, e.g., Clark and Fujimoto (1991).

311

14. Clark and Fujimoto (1991), for instance, found that Japanese automobile companies not only tended to overlap product and process engineering to a greater extent than U.S. and European firms, but also had faster process engineering cycles.

15. "How J&J's Foresight Made Contact Lenses Pay," *Business Week,* 4 May 1992, p. 132.

16. See, e.g., Jean-Jacques Servan-Schreiber (1968).

17. National Science Foundation, *Science and Engineering Indicators 1993.*

18. Scherer (1992, p. 1), notes:

> By 1980, it was clear that America was far from having a monopoly on industrial science and technology. Other nations did catch up. Indeed, they did more than catch up. Their industries moved visibly ahead in automobile design and quality, steelmaking technology, consumer electronics, shipbuilding, textile machinery, general-purpose numerically controlled machine tools, copying machines, ceramics, high-voltage electrical transmission and rectifying apparatus, nuclear power reactors, industrial enzymes, and much else.

19. *Advanced Processing of Electronic Materials in the United States and Japan: A State of the Art Review Conducted by the Panel on Materials Science of the National Research Council* (Washington, DC: National Academy Press, 1986).

20. Various studies have documented a dramatic increase in the number of technological collaborations between U.S. and foreign firms (see, e.g., Mowery 1988) during the 1980s.

21. Some of the Swiss and German pharmaceutical companies have ancestries dating to the eighteenth century.

22. With the exception of Iansiti's (1995) work on mainframe computer chip modules and Henderson and Cockburn's (1992) work on research productivity in pharmaceuticals, most work on development has drawn data from less technologically uncertain environments, such as automobiles (e.g., Clark and Fujimoto 1991).

23. Pharmaceutical development projects are often terminated because of the product's failure to demonstrate safety or efficacy in clinical trials. Since these failures are unrelated to process development, they do not introduce sampling biases. Although difficulties with process development can seriously delay project schedules, it is extremely rare for such problems to lead to outright termination of the entire project.

Chapter 2

1. A growing body of field-generated research on product development performance has successfully traversed and integrated the details and the general patterns; see, for example, Clark and Fujimoto (1991), Henderson and Cockburn (1992), Iansiti (1995), and von Hippel and Tyre (1995). These studies have been influential to the current research because they provided not only an inspirational "proof of existence," but also methodological guidance for how to proceed.

2. See Wright (1936), Hirsch (1952), Alchian (1959), Arrow (1962), Hirschman (1964), and Lieberman (1984).

3. Thus, in work on the learning experienced by Boeing's Plant #2 during the production of the B-17, Mishina found that productivity increased most when the plant encountered capacity constraints and was forced to increase scale (without physically expanding the plant). In other words, learning was a response to a capacity problem. Von Hippel and Tyre (1995) found that, when new production equipment was introduced into a plant, problem solving was triggered by mismatches between the equipment's design and the requirements of the actual environment. Learning, in their context, was a response to unanticipated problems in equipment design.

4. Von Hippel (1976, 1988) has written extensively on the role of users in the innovation process.

5. See "BMW: The 7-Series Project (A)" (HBS Case 9-692-083).

6. There is growing evidence that differences in manufacturing performance across factories and firms are largely attributable to the "software" (the procedures) rather than the "hardware" (the equipment). See, for example, Hayes and Clark (1985), Garvin (1988), and Upton (1995).

7. See, for example, Stobaugh (1988).

8. See, e.g., Clark and Fujimoto (1991) and Ulrich and Eppinger (1995).

9. Adler and Clark (1991) develop a model of the learning curve that explicitly differentiates between autonomous "first-order" and induced "second-order" learning effects (such as the improvements that take place as a result of engineering change orders or worker training).

10. See, among others, Bowen et al. (1994).

11. Adler and Clark (1991) and von Hippel (1994).

12. See "McDonald's Corporation 1992: Operations, Flexibility, and the Environment" (HBS Case 9-693-028, p. 5).

13. Von Hippel and Tyre (1995, p. 25).

14. "Pilkington Float Glass—1955" (HBS Case 9-695-024).

15. Because of uncertainty, in practice these targets are often framed as ranges rather than discrete points (such as "Cost should be between $10 and $15 per unit").

16. A controversial issue within the economics of R&D literature is whether it makes sense to model a firm's R&D choices in an optimization framework. This issue is well beyond the scope of this work. For convenience, we will use terms such as *optimal* and *optimizing* when describing choices. Here, however, it matters little whether firms are actually optimizing or "satisficing."

17. Viewing product and process development in terms of problem solving has a long history in the innovation and organization literature. See, for example, Allen (1966), Frischmuth and Allen (1969), Simon (1978), Clark and Fujimoto (1991), Iansiti and Clark (1994), and von Hippel (1994).

18. Wheelwright and Clark (1992) suggest that the role of prototyping is so critical to

the development process that it is helpful to view development projects as a series of "design-build-test" cycles.

19 This practice of using computers to test product designs has been referred to as "virtual prototyping" (see Garcia and Gocke 1994).

20. For simplicity, we will repress the added complication that one can have observational errors even in the laboratory because of instrument calibration or other factors. Thus, the true $L(p)$ might differ from the observed $L(p)$.

21. For example, in the automobile case, investments in production tooling for the entire car could cost nearly $100 million. If designs change, the tooling becomes obsolete and must be replaced.

22. In chemical processes, safety issues can also increase the cost of full-scale experiments.

23. See, for example, Teece (1982) and Kogut and Zander (1992). Winter (1987) developed an expanded taxonomy of knowledge, which included the additional dimensions of teachability, observability in use, complexity, and links to other components of a system.

24. Bohn and Jaikumar's (1989) "stages of knowledge" framework provides a useful taxonomy for differentiating knowledge along this dimension.

25. This would essentially correspond to "Stage 8" in Bohn and Jaikumar's framework.

26. Dimensional analysis can be used to map experimental observations across scales; to do dimensional analysis, however, one needs to know the underlying scale effects.

27. On the role of scientific knowledge in supporting efficient R&D, see Nelson (1982).

Chapter 3

1. See, for example, Tushman and Anderson (1986), Henderson and Clark (1990), and Christensen (1992).

2. Clymer (1975, p. 138).

3. On the early history of penicillin research and production, see *Economic Report on Antibiotic Manufacture* (Federal Trade Commission, 1957).

4. On the concept of dominant designs and their impact on competition, see Abernathy and Utterback (1978), Utterback and Suarez (1993), and Utterback (1994). A related concept is the design hierarchy outlined by Clark (1985).

5. In 1943, a new strain of penicillin mold 100 times more productive than the original Fleming mold was found (literally). Bombarding this strain with X rays created a mutant strain that increased yield fivefold (Federal Trade Commission, 1957, p. 5).

6. Barber and Kang (1991), for example, found that the corrected average return on investment for 88 drug companies between 1976 and 1987 exceeded benchmarks for two control groups by an average of 2 or 3 percentage points.

7. Rogaine, a popular treatment for male pattern baldness, for example, was initially

tested in humans as an antihypertensive agent. During clinical trials, the drug proved ineffective in lowering high blood pressure, but researchers noticed that some patients experienced an interesting side effect: they began to grow hair on their scalps.

8. *Medical and Healthcare Marketplace Guide,* 1993, p. 34.

9. The Omnibus Budget Reconciliation Act of 1990 requires rebates of 15.7 percent of the average manufacturer's price or the average manufacturer's price minus the best price in the market, whichever is greater. Additional rebates are required on drugs with price increases exceeding the rate of inflation.

10. "Industry Focuses on Disease," *Representative,* September 1994, p. 1.

11. Under Waxman-Hatch, the life of drug patents can be extended up to five years to compensate for regulatory delay. The total period of exclusivity, including the original patent life, cannot exceed fourteen years.

12. *Standard and Poor's Industry Survey on Health Care,* 16 December 1993, p. H4.

13. *Wall Street Journal,* 18 January 1995, p. B4.

14. Henderson (1994), for example, notes that in 1992 there were more than 80,000 papers published in the field of cardiovascular pharmacology and biochemistry alone.

15. The Herfindahl Index is a common measure of competitive intensity in industries. It is calculated by summing the squares of market shares of all competitors in the market; the closer the Herfindahl Index is to 1, the less competitive the market.

16. For example, in 1976 the cost of successfully developing a new drug (which also includes the development costs of the many failed attempts) was estimated at $54 million (Hansen 1979). A more recent estimate using a similar methodology (Office of Technology Assessment 1992) found the cost had risen to approximately $360 million.

17. "A Modern Smokestack Industry," *Economist,* 14 November 1992, p. 84. This estimate is consistent with data available from the largest five companies with virtually all their sales from pharmaceuticals in 1993: Merck (21 percent), Glaxo (13 percent), Lilly (25 percent), Rhone Poulenc (29 percent), Marrion Merrel Dow (23 percent).

18. Michael Boss, "Companies Can Find a Competitive Edge in Their Choice of a Manufacturing Strategy," *Genetic Engineering News,* July–August 1990, p. 4.

Chapter 4

1. The FDA requires that all drug products be subjected to stability tests to determine how quickly the active ingredient degrades. These stability tests must be conducted on product samples produced by a process which is essentially the same as that which will be used to produce the drug commercially.

2. The data presented in this section were collected and analyzed by four Harvard

MBA students (Class of 1994) as part of a field study project under the author's supervision.

3. This number was consistent with Lieberman's (1984) analysis of thirty-four chemical products, which revealed that, on average, a doubling of plant capacity in the chemical industry resulted in an 11 percent reduction in unit costs. Because the plants generally were operating near full capacity, this was approximately a doubling in production volume.

4. Yield comprises two components: fermentation (the output of active ingredient per liter of fermentation broth) and recovery (the amount of active ingredient recovered from the broth). Multiplying these two components gives an overall measure of yield.

5. Mishina (1991) finds a similar pattern in a detailed analysis of the history of the B-29 production.

6. Drugs are chemical entities, so the characteristics of the product are determined by the process. This is why regulatory authorities concern themselves with the particulars of the manufacturing process. Companies must prove that their process is capable of consistently producing the specified product. For biotechnology products, regulations are even more restrictive. The nature of the interaction of product and process technology for proteins is not as well understood as it is for smaller chemical entities. As a result, it is difficult to change the process, the equipment, or even the scale of production and demonstrate that exactly the same product is being produced. Most proteins are so complex that a full characterization of the product is virtually impossible. Thus, the FDA division responsible for biotechnology products (the Office of Biologics) requires that companies manufacture a substantial portion of their Phase III test material in the same facility that will be used for commercial manufacture. Substantial changes in the process require additional clinical trials ("cross-over studies") to demonstrate that the product made by the new process is clinically equivalent to that made with the old process.

7. Analysis based on a sample of ninety-three new chemical entities first entering human testing between 1970 and 1982.

8. Information on this project is drawn from Ernst and Young (1994) and Forbes (1994).

9. These classes were selected for two reasons. First, each represents an important therapeutic advance, and they are major product innovations. However, more practically, the initial inventions of these classes occurred in the early 1970s—the time frame for which computerized patent files are available. In order to track a drug innovation life cycle from its inception, we needed to choose drug classes born in the early 1970s.

10. "Merck Joins Roche Unit in Offering Test Drug Free to Some AIDS Patients," *Wall Street Journal*, 17 July 1995, p. B3.

11. Jeffrey Young, "Lefties, Righties, and Anxieties," *Forbes*, 19 July 1993, pp. 208–209.

12. Under U.S. patent law, an isomerically pure form of a molecule can be patented even if the isomerically mixed version has been patented by someone else.

13. Audrey Choi, "Lifting the Side Effects Out of the Drug," *Wall Street Journal,* 11 November 1995, p. B1.

14. Toxicology studies are conducted on laboratory animals to determine side effects; because they must be conducted prior to the start of human clinical trials, they are on the critical path for the project. As a point of comparison, the average lead time for this phase on Atlantic's previous six projects was eleven months (with a minimum of three months and a maximum of twenty-one).

Chapter 5

1. The schematic would be slightly different at the initial discovery phases for a biotechnology-based protein, but the essential nature of the process is virtually identical; for purposes of exposition, only the chemical entity is shown.

2. X-ray crystallography and NMR spectroscopy are critical research tools for companies engaged in "structure-based design" of drugs, whereby one first achieves a detailed understanding of the molecular structure of a receptor involved in a particular disease, and then tries to design the molecule to "fit" that receptor in order to either catalyze or inhibit a specific reaction from taking place inside the body.

3. In most drug products, the active chemical ingredient, although the most expensive component, represents only a small fraction of the total volume of material. Although the buffer ingredients themselves have no direct therapeutic effect, the choice can critically affect how quickly the active ingredient is absorbed and metabolized.

4. With permission from the FDA, some phases can be combined. This often happens when a drug is being developed to treat a life-threatening condition for which there is no alternative treatment.

5. The issue of safety during Phase I is relative; for conditions such as AIDS, for example, afflicted patients may be used rather than healthy volunteers, and the threshold for what would be considered an unacceptable side effect is high.

6. For a new chemical entity, this application is referred to as a New Drug Application (NDA); for biotechnology-based products, the application is called a Product Licensing Application. Biotechnology companies also must file an Establishment Licensing Application with the FDA to gain approval of the manufacturing plant.

7. The number of options generated varies across molecules and projects; some molecules offer few possible options.

8. A side reaction refers to the reaction of by-products from another reaction.

9. For a discussion of how the physical environment can affect problem solving, see von Hippel and Tyre (1995).

10. Insulin was extracted from pulverized pig pancreases; factor VIII was purified from human blood; HGH was extracted from the pituitary glands of human cadavers.

11. There is also a regulatory issue. Because the genetics of the cell directly affect the nature of the product, changes in the cell line after the commencement of clinical trials may require additional analytical or clinical work to demonstrate equivalency.

12. Swanson, R. (1986), "People Make Decisions as Owners," Interview with Arthur Young High Technology Group, *Biotech 86: At the Crossroads: A Survey of an Industry in Evolution* (cited in McKelvey 1994).

13. The concept of tacit knowledge was first articulated by Polanyi (1959); its impact on technology transfer was examined by Teece (1976).

Chapter 6

1. See, for example, Clark and Fujimoto (1991) on the automobile industry and Iansiti (1995) on mainframe computers.

2. See, for example, Clark and Fujimoto (1991) and Iansiti (1995).

3. On the issue of partitioning in problem solving, see von Hippel (1990).

4. This difference was statistically significant at $p < .09$.

5. For example, good data were available on the total number of hours spent from the start of process research to the start of pilot development, and from the start of pilot development to the start of technology transfer. However, it generally was not possible to isolate the person-hours invested by process researchers during the pilot development stage. In many cases, a company's tracking systems did not make the distinction because it was not considered meaningful. For instance, if a process researcher were called to help out on a project during pilot development or the technology transfer phase, it may not really matter that those person-hours came from someone officially employed by the process research group. What does matter for the purposes of this study is the total number of hours invested at different phases (regardless of which personnel were contributing those hours).

Chapter 7

1. See, for example, von Hippel and Tyre (1995) or Thomke (1995).

2. See, for example, Dewhurst and Boothroyd (1987), Whitney (1988), and Ulrich and Eppinger (1995, ch. 9).

3. An exception is Clark and Fujimoto (1991), who examine the linkage between characteristics of high-quality development in automobiles and manufacturing performance.

4. See Phadke (1989), Clausing (1993), and Ulrich and Eppinger (1995).

5. In some cases, companies refused to release data on manufacturing costs; in others, management conceded that the data from their cost accounting systems were not particularly good reflections of actual production costs. Finally, even where pristine

cost data were available on individual products, comparing costs across highly heterogeneous products is problematic.

6. Despite the small sample, the relationship is statistically significant at $p = .01$.

7. Given the highly sensitive nature of manufacturing cost data in the drug industry, this was the only company willing to share such information across a broad array of products. For purposes of confidentiality, data have been presented in indexed form (all starting manufacturing costs = 100).

8. Upton's (1995) framework, originally developed for manufacturing operations, identifies three basic types of flexibility: range flexibility (the cope of change that can be made), mobility flexibility (the speed with which any given change can be made), and uniformity of performance (the impact of a change on the performance of the process).

9. See, for example, Wheelwright and Clark (1992).

10. This theme is echoed in the literature on product development and quality in manufacturing. On quality in product development, see Clark and Fujimoto (1991), Clausing (1993), and Ulrich and Eppinger (1995).

11. For a general discussion of this issue, see Thomke (1995).

12. For a formal model of design iteration with respect to the timing of commitments, see Smith and Eppinger (1992) and Krishnan et al. (1993).

Chapter 8

1. The idea that firm-specific knowledge relates to competitive performance is well developed in the literature on resource-based views of firms (Penrose 1959, Teece 1982, Wernerfelt 1984, Teece and Pisano 1994).

2. An exception is Iansiti and Clark (1994).

3. Exceptions include Iansiti and Clark (1994) and Iansiti (1995).

4. For a useful review and contribution, see Levitt and March (1988); see also Cyert and March (1963), Argyris and Schön (1978), Levinthal and March (1981), and Nelson and Winter (1982).

5. Iansiti and Clark (1994) develop a similar perspective. However, their framework focuses on how integration across projects of the same generation influences capabilities for development in future generations. The framework here does not address the issue of cross-project integration, but instead revolves around the impact of individual projects on the knowledge base available for future projects.

6. On the concept of tacit knowledge, see Polanyi (1958), Teece (1977), and Kogut and Zander (1992).

7. See, e.g., Levinthal and March (1981), Nelson and Winter (1982), and Levitt and March (1988).

8. Models of organizational learning as a search include Levinthal and March (1981) and Nelson and Winter (1982).

9. The issue of organizational inertia has a vast literature but takes its strongest form

in ecological approaches to organizations. See, for example, Hannan and Freeman (1989) and Hannan and Carroll (1992).

10. Schumpeter (1934), Winter (1971), Levinthal and March (1981), and March (1991).

11. For a discussion of factories as laboratories, see Leonard-Barton (1992).

12. In the "stages of knowledge" framework developed by Bohn and Jaikumar (1989), the very first stage of knowledge is having the ability to distinguish between good and bad output.

13. The distinction between "know-how" and "know-why" has a long history in the literature on process control and manufacturing improvement; see Bohn and Jaikumaar (1989) and Leonard-Barton (1995).

14. Ironically, degradation of the protein was not the root cause of the problem. In fact, further analysis of the animal test data indicated there never was a problem with the product—it was therapeutically active. One scientist noted that "this error was fortuitous because it allowed us to identify and solve the degradation problem."

15. See Bohn and Jaikumar (1989) and Leonard-Barton (1995) on the topic of know-how and know-why.

16. There is a good deal of literature supporting the idea that organizations store knowledge in the patterns of interactions and behavior that cut across individual employees. Nelson and Winter (1982) refer to these patterns as "organizational routines" and liken them to the genes of biological organisms (see especially chapter 4).

Chapter 9

1. The fact that Eli Lilly participated in the development of these two teaching cases does not necessarily imply that the company participated in the main study on which this book is based.

2. Description based on "Eli Lilly and Company: Manufacturing Process Technology Strategy (1991)," (HBS Case 9-692-056). The analysis and discussion are based on the teaching note for this case (5-692-109).

3. Description based on "Eli Lilly and Company: The Flexible Facility Decision (1993)" (HBS Case 9-694-074). Analysis and discussion are based on the teaching note for this case (5-696-041).

4. On this issue, see Jordan and Graves (1995).

5. Description of this situation is based on "Nucleon, Inc." (HBS Case 9-692-041), and analysis and discussion based on the teaching note for this case (5-692-095).

6. Lest one think this leaves the plant with a trivial aspect of process development, it should be kept in mind that equipment up-time is perhaps the single most important factor driving differences in the economic performance of complex, capital-intensive processes.

7. For a discussion of the roles and importance of prototypes in development, see Clark and Fujimoto (1991), Bowen et al. (1994), and Ulrich and Eppinger (1995).

8. "BMW: The 7-Series Project (A)," (HBS Case 9-692-083). Analysis and discussion are based on the teaching note for this case, 5-692-094.

9. For a discussion of the definitions of prototype quality, see Clark and Fujimoto (1991).

10. There is a growing literature on evaluating investments in terms of options value. See, e.g., Kester (1984), Baldwin and Clark (1993), and Dixit and Pindyck (1994).

11. In Nelson and Winter's (1982) evolutionary theory of the firm, the capabilities of an organization are rooted in organizational "routines," which they define as regular and predictable patterns of behavior.

Chapter 10

1. "The Boeing 767: From Concept to Production (A)" (HBS Case 9-688-040).

2. The second dimension of knowledge is essentially the dimension of focus in Bohn and Jaikumar's "stages of knowledge" framework (1989).

3. Interestingly, historical accounts of chemical process development in the nineteenth and early twentieth centuries reveal that it looked much like biotechnology today in terms of requiring extensive, full-scale trial and error (Haber 1958, Enos 1962, Freeman 1982).

4. University research in basic science, for example, would seem to play a critical role in laying down the scientific principles that support deductive learning strategies. This clearly was the case for chemical synthesis, where universities played a strong part in basic chemistry research and, later, chemical engineering.

5. Clark and Fujimoto (1991, p. 24) describe the symmetry between product and process design in terms of linkages to future customers.

6. See Garcia and Gocke (1994).

7. Clearly, there are many instances where safety concerns dictate that firms test prototypes under simulated conditions. Drug companies initially test drugs on laboratory animals before they are given to human patients; similarly, auto companies conduct safety tests with crash test dummies under laboratory conditions rather than with real people on real roads.

8. See, for example, Clark and Fujimoto (1991) on automobiles, Schoonhoven et al. (1990) and Iansiti (1995) on mainframe computers, Henderson and Cockburn (1992) on synthetic drugs, and von Hippel (1990) on scientific instruments.

9. Cyert and March (1963) first discussed the idea that organizational behavior tended to be influenced by "standard operating procedures" rather than explicit optimization. Nelson and Winter (1982) developed a theory of the firm based on the idea that organizational processes are akin to the "genes" of firms; they regulate behavior and tend to replicate over time.

10. Wheelwright and Clark (1995) propose using product development as a framework for implementing organizational change.
11. There is a vast collection of literature on process innovation and improvement in the context of mature industries; perhaps the most comprehensive picture is provided by Hollander's (1965) study of DuPont's rayon plants.
12. On the role of systems-level knowledge in development, see Iansiti (1995).

REFERENCES

Abernathy, William J. 1978. *The Productivity Dilemma*. Baltimore, MD: The Johns Hopkins University Press.

Abernathy, William J., and Kim B. Clark. 1985. "Innovation: Mapping the Winds of Creative Destruction." *Research Policy* 14:3–22.

Abernathy, William J., and James M. Utterback. 1978. "Patterns of Industrial Innovation." *Technology Review* 80, no. 7 (June–July):2–9.

Adler, Paul, and Kim B. Clark. 1991. "Behind the Learning Curve." *Management Science* 37, no. 3 (March):267–281.

Alchian, A. 1959. "Costs and Output." In *The Allocation of Economic Resources: Essays in Honor of B. F. Halley,* edited by M. Abramovitz. Stanford, CA: Stanford University Press.

Allen, Thomas J. 1966. "Studies of the Problem-Solving Process in Engineering Design." *IEEE Transactions on Engineering Management* EM-13, no. 2 (June):72–83.

Allen, Thomas J. 1977. *Managing the Flow of Technology: Technology Transfer and the Dissemination of Technological Information Within the R&D Organization*. Cambridge, MA: MIT Press.

Argyris, Chris and D. Schön (1978). *Organizational Learning*. Reading, MA: Addison-Wesley.

Arrow, Kenneth J. 1962. "The Economic Implications of Learning by Doing." *Review of Economic Studies* 29 (April):166–170.

Arthur Young High Technology Group. 1986. *Biotech 86: At the Crossroads—A Survey of an Industry*. San Francisco: Arthur Young.

Bader, Fredric. 1992. "Manufacturing Costs of Biotechnology Derived Pharmaceuticals." *Proceedings of Workshop on Biotechnology,* Center for the Study of Drug Development, Tufts University.

Baldwin, Carliss Y., and Kim B. Clark. 1993. "Modularity and Real Options." Harvard Business School Working Paper 93–026.

Barber, William, and S. H. Kang. 1991. "Accounting Based Measures as Estimates of Economic Rates of Return: An Empirical Study of the U.S. Pharmaceutical Industry." Working Paper, U.S. Office of Technology Assessment.

Bienz-Tadmor, Briggitta, and Jeffrey S. Brown. 1994. "Biopharmaceuticals and Conventional Drugs: Comparing Development Times." *BioPharm* 7, no. 2:44–49.

"BMW: The 7-Series Project (A)." 1992. Harvard Business School Case 9–692–083; Teaching Note 5–692–094.

"The Boeing 767: From Concept to Production (A)." 1988. Harvard Business School Case 9–688–040.

Bohn, Roger. E., and Ramchandran Jaikumar. 1989. "The Dynamic Approach: An Alternative Paradigm for Operations Management." Harvard Business School Working Paper.

Boss, Michael. 1990. "Companies Can Find a Competitive Edge in Their Choice of a Manufacturing Strategy." *Genetic Engineering News* (July–August):4.

Boston Consulting Group. 1993. "The Changing Environment for U.S. Pharmaceuticals." Boston, MA: Boston Consulting Group.

Bowen, H. Kent, Kim B. Clark, Charles A. Holloway, and Steven C. Wheelwright, eds. 1994. *The Perpetual Enterprise Machine*. New York: Oxford University Press.

Burns, T., and George M. Stalker. 1961. *The Management of Innovation*. London: Tavistock Publications.

Burrill, G. Steven, and Kenneth B. Lee (1993). *Biotech 94: Long-Term Value, Short-Term Hurdles*. San Francisco: Ernst & Young.

Business Week. 1990. "How a $4 Razor Ends Up Costing $300 Million." (29 January):62.

Business Week. 1992. "How J&J's Foresight Made Contact Lenses Pay." (4 May):132.

Christensen, Clayton. 1992. "Exploring the Limits of the Technology S-Curve: Part II: Architectural Technologies." *Production and Operations Management* 1, no. 4:334–357.

Clark, Kim B. 1985. "The Interaction of Design Hierarchies and Market Concepts in Technological Evolution." *Research Policy* 14, no. 5 (October):235–251.

Clark, Kim B., and Takahiro Fujimoto. 1991. *Product Development Performance: Strategy, Organization, and Management in the World Auto Industry*. Boston, MA: Harvard Business School Press.

Clausing, Don. 1993. *Total Quality Development: A Step-by-Step Guide to World Class Concurrent Engineering*. New York: ASME Press.

Clymer, H. A. 1975. "The Economic and Regulatory Climate: U.S. and Overseas Trends." In *Drug Development and Marketing*, edited by R. B. Helms. Washington, D.C.: American Enterprise Institute.

Cohen, Wesley, and Daniel Levinthal. 1990. "Absorptive Capacity: A New Perspective on Learning and Innovation." *Administrative Science Quarterly* 35, no. 1:128–152.

Cyert, R. M., and J. G. March. 1963. *A Behavioral Theory of the Firm*. Englewood Cliffs, NJ: Prentice-Hall.

Dewhurst, Peter, and Geoffrey Boothroyd. 1987. "Design for Assembly in Action." *Assembly Engineering* 30, no. 1 (January).

DiMasi, Joseph A., Ronald W. Hansen, Henry G. Grabowski, and Louis Lasagna. 1991. "Cost of Innovation in the Pharmaceutical Industry." *Journal of Health Economics* 10:107–142.

DiMasi, Joseph A., Ronald W. Hansen, Henry G. Grabowski, and Louis Lasagna. 1995. "Research and Development Costs for New Drugs by Therapeutic Category." *PharmacoEconomics* 7, no. 2:152–169.

DiMasi, Joseph A., Mark A. Seibring, and Louis Lasagna. 1994. "New Drug Development in the United States from 1963–1992." *Clinical Pharmacology Therapeutics* 55, no. 6:609–622.

Dixit, Avinash K., and Robert S. Pindyck. 1994. *Investment Under Uncertainty.* Princeton, NJ: Princeton University Press.

The Economist. 1992. "A Modern Smokestack Industry." (14–20 November):84.

"Eli Lilly and Company: Flexible Facility (1993)." Harvard Business School Case 9–694–074; Teaching Note 5–696–041.

"Eli Lilly and Company: Process Technology Strategy (1991)." Harvard Business School Case 9–692–056; Teaching Note 5–692–109.

Enos, J. L. 1962. *Petroleum Progress and Profits: A History of Process Innovation.* Cambridge, MA: MIT Press.

Federal Trade Commission. 1957. *Economic Report on Antibiotic Manufacture.* Washington, D.C.: U.S. Government Printing Office.

Fine, Charles. 1986. "Quality Improvement and Learning in Productive Systems." *Management Science* 32, no. 10:1301–1315.

Flaherty, Thérèse M. 1992. "Manufacturing and Firm Performance in Technology-Intensive Industries: U.S. and Japanese DRAM Experience." Mimeo.

Forbes. 1991. "We Had to Change the Playing Field." (4 February):82–86.

Forbes. 1993. "Lefties, Righties, and Anxieties." (19 July):208–209.

Forbes. 1994. "Calculated Risks." (9 May):178–180.

Fortune. 1994. "You'll Never Guess Who Really Makes. . . ." (3 October):124–128.

Freeman, Christopher. 1982. *The Economics of Industrial Innovation.* London: Frances Pinter.

Frischmuth, D. S., and Thomas J. Allen. 1969. "A Model for the Description and Evaluation of Technical Problem Solving." *IEEE Transactions on Engineering Management* EM-16, no. 2:58–64.

Gambardella, Alfonso. 1995. *Science and Innovation: The U.S. Pharmaceutical Industry During the 1980s.* Cambridge: Cambridge University Press.

Garcia, A. B., and Johnson Gocke. 1994. *Virtual Prototyping: Concept to Production.* Fort Belvoir, VA: Defense Systems Management College Press.

Garvin, David A. 1988. *Managing Quality.* New York: Free Press.

Garvin, David A. 1992. *Operations Strategy: Text and Cases.* Englewood Cliffs, NJ: Prentice-Hall.

Garvin, David A. 1994. "The Processes of Organization and Management." Harvard Business School Working Paper 94–084.

Haber, L. 1958. *The Chemical Industry During the Nineteenth Century.* Oxford: Oxford University Press.

Hannan, Michael T., and Glenn Carroll. 1992. *Dynamics of Organizational Populations: Density, Legitimization and Competition.* New York: Oxford University Press.

Hannan, Michael T., and John Freeman. 1989. *Organizational Ecology.* Cambridge, MA: Belknap Press.

Hansen, Ronald W. 1979. "The Pharmaceutical Development Process: Estimates of Current Development Costs and Times and the Effects of Regulatory Changes." In *Issues in Pharmaceutical Economics,* edited by Chien Ri. Lexington, MA: Lexington Books.

Hatch, Nile W., and David C. Mowery. 1994. "Process Innovation and Learning by Doing in Semiconductor Manufacturing." Haas School of Business, University of California at Berkeley, CCC Working Paper # 94–17.

Hayes, Robert H., and Kim B. Clark. 1985. "Exploring the Sources of Productivity Differences at the Factory Level." In *The Uneasy Alliance: Managing the Productivity-Technology Dilemma,* edited by Kim B. Clark, Robert H. Hayes, and Christopher Lorenz. Boston, MA: Harvard Business School Press.

Hayes, Robert H., and Steven C. Wheelwright. 1984. *Restoring Our Competitive Edge: Competing Through Manufacturing.* New York: John Wiley & Sons.

Hayes, Robert H., Steven C. Wheelwright, and Kim B. Clark. 1988. *Dynamic Manufacturing: Creating the Learning Organization.* New York: Free Press.

Henderson, Rebecca M. 1994. "The Evolution of Integrative Capability: Innovation in Cardiovascular Drug Discovery." *Industrial and Corporate Change* 3, no. 3:607–630.

Henderson, Rebecca M., and Kim B. Clark. 1990. "Architectural Innovation: The Reconfiguration of Existing Product Technologies and the Failure of Established Firms." *Administrative Science Quarterly* 35:9–30.

Henderson, Rebecca M., and Ian Cockburn. 1992. "Scale, Scope and Spillovers: Research Strategy and Research Productivity in the Pharmaceutical Industry." Paper presented at the Meetings of the American Economic Association.

Hirsch, W. 1952. "Manufacturing Progress Function." *Review of Economics and Statistics* 34 (May):143–155.

Hirschmann, W. 1964. "Profiting from the Learning Curve." *Harvard Business Review* 42, no. 1:125–139.

Hollander, S. 1965. *The Sources of Increased Efficiency: A Study of the DuPont Rayon Plants.* Cambridge, MA: MIT Press.

Iansiti, Marco. 1995. "Technology Integration: Managing Technological Evolution in a Complex Environment." *Research Policy* 24:521–542.

Iansiti, Marco, and Kim B. Clark. 1994. "Integration and Dynamic Capability: Evidence from Product Development in Automobiles and Mainframe Computers." *Industrial and Corporate Change* 3, no. 3:557–606.

Imai, K., I. Nonaka, and H. Takeuchi. 1985. "Managing the New Product Development Process: How Japanese Companies Learn and Unlearn." In *The Uneasy Alliance: Managing the Productivity-Technology Dilemma,* edited by Kim B. Clark, Robert H. Hayes, and Christopher Lorenz. Boston, MA: Harvard Business School Press.

"ITT Automotive: Global Manufacturing Strategy (1994)." Harvard Business School Case 9–695–002; Teaching Note 5–696–040.

Jordan, William C., and Stephen C. Graves. 1995. "Principles on the Benefits of Manufacturing Process Flexibility." *Management Science* 41, no. 4 (April):577–594.

Kester, W. Carl. 1984. "Today's Options for Tomorrow's Growth." *Harvard Business Review* (March–April):153–160.

Kogut, Bruce, and Uday Zander. 1992. "Knowledge of Firm, Combinative Capabilities, and the Replication of Technology." *Organization Science* 3:383–397.

Kolassa, M. 1993. "Reductions in Pharmaceutical Price Growth: An Assessment of List Price Changes in the U.S. Pharmaceutical Market 1989–1992." Working Paper, The Pharmaceutical Marketing and Management Research Program, Research Institute of Pharmaceutical Sciences, The University of Mississippi.

Kolassa, M., and B. F. Banahan III. 1995. "Growing Competition in the Pharmaceutical Industry: A Response to the PRIME Institute Report." Technical Report No. PMM 95–001, The Pharmaceutical Marketing and Management Research Program, Research Institute of Pharmaceutical Sciences, The University of Mississippi.

Krishnan, Viswanathan, Steven Eppinger, and Daniel Whitney. 1993. "A Model-Based Framework to Overlap Product Development Activities." MIT Sloan School of Management Working Paper #3635–93–MSA.

Langlykke, Asger F. 1970. "The Engineer and the Biologist." *The History of Penicillin Production.* Chemical Engineering Progress, Symposium Series 100, New York: American Institute of Chemical Engineers.

Lee, Kenneth, and G. Steven Burrill. 1994. "Biotech 95: Reform, Restructure, Renewal." Palo Alto: Ernst & Young.

Leonard-Barton, Dorothy. 1988. "Implementation as Mutual Adaptation of Technology and Organization." *Research Policy* 17:251–267.

Leonard-Barton, Dorothy. 1992. "The Factory as a Learning Laboratory." *Sloan Management Review* 34, no. 1 (Fall):23–38.

Leonard-Barton, Dorothy. 1995. *Wellsprings of Knowledge.* Boston, MA: Harvard Business School Press.

Levin, Richard C., Alvin K. Klevorick, Richard R. Nelson, and Sidney G. Winter. 1987. "Appropriating Returns from Industrial R&D." *Brookings Papers on Economic Activity:*783–820.

Levinthal, Daniel, and James March. 1981. "A Model of Adaptive Organizational Search." *Journal of Economic Behavior and Organization* 2:307–333.

Levitt, B., and J. March. 1988. "Organizational Learning." *Annual Review of Sociology* 14:319–340.

Lieberman, Marvin. 1984. "The Learning Curve and Pricing in the Chemical Process-ing Industries." *Rand Journal of Economics* 15, no. 2 (Summer):213–228.

Lorenz, Christopher. 1986. *The Design Dimension: Product Strategy and the Challenge of Global Marketing.* New York: Blackwell.

Mahoney, T. 1959. *The Merchants of Life.* New York: Harper & Brothers.

March, James G. 1991. "Exploration and Exploitation in Organizational Learning." *Organizational Science* 2, no. 1:71–87.

"McDonald's Corporation 1992: Operations, Flexibility, and the Environment." Har-vard Business School Case 9–693–028.

McKelvey, M. 1994. "Evolutionary Innovation." PhD Thesis, Linkopings Universitet, Sweden.

Medical and Healthcare Marketplace Guide. 1993. 9th ed. MLR Biomedical Information Services.

Metalworking News. 1990. "Gillette Set to Go on Laser-made Sensor Razor." (Jan-uary):1.

Mishina, K. 1992. "Learning by New Experiences." Harvard Business School Working Paper 92-084.

Mowery, David C., ed. 1988. *International Collaborative Ventures in U.S. Manufacturing.* Cambridge, MA: Ballinger.

National Research Council. 1986. *Advanced Processing of Electronic Materials in the United States and Japan: A State of the Art Review Conducted by the Panel on Materials Science of the National Research Council.* Washington, D.C.: National Academy Press.

National Science Foundation. 1993. *Science and Engineering Indicators.* Washington, D.C.: USGPO.

Nelson, Richard. 1982. "The Role of Knowledge in R&D Efficiency." *Quarterly Journal of Economics* (August):453–470.

Nelson, Richard. 1984. *High Technology Policies.* Washington, D.C: American Enter-prise Institute.

Nelson, Richard R., and Sidney G. Winter. 1977. "In Search of Useful Theory of Innovation." *Research Policy* 5:36–76.

Nelson, Richard R., and Sidney G. Winter. 1982. *An Evolutionary Theory of Economic Change.* Cambridge, MA: Harvard University Press.

Nevins, James L., Daniel E. Whitney, and Thomas L. DeFazio. 1989. *Concurrent Design of Products and Processes: A Strategy for the Next Generation in Manufacturing.* New York: McGraw-Hill.

Newell, A., and Herbert Simon. 1972. *Human Problem Solving.* Englewood Cliffs, NJ: Prentice-Hall.

"Nucleon, Inc." Harvard Business School Case 6–692–041; Teaching Note 5–692–095.

Office of Technology Assessment. 1992. *Pharmaceutical R&D: Costs, Risks, and Rewards.* Washington D.C.: U.S. Government Printing Office.

Parexels' Pharmaceutical R&D Statistical Sourcebook. 1995.

Pavitt, K. 1984. "Sectoral Patterns of Technical Change: Towards a Taxonomy and a Theory." *Research Policy* 13:343–373.

Penrose, Edith. 1959. *Theory of the Growth of the Firm*. London: Basil Blackwell.

Phadke, Madhav S. 1989. *Quality Engineering Using Robust Design*. Englewood Cliffs, NJ: Prentice-Hall.

Pharmaceutical Research and Manufacturers Association. Various years. *U.S. Pharmaceutical R&D (PhRMA) Annual Survey*.

"Pilkington Float Glass—1955." Harvard Business School Case 9–695–024.

Pisano, Gary P. 1990. "The R&D Boundaries of the Firm: An Empirical Analysis." *Administrative Science Quarterly* 35, no. 1:153–176.

Pisano, Gary P., and Paul Y. Mang. 1992. "Manufacturing, Firm Boundaries, and the Protection of Intellectual Property." Harvard Business School Working Paper 92–048.

Pisano, Gary P., and Paul Y. Mang. 1993. "Collaborative Product Development and the Market for Know-How: Strategies and Structures in the Biotechnology Industry." In *Research on Technological Innovation, Management and Policy*, vol. 5, edited by Richard S. Rosenbloom and Robert Burgelman. Greenwich, CT: JAI Press.

Pisano, Gary P., and Steven C. Wheelwright. 1995. "The New Logic of High-Tech R&D." *Harvard Business Review* 73 (September–October):93–105

Polanyi, Michael. 1958. *Personal Knowledge: Towards a Post-Critical Philosophy*. Chicago, IL: University of Chicago Press.

Rapping, L. 1965. "Learning and the World War II Production Functions." *Review of Economics and Statistics* 48 (February):98–112.

Reinertsen, Donald. 1992. "The Mythology of Speed." *Machine Design* (26 March).

Representative. 1994. "Industry Focuses on Disease." Vol. 24, no. 9 (September):1.

Rosenberg, Nathan. 1982. *Inside the Black Box: Technology and Economics*. New York: Cambridge University Press.

Rumelt, Richard P. 1984. "Towards a Strategic Theory of the Firm." In *Competitive Strategic Management*, edited by R. B. Lamb. Englewood Cliffs, NJ: Prentice-Hall.

Scherer, F. M. 1992. *International High-Technology Competition*. Cambridge, MA: Harvard University Press.

Schmenner, Roger W. 1987. *Production and Operations Management: Concepts and Situations*, 3d ed. Chicago, IL: Science Research Associates.

Schoonhoven, Claudia, Kathleen M. Eisenhardt, and Katherine Lyman. 1990. "Speeding Products to Market: Waiting Time to First Product Introduction in New Firms." *Administrative Science Quarterly* 35, no. 1:177–207.

Schumpeter, Joseph. 1934. *Theory of Economic Development*. Cambridge, MA: Harvard University Press.

SCRIP's Yearbook. 1994. London: PJB Publications Ltd.

Servan-Schreiber, Jean-Jacques. 1968. *The American Challenge*. New York: Athenaeum.

Simon, H. 1978. "Rationality as Process and as Product of Thought." *American Economic Review* 69, no. 5:573–583.

Smith, Robert, and Steven Eppinger. 1992. "Identifying Controlling Features of Engineering Design Iterations." MIT Sloan School of Management Working Paper #3348–91-MS.

Stalk, George, Jr. 1988. "Time—The Next Source of Competitive Advantage." *Harvard Business Review* 66 (July–August):41–51.

Standard and Poor's Industry Survey on Health Care. 1993. New York.

Statman, Meir. 1983. *Competition in the Pharmaceutical Industry: The Declining Profitability of Drug Innovation.* Washington D.C.: American Enterprise Institute.

Stobaugh, Robert. 1988. *Innovation and Competition: The Global Management of Petroleum Products.* Boston, MA: Harvard Business School Press.

Teece, David J. 1976. *The Multinational Corporation and the Resource Cost of International Technology Transfer.* Cambridge, MA: Ballinger.

Teece, David J. 1977. "Technology Transfer by Multinational Firms: The Resource Cost of Transferring Technological Know-How." *Economic Journal* 87:242–261.

Teece, David J. 1982. "Towards an Economic Theory of the Multi-Product Firm." *Journal of Economic Behavior and Organization* 3:39–63.

Teece, David J. 1986. "Profiting from Technological Innovation: Implications for Integrating, Collaborating, Licensing, and Public Policy." *Research Policy* 15, no. 6:285–305.

Teece, David J., and Gary P. Pisano. 1994. "Dynamic Capabilities: An Introduction." *Industrial and Corporate Change* 3, no. 3:538–556.

Thomke, Stefan. 1995. "The Economics of Experimentation in the Design of New Products and Processes." Unpublished PhD thesis, Massachusetts Institute of Technology.

Tushman, Michael L., and Philip Anderson. 1986. "Technological Discontinuities and Organizational Environments." *Administrative Science Quarterly* 31, no. 1:439–465.

Tyre, Marcie, and Eric von Hippel. 1993. "The Situated Nature of Adaptive Learning in Organizations." MIT Sloan School of Management Working Paper #BPS-3568–93.

Ulrich, Karl, and Steven Eppinger. 1995. *Product Design and Development.* New York: McGraw-Hill.

Upton, David. M. 1994. "The Management of Manufacturing Flexibility." *California Management Review* 36, no. 2 (Winter):72–89

Upton, David M. 1995. "Flexibility as Process Mobility: The Management of Plant Capabilities for Quick Response Manufacturing." *Journal of Operations Management*:205–224.

Utterback, James M. 1994. *Mastering the Dynamics of Innovations.* Boston, MA: Harvard Business School Press.

Utterback, James M., and Fernando F. Suarez. 1993. "Innovation, Competition, and Industry Structure." *Research Policy* 22, no. 1:1–21.

Von Hippel, Eric. 1976. "The Dominant Role of Users in the Scientific Instrument Innovation Process." *Research Policy* 5:212–239.

Von Hippel, Eric. 1988. *The Sources of Innovation.* New York: Oxford University Press.

Von Hippel, Eric. 1990. "Task Partitioning: An Innovation Process Variable." *Research Policy* 19:407–418.

Von Hippel, Eric. 1994. "'Sticky Information' and the Locus of Problem-Solving." *Management Science* 40, no. 4 (April):429–439.

Von Hippel, Eric, and Marcie Tyre. 1995. "How the 'Learning by Doing' Is Done: Problem Identification in Novel Process Equipment." *Research Policy* 24, no. 1:1–12.

Wall Street Journal. 1992. "Electronics Industry in Japan Hits Limits After Spectacular Rise." (28 April):A1, A16.

Wall Street Journal. 1995a. "Bestselling Drugs Held Off Low-Cost Challengers in '94." (18 January):B4.

Wall Street Journal. 1995b. "Merck Joins Roche Unit in Offering Test Drug Free to Some AIDS Patients." (17 July):B3.

Wall Street Journal. 1995c. "Lifting the Side Effects Out of the Drug." (11 November):B1.

Wernerfelt, Berger. 1984. "A Resource-Based View of the Firm." *Strategic Management Journal* 5:171–180.

Wheelwright, Steven C., and Kim B. Clark. 1992. *Revolutionizing Product Development*. New York: Free Press.

Wheelwright, Steven C., and Kim B. Clark. 1995. *Leading Product Development*. New York: Free Press.

Whitney, Daniel. 1988. "Manufacturing by Design." *Harvard Business Review* 66 (July–August):83–91.

Winter, Sidney G. 1971. "Satisficing, Selection and the Innovating Remnant." *Quarterly Journal of Economics* 85:237–261.

Winter, Sidney G. 1987. "Knowledge and Competence as Strategic Assets." In *The Competitive Challenge*, edited by D. J. Teece. Cambridge, MA: Ballinger Publishing Company.

Womack, James, Daniel Jones, and D. Roos. 1990. *The Machine That Changed the World*. New York: Macmillan.

Wright, T. P. 1936. "Factors Affecting the Cost of Airplanes." *Journal of Aeronautical Science* 3 (February):122–128.

INDEX

ABOUT THE AUTHOR

Gary P. Pisano is an associate professor at the Harvard Business School in the technology and operations management area, where he specializes in manufacturing strategy and development of new process technology. His other research interests include vertical integration, joint ventures, and supplier relations. He is currently undertaking research on strategies to improve the quality and efficiency of healthcare. Professor Pisano has consulted to a number of organizations in the healthcare industry and has written widely on R&D, process development, and manufacturing strategy. His articles have appeared in the *Harvard Business Review, Strategic Management Journal,* and *Administrative Science Quarterly.* Professor Pisano is a coauthor with Robert Hayes and David Upton of *Strategic Operations: Competing Through Capabilities* and is a coeditor with Robert Hayes of *Manufacturing Renaissance* (HBS Press).